Return to Berry Meadow
and Other Stories of Our People

Richard Scheuerman, Editor

Published by the
American Historical Society of Germans from Russia (AHSGR)
631 "D" Street
Lincoln, Nebraska 68502-1199

Printed by
Augstums Printing Service, Inc.
1621 South 17th Street
Lincoln, Nebraska 68502-2698

For Mary, Karl, and Leigh
To know from whence we've come

TABLE OF CONTENTS

LIST OF PHOTOGRAPHS

LIST OF MAPS

PREFACE

The efforts of many individuals throughout the world have yielded this harvest of stories and articles about a group of people whose heritage is rooted in the black earth of Russia's Volga region. Among the thousands of German colonists who immigrated to this area in the 1760s, several dozen families from Hessen's scenic Vogelsberg district were directed to a wooden valley on the northern periphery of the colonial enclave established by Catherine the Great. In this special place they founded the village of Yagodnaya Polyana, or Berry Meadow, that remained an outpost of Old World German culture well into the twentieth century. Policies that the Russian government directed against some of its non-Slavic minorities in the late 1800s induced tens of thousands of Russia's Germans to immigrate to North America.

This book is based on oral histories and original sources drawn from all these places—Germany, Russia, Canada, and the United States. Access provided to the authors by the following individuals and institutions have made this collection possible: Henny Hysky of the Volgelsberg Heimat Museum, Schotten, Germany, and the Buedingen Castle Archives in Buedingen; Dr. Igor Plehve, Saratov State University; John Guido and Larry Stark, Holland Library Archives, Pullman, Washington; Rev. Horst Gutsche, Calgary, Alberta; and Kathy Schultz, JoAnn Kuhr, and Richard Rye of the American Historical Society of Germans from Russia in Lincoln, Nebraska.

I am deeply grateful to Selma Muller for her translations of the Basenau, Eurich, and Luft articles, and to Sergei Bondar for his translation of Olga Litzenberger's dramatic account of Asian exile, "Enduring the Soviet Experience," and for translating the Popov and Gonyasinsky reports from archaic Russian. The Kromm and Wuertz articles were translated by the late Rev. Fred Schnaible. I am also indebted to the families of the late Anna Weitz, Endicott, Washington; Catherine Luft, Sheboygan, Wisconsin; and Susan Yungman, Pine Island, New York; for permission to share their stories. Sandra Stelter, Mr. and Mrs. John Scheirman, Mr. and Mrs. Alfred Poffenroth, Roy Kaiser, and the families of Nyal and Ed Scheuerman are also thanked for their valued contributions and friendship.

I am especially indebted to Dr. Nancy Holland, Trinity College, for her patient nurturing of this work and extensive proofreading, to Leona Pfeifer, chair of the A.H.S.G.R. editorial committee, and to Julie Lust for preparing the manuscript. I also gratefully acknowledge the advice and encouragement of Dr. Tim Kloberdanz, William Scheirman, and Dr. Tim McCarthy. Alexei Kuryaev and Yergenii Kunitsyn made possible my first visit to Yagodnaya Polyana under difficult circumstances where we have been hosted graciously by the families of George and Victor Scheuerman on several occasions since that time. My initial journey to the Volga in 1991 allowed the first glimpse of the old colonies by a Westerner since the 1920s and was permitted only through the intervention of the Honorable Y. I. Kazantsev, Russian Deputy Minister of Education, who has undertaken great personal sacrifice with other brave souls in Russia to lead the nation out of its often troubled past and promote progressive change through education. The photographs that appear in this book were taken on a subsequent trip to the village in July, 1993.

I am especially mindful of the abiding support given by parents, Don and Mary Scheuerman, and by my wife, Lois, that allowed me to "return to Berry Meadow" on behalf of all those who had long sought to learn the fate of this special place and those people who first called it home.

Richard Scheuerman
St. John, Washington
March 26, 1995

VOGELSBERG:
THE ORIGINAL HOMELAND

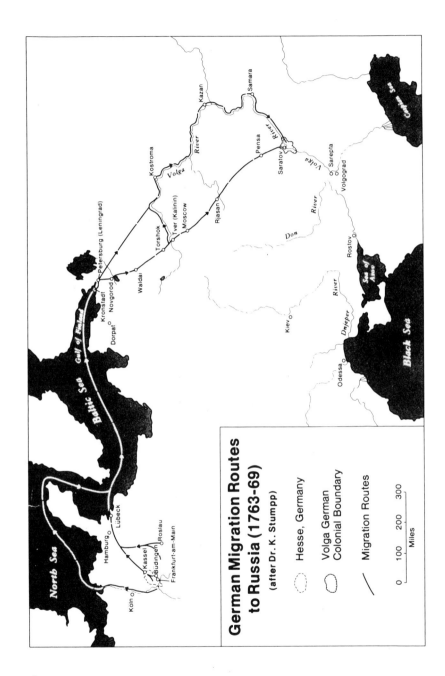

German Migration Routes to Russia (1763-69)

(after Dr. K. Stumpp)

Hesse, Germany

Volga German
Colonial Boundary

Migration Routes

Miles
0   100   200   300

Caspian Sea

Samara

Kazan

Volga River

Kostroma

Volga

Pensa

Saratov River

Sarepta

Volgograd

Volga

Petersburg (Leningrad)

Torshok

Tver (Kalinin)

Moscow

Rjasan

Don River

Kronstadt

Novgorod

Waldai

Dorpat

Kiev

Dnieper River

Rostov

Sea of Azov

Gulf of Finland

Baltic Sea

Odessa

Black Sea

Lübeck

Hamburg

Kassel

Büdingen

Roslau

Frankfurt-am-Main

Köln

North Sea

2

A History of the Vogelsberg and Town of Schotten
by Karl-Heinz Basenau

The "Heart of the Vogelsberg" is what the old town of Schotten calls itself. It lies nestled in the upper Nidda Valley with beautiful viewpoints, healthy air and well-preserved monuments. It is called the "Heart of the Vogelsberg"—not because of its central geographical location, but because of its reputation as the economic center for most of the villages in the high Vogelsberg. Until 1938, Schotten was the district or county seat, belonging to the rural district of Buedingen. Since the government reform it has been part of the Vogelsberg district which is also famous for its racing and health resorts which are well known far beyond the boundaries of Hesse as popular destination spots.

If we take a look at the history of the city, we can reach back to the ninth century. The beginning of the place was a farm which first grew into a village and then in 1354 was granted rights of a town. Because of its cold climate, however, it took a long time to be settled. It is generally accepted that Schotten is connected with the founding of the Irish-Scottish mission of the pre-Boniface era. With a charter dated in the year 778, the Abbott Beatus presented the Schotten cloister of Hanau at Strassburg, situated on an island in the Rhine River, to this his cathedral, eight churches in the Upper Hessen area and specified all but one of them by name: the Church in the Licher Mark, Church in Hofe Zu Wiesech, Church in Sternbach, Bauernheim, Rodheim, Horloff, and "in Buchonia." St. Michael's Church is situated in Buchenland on the plain in Schotten. Not far from this vanished original church, the St. Mary's Cathedral was erected, which as time passed, alternated with the older St. Michael's Cathedral and finally became City Church. In the Charter referred to, a church is mentioned as "*zu den Schotten in Buchonia*" ("in Scot's ecclesia in Buchonia") and a "*Godestal.*" The name of the village Gotzen above Schotten reminds one of the Christian Mission which made a *Gotzen* (idol) into a *Gottestal* ("God's Valley").

According to legend, a half-hour by foot above Schotten at the summit there stood a huge image of an idol named Lug. For this reason the place is called *Heilung*. The upper part of the image was a large oxen head which was hollow on the inside and glowed at night. This Lug is supposed to have been one of our ancestors' venerated land-gods. Legend claims that the name of the village Gotzen is derived from this holy place, that this name had at one time been "*Gotzenhain bei den drei Linden.*" Gotzenhain means "idol grove."

The founding of the church and the city of Schotten by Scottish monks is further verified by an old Latin charter, which was found in the knob in the church spire, when the church was renovated. Translated, it says: "In the year 1015, after the birth of our Lord Jesus Christ, during the rule of the king, who had the nickname 'the Lame One' [Kaiser Heinrich II, 1002-1024], two sisters born in Scotland, one of whom was named Rosamunde, the other Demudis, began the building of this city and our first Schotten church."

According to the legend, two kings' daughters from Scotland wanted to convert the heathen living in "Buchonia," on the west side of Vogelsberg in order to save their souls from eternal damnation. In their traveling they came to the banks of a stream named Nidda. Here they became witnesses to strange events. Suddenly a wolf came tearing out of the woods in order to capture the two fawns of a doe, who was grazing along the edge of the stream. The doe valiantly defended her young and threw him into the Nidda. The torrential stream carried the beast away. A bit later, the princesses spied a snake who wanted to steal some baby song-birds on a tree. But the mother bird courageously flew at her and picked out her eyes. The snake lost her sense of direction, fell from the tree into the Nidda, and was carried away downstream.

The two princesses were named Rosamund and Dichamund. They were deeply impressed by the courage of the weak in deepest distress. They decided to rest in the place of these events. During the night the Lord appeared to them as they slept. When, the next morning, two heathen princes appeared to chide them about their disrespect to their old idols, one of them said: "You want to rob us of our belief, therefore you must die! But we will give you a chance to try your strength with us in a fight, then we will see whose God is the strongest." The weak Dichamund was the first to accept the challenge. When the first heathen prince started for her, suddenly a falcon darted from the sky and, with his claws and bill, destroyed his eyes. Dichamund touched him with her stick, her only weapon, and he immediately breathed his last. The second prince suffered the same fate when he came near Rosamund. The bird flew away. All the attendants of the princes were filled with horror and allowed themselves to be baptized. The king's daughters stayed in that place where the Lord had helped them so wondrously and founded a settlement. Later this was named Schotten in memory of the Scottish princesses. The falcon was chosen to be on the coat of arms of Schotten.

The inhabitants of the surrounding villages went to the little church of the Schotten monks in the upper Nidda valley on Sundays. They built their houses "to the Schotten" during the course of centuries; was better life "in the Schotten" than in the little villages scattered around which had been forsaken and gradually decayed. As examples, there was Giesenhagen on the slope of Gieselstein in the Giertal Gera, then Vockenhain and Salckenrod on the slope of the Niedwald. Below Schotten, during the Middle Ages, there were the villages Nubel and Elbesshausen with a church shared by both: the St. George Church, which was served by a priest from Wingershausen. When the people of both villages moved away, the chapel became neglected. It was situated above the highest intersection of the former railway line Nidda-Schotten, at the edge of the *"Spiep"* where the Nidda reservoir is today. At the time when the railway was built in 1888, the foundations could still be faintly seen. A very ancient, huge thirty-eight centimeter long key was found.

In 1318, when Eberhard von Brauberg made an agreement with the inns in Schweinberg regarding *"Peterlinge"* (bondmen with special rights) in the courts of Bobenhausen II, Felda and Oberohmen, there appeared first of all as witness a village mayor, Konrad zu Schotten. This proves that Schotten, already in the Breuberger time, had risen to be a town with a court of justice. When in 1293 a quarrel arose over ownership of a monastery in Echzell and had to be settled in court there appeared, among others, as arbiter a *"plebanus in Scotis,"* priest of the people (*Leut priester*) in Schotten. The two last Breuberger, Eberhard Reitz III and his uncle Amos, had died before April 4, 1323 without leaving heirs. Each had a daughter through whom the property came to the sons-in-law. The former was married to Konrad von Weinberg and after that to Gottfried VI von Eppenstein. The Breuberger, in spite of splitting up into two tribes, had always conducted their business together in regard to the property. Until its dissolution, the seat of government was the Altenburg, the only castle in Schotten.

The archives of the Schotten parish preserves a letter of indulgence or dispensation dated February 3, 1330 from Avignon by Pope John XXII in which the pilgrims to the church of Holy St. Michael and to the chapel of the Holy Virgin were granted a letter of indulgence of forty days. This letter was verified anew by Pope Clemens VI from Avignon, the residence of the Pope at that time, in the year 1351. At this time, the churches were named the Parish Church of St. Michael and Mary's Church or Our Dear Lady's Cathedral or Minster. The stories of the Schotten miracles of Mary and the letters of indulgence brought the village Schotten many pilgrims and this brought to it an upswing and economic success.

The people of Schotten profited from the building of the church and the sovereign authority. So Lukarde (from Eppstein in Taunus) was able, shortly after 1310, to redeem Court Schotten which her father Eberhard Reitz III von Breuberg had mortgaged on February 3, 1345 to Count Otto von Waldeck for 800 pounds of heller (1 heller = less than 1 copper cent). A "farthing" at that time was less than one copper cent. Konrad von Trimberg (named for the ancestral Trimberg near Wurzburg) had, on April 7, mortgaged the Court Schotten to Hermann von Libberg. Both lines had the right to settle. The two city gentlemen most likely never resided in Schotten since it was too remote. In those times, it was the custom to use distant property to mortgage. After the division among the Breuberger heirs, the second burg, the Eppstein Castle, was built.

In 1354, the village of Schotten received the right to be called a city *(civitas)*. Since the Masters of Trimberg and Eppenstein remained faithful to

Kaiser Karl IV, and had supported him in the struggle to return his imperial dignity, he gave their Schotten property city rights. In the ancient charter dated January 4, 1354, it states: "Out of their common village at Schotten, they are to build a market and town in the Mentzer (Mainzer) Bisthum and a fortress and battlements, moats, towers, etc." The town, of this herein named Konrad von Trimberg, is to have all rights and privileges like "our town" Friddeburg (Friedberg). On January 6, 1356 the second charter was made in Nuremberg, in favor of the occupants, Konrad von Trimberg and Eberhard von Eppenstein. Both received the right to enlarge their town patterned after the town of Frankfurt, with all legal authority. So to the fortifications were added the weekly market, whose customers were promised free escort. Their lordships received all jurisdiction over lower and higher court, criminal court, jail and gallows. A city coat of arms was made: a white falcon sitting on a branch (today a cliff) on a blue background. The castle, the old fortress with its trenches, still reminds one of the old fortifications of long ago even after the lower and upper gates were torn down last century.

During the 1470s, in the line of succession by inheritance, and by mortgage, two nobles rose to power in Schotten; the Lords von Rodenstein and von Schweinsberg. From their castles in Schotten, they engaged in what was considered the almost honorable business at that time of highway robbery. Already ten years after the town had been granted and honored with a charter (1364), Konrad von Trimberg mortgaged his share for 1550 gulden in gold to the taverns of Schweinsberg, which had at their disposal in the neighboring Ulfa, a castle with land and sat as lords at the Ziegenheinischen Castle Stornfels. The other half of Schotten, where the cathedral stands, Eberhard von Eppenstein exchanged for 1500 gold gulden in 1377 to Johann, Master of Rodenstein. The Eppenstein seat of government was the castle. The taverns were situated on the so-called "Altenburg."

The Rodensteiners came with their servant Peter von Schwanheim to Schotten which had a feud with the city of Mainz. The feud and "robbery and seizure" on the kingdom's streets forced the merchants and also the towns into bearing arms against the murders' and robbers' (*Mordkauten* and *Raubnester*) castles like Schotten and other places. The Rhine Cities' Union, under leadership of the Archbishop Adolph (von Nassau) from Mainz with his assault troops laid siege to Schotten on January 21, 1382 with the whole Cities' Union army from the cities Mainz, Strassburg, Speyer, Frankfurt, Worms, Hagenau, and others. A thousand marksmen and five-hundred weapons (the lowest units of the feudal army armed with spears) for a total of 2500 armed men. By January 24th, the city was conquered. The fortifications had to be razed, both castles destroyed clear down to the foundation.

The castle was rebuilt beginning in 1403. The *Altenburg* (Old Castle) was built anew by the Masters of Guenderrode out of wood. Only upon the pleas of the Schotten citizens did they give up plans for also destroying the Liebfrauenkirche, to which the robber barons had fled as their last bulwark.

6

According to an ancient record, an oath had to be given that never again would it be used as a stronghold or else all the population would be moved to Mainz. A city wall as strong as before was never built again. Walls, trenches, and palisades were replaced later but these again made room for progress in war technology.

Destruction of the *Altenburg* gave the Hessian Landgrave (Count) Hermann the Scholar welcome opportunity to intervene, because it had been the center of his vassals—the innkeepers. On March 9, 1382 he filed a complaint with the city of Frankfurt because of the damage done to his vassals because of the Rodensteiners in Schotten. The Eppstein or Schweinsberger half of the town was later mortgaged to the Barons von Riedesel for the sum of 2516 gold florins. The head of this clan (*Stammvater*) was Hermann Herr zu Eisenbach who lived with his wife in the city. He died in 1463 and was entombed with his wife in the choir section of the church. The sons Hermann and Georg came into possession of this property. In 1479 they must have sold their rights to Landgrave Wilhelm von Hessen. An old document of 1538 names the Hessian hereditary Marshal Johannes von Riedesel *Lehnherr* (feudal master) of the pastorage Schotten. Also the Trimberg or Rodenstein city half (*Stadthaelfte*) soon passed into Hessian ownership. Landgrave Hermann gave permission to Johann von Rodenstein and Lipberg to rebuild the castle and granted them a building loan of 2400 gulden in 1403, over which they gave him an exact account. After him the next Hessian magistrate or administrator in Schotten was Wolf Schenk zu Schweinsberg. In 1407 he was succeeded by Eckhard Waise von Feuerbach.

Fritz Sauer, on whose research this report is essentially based, assumes that this year was the time when the transfer of all of Schotten to Hessen took place because when Landgrave Ludwig von Hessen confirmed to the city of Schotten its privileges and rights on June 23, 1454, he refers to a letter with which his father Landgrave Hermann the Scholar confirmed that the mayor, council, and the whole parish of Schotten were assured their old freedoms, customs, and ancestry. Since Landgrave Hermann the Scholar died in 1413, this letter of confirmation must have been sent before this to Schotten. "The appointment of Eckhard Waise von Feuerbach to be Administrator or Magistrate of Hesse was shortly before." Since then Schotten has constantly remained a Hessian possession. At the death of Philip the Magnanimous, the town became inheritance of a Count von Dietz, but fell in 1583, by a trade with Wilhelm von Hessen-Kassel, to Hessen-Darmstadt. In the middle of the sixteenth century, the faithful Chancellor Thilemann von Guenderrode was given the old castle and some larger pieces of real estate on feudal tenure as a reward. The landgrave deputy administrators with the other officials also had their places in the castle. The jurisdiction comprised Rainrod, Betzenrod, Goetzen, Rudingshain, Mickelbach, Breungeshain, and the Kiliansherberge. The next higher authority was the magistrate in Nidda.

Berry Meadow Welcome: Black Bread and Salt

In the Thirty Years' War, Schotten also was afflicted by plundering, epidemics and contributions (levied) for the cost of war. In 1622, Colonel Carpezon laid a heavy burden on the town, taxing them 2200 talers. From 1636 there is a report that the commander from Hanau ordered Lieutenant Severing to conduct plundering. After a Schotten citizen had shot the lieutenant the troops carried on terribly among the people. The introduction to a report of a pestilence breaking out in 1625 reads: "On January the 13th, in the year 1625, God the Almighty has afflicted us, because of the Schotten incident and our great sin, with the punishment of pestilence. When before, in 1619, our dear God not alone this but also other parts of the land, gave a sign in a huge comet in the form of a fiery rod, so we could see it and, if we did not improve and do penance, we would be punished. But since the people paid little attention but were like those in Sodom and Gomorrah, and continued in their sins, without listening to the teachers and preachers who did all they could to get them to repent, but they paid little attention so the Almighty God was forced to let punishment come over Germany, such as in the Riedeselish country and all around for five long years the people carried on war, robbed people, so that no one dared to leave home farther than a half mile from home—so that in the year 1622 Duke Christian von Braunschweig [Brunswick] with his strong army went all over the kingdom of Hesse, doing great damage, especially in Schotten, Gericht, Burkhards, Cranfeld, and all over the Vogelsberg—torturing the poor people, plundering, and brought them to utter ruin, also the domain of Schotten they robbed of 2000 talers."

It took a long time for the town Schotten and vicinity to recover from the damage, cruelties, hunger, and pestilence! No wonder that many a village in Vogelsberg became deserted as, for example, Ekhardts and Diedenhein (near Eschenrod), Reifentshain (near Eichelsachsen), Nubel and Elbershausen, and Ruthardshausen between Schotten and Lauback with its still preserved ruins of the church on the "*Kirchberg*" (in the woods by the hunting lodge). If these places all went to ruin in the Thirty Years' War or were deserted before is uncertain with most of them. Many in Vogelsberg were settlements that failed. In the Middle Ages the number of settlements was more than double that of today. Many failed because of bad soil conditions, position on the winter side, bad weather, or damage to crops by wild animals. Also the feeling of loneliness may have played a role in the tiny mountain villages. At the beginning of the eighteenth century, Upper Hesse experienced a very great wave of emigration. Many farmers left their home without permission. The main reason of this farmer flight was perhaps the unrestrained passion for hunting of the then Darmstadt Landgraves. The wildlife could increase to a great extent because it had to be saved for the princely hunt. The farmers had to stand by, doing nothing, watching wild boars, deer, and fawns graze in their fields and meadows or observing how a hunt on horseback by the nobles with hounds, ruined the crops. The Manor Zwiefalten was quite close to a hunting castle of Landgrave Ernst Ludwig (1678-1739). Not until the last Landgrave,

Ludwig IX, who had no interest in hunting, did conditions improve. In 1770 the inventory of the hunting castle was auctioned and in 1829 Zwiefalten with all its land was sold.

A complete report of 1608-1729 gives information about the city government at this time and indicates economic progress. Craft guilds began and the chief *Burgermeister* and assistant, council members, wine masters, city host, brewmaster, water master *(Bornmeister)* city clerk, meat and bread inspectors, fire and wood inspectors, city employees, and night watchmen, lived and worked for the welfare of the citizens. The Schotten City Hall of about 1512, a stately "panelling or framework style" building still houses the city government today. The "panelling" was hidden under trimming for a long time but in 1902 was discovered and laid open, also considerably expanded in the old style by Wilhelm Jost. In 1590 in the City Hall, under the Rathaus, hung leather buckets and ladders for fighting fires, pick axes and hammers for road construction, and marketing scales to weigh flour, hay and wool. In the Rathaus attic *(Boden)* the official fruit measures were stored—the *Meste,* Half-Meste (wooden buckets) and hand ladle *(Sechter).*

In 1777 the spartan "large Council Chamber" had fifteen arm chairs, two benches, "a new green carpet over three tables," and as wall-decor, three portraits of princes and a mirror. Business was conducted in the "little room" next to the council chamber. Tin plates, salt shakers, spoons, earthenware drinking mugs, and brass candle sticks indicate that the large Council Chamber was also a banquet hall for the Council families. Beginning in 1734 a newly-built city inn or restaurant served for such occasions. Beginning in 1491 the City Hall was also the Courthouse. Proceedings were held in the large room and announced in the hall. If the prison *(Stock)* was located here is not known. The whipping-post with the iron neck-band was located on the southwest corner post of the City Hall. In 1361, the *Spilhus,* which served as Court House, City Hall and market, was located on the same place. An exact date of the tearing down the old one and building of the new could not be ascertained.

Finally, mention must be made of the introduction of the Reformation in Schotten. By 1527 (1526 in Nidda) it had taken firm hold. The last Catholic clergyman, named Frasch, was relieved by the first Evangelical Johannes Heil. There were at first two parishes with a First Pastor or Metropolitan and Chaplain or Diakon, helper of the first pastor but independent, caring for Rainrods and Rudinghains. Not until the eighteenth century (1731) did the two pastors become independent spiritual advisors and co-pastors in the city church.

A History of Old Nidda
by Georg Eurich (1986)

In the eleventh and twelfth centuries the County of Nidda was ruled by the Counts of Malsburg-Nidda. No one today knows the exact boundaries of that time and precise origin of this family. Here again old legends surface. It is said that during the time of Charlemagne this dynasty enjoyed a period of great splendor and the influence of the nobility allegedly reached to Saxony. Zienenberg is presumed to have been the headquarters. Where the rulers in Nidda resided and ruled is unknown especially since according to folklore, the presumed place, "Altenburg," cannot be determined because there are no traces of any earlier buildings to be found.

After the ruling house had not brought forth a male heir, the Earldom of Nidda at the turn of the thirteenth century fell to the County of Ziegenhain. In 1450, after major inheritance quarrels broke out, Nidda was debarred from rule in Hesse. By 1500, however, some officials were put into office to help develop the country. There were office holders by the name Krieg, who were closely affiliated with Nidda and Bad Salzhausen through inheritance and worked in successive generations to bring about harmony in Nidda. They represented Napoleon's interests, one of which was the designation of Nidda for the ruling Duke of the Grand Duchy of Hesse.

There are many legends from the Nidda area. Jacob Grimm was interested for good reason in all the stories from the land between Vogelsberg and Wetterau. Perhaps he also had the legends "Little Money-fine," "The White Lady," "The Little Gray Man" and "The Headless White Horse," told to him. The best known tale that deals with the origin of Nidda in the twelfth century rests on a relationship between poetry and Count Berthold, who is said to have lived on the Altenburg, on a hill above present Nidda's part of the city called Kohden. He had made himself unpopular with the Kaiser at that time. During the time the Kaiser was lingering in Italy for the crowning, Count Berthold together with other neighboring houses of nobility carried on a war and marauding expeditions against the Archbishop of Mainz. These warmongers, with Count Herrmann who was the Count of the Palatinate on the Rhine at the head, were to appear before the Reichstag in Worms and give an account of their acts.

Berthold, who feared punishment for this offense and for yet other grievous transgressions which had not yet been brought up, stayed away from the Reichstag. He was then besieged in his castle by the emperor's troops.

After his resistance became hopeless, his sly countess begged the leader of the troops for safe conduct from the castle. She wanted to ride on a donkey and take along only what she especially treasured. It was agreed. The enemy commander-in-chief realized her trick too late—for on the back of the donkey sat her three children and the Countess herself carried the robber Berthold into the swampy valley. In the middle of the swamp, the gray animal sank so deep down, it did not want to go any further. In despair, the Countess cried out, "Little donkey, nid da, nid da." (nid = *nicht*, "not"; *da* = "here"). According to her vow, she wanted to build a new castle where the donkey would stop. So, in this place a new aristocratic residence was built and, close by, little by little, Nidda was built. Of course, Count Berthold of his own free will, after fulfilling certain conditions, put himself into the hands of the Kaiser. His punishment was not particularly severe.

Almost every place where the seed of Christendom sprouted early, the church created a platform for influence and might. It must have been similar beneath the cross of the Johannites in Nidda. The great monument that serves as the sign of the city, St. John's Tower, looks out over many roofs like a slightly stooped watchman. In 1187, so it states in an old document, the infamous Count Berthold of Nidda gave the parish of Nidda plus the many farms that were scattered far and near around Nidda, to the mighty St. John's Order. Whether this Count Berthold had lived in and around Nidda earlier has not been verified. The monastery and a St. John's estate that was located directly near today's St. John's Tower, together with a smaller and earlier church, a graveyard and garden formed a closed entity which could have been at the edges of the former old town of Nidda. The drawings of this monastery are exact and show only a few gaps. From this beginning, one can see that the increase of money, maladministration and disputes with the secular authority run like a red thread through the history of the Nidda Johannites.

The many sister churches which, in part, still exist today in and outside the large congregation of Nidda, give visible proof of the former power and strength; however magnificent these churches with their beautifully decorated interiors appear, they are not comparable with the former Nidda Johannite Church of which only the tower remains.

The Order of St. John was dissolved during the Reformation, since the government of that time turned toward the Lutheran teaching and the Confession of Faith of the citizens was determined by the belief of the Nidda Count in power. There are stories, not verified, that Luther's trip to Worms had taken him also past St. John's Monastery in Nidda. Famous men, for example, Dr. Johannes Pistorius of Nidda, Superintendent of Hesse and his son who was also a jurist, Theologian and Father Confessor to Kaiser Rudolf II, writers and other well known and educated persons serve as proof that already in the fifteenth and sixteenth centuries there must have been an excellent school in Nidda. Today, after centuries full of dissention and distrust, almost all known Christian confessions are living in good harmony in Nidda.

12

The hunting societies of nobility often carried on their scandalous conduct in the land of Nidda. Always when a Hessian count was seized with hunting fever—and that was not seldom, a cry of despair went throughout the peasantry. Now compulsory service, added tax, and destruction of all their crops was ahead of them. Distress knocked on the doors of the farmers again. Trade and travel routes had to be changed from one day to another and paths in the woods were barricaded. Fleeing from house and farm was the last act of despair for many farmers. Above all, under Ludwig VIII, who had led his land of Hesse to financial ruin, the common people had to suffer bitterly. The hunting passion of this ruler can be seen today if one looks at voluminous notes and confiscated hunting trophies which plainly confirm that especially in the district around Ulfa and Eicheldorf there was considerable hunting by the nobility. Deep trenches that were dug so wild game could be caught are still around Ulfa.

Not until the Thirty Years' War (1618-1648) did Niddaland really suffer severely. Many sketches have been found depicting the people's plight. The overcrowded city was protected by a fortress with walls, palisades formed in ditches and defense towers. There are estimates that up to 7,000 people at that time lived in Nidda and sought refuge in the city. An imperial corps with several hundred soldiers who attacked the city were easily warded off by the Hessian's Captain Blum with several hundred of his men. In the tragic year 1635, however, the need for food and help in sickness must have been beyond description. It is estimated that at least 2,000 died of pestilence. Besides the 2,000 royal troops, who were noted as plunderers, the city had to suffer under the French, Weimanian, Swedish and Bavarian marauders and troop contingents.

St. John's Church in Nidda is said to have been devastated in 1642 by the Bavarian General Wahlen who had set up his headquarters in town so he could destroy it. The Swedes, who took over the city after the Bavarians, continued a horrible devastation. After the end of the Thirty Years' War, the entire city was in a pitiful condition. But the time of peace did not last long, because the French in Hesse toward the end of the century were at war and the Nidda Castle served as a sanctuary for a brief time. Finally the Saxons drove the French from Wetterau. In 1735 the troops from Hannover established their winter quarters in Nidda. The Seven Years' War (1756-1763) again brought all kinds of horror for the Niddaland with the French to strip the Hessian people of anything they had!

With need and misery tied into an insoluble knot, the poor were driven far away. Particularly, in Hesse under the pressure of its landgrave, the people had to suffer considerably. The farmers felt the injustice doubly at the time as senseless hunting had destroyed fields, harvests had been trampled down, servile labor enforced and, part of whatever the people raised, had to be surrendered. To this was added the division of land for heirs. These circumstances caused people to emigrate because they lost their foothold. Just in the immigration list of the German village in Russia, Yagodnaya Polyana (Berry Field), one finds under the date of September 16, 1767 the names of fifty-two families from the region of present Nidda.

The Journey to the Volga from Eichelsdorf and the Vogelsberg
by Wilhelm Wuertz

In Oberhessen is the wonderful little city of Buedingen. Thick walls, stubborn towers and secure gates protect high gabled frame houses which sit on crooked, angular streets. How crowded it must have been in the summer of 1766! Hundreds upon hundreds of strangers filled every spare room. All were glad to be leaving their old homeland, and longed for the still distant new home. Commissars of the Russian Empress Catherine the Great, had been living in Buedingen for months. This city was the capital of Isenburg and any commissar who dared cross over into neighboring Hesse would certainly have been arrested. The landgraf did not want to lose even one of his subjects. All farmers were to stay, serve the graf, tithe and pay taxes. And how gladly all would have stayed if conditions had not been so dire in the German homeland. The Frenchman had come every year and searched, taken the last sack of fruit from the hiding place in Steinhaufen and Hecken, and bloodied the farmers during the Seven Years' War (1756-1763). Frederick the Great had asserted himself against his enemies and the Seven Years' War (1756-1763) was over, but the aftermath, not only Prussia but other countries in Germany suffered. The major conflict escaped Oberhessen; only small bands had some conflict with the French. The need really was economic, since money became scarcer. Trade and commerce were very subdued for a long time. Crop failure, lack of money in the land, and higher taxes to help the country get back on its feet took their toll. Dividing the land for inheritance purposes made the parcels of land ever smaller, and even diligence no longer spelled success. The soldiers home from the war could not reconcile themselves to these conditions.

The hunting mania of the landgrafs Ernst Ludwig and his son Ludwig VIII also exacerbated this problem. Landgraf Ernst Ludwig (1678-1739) had the hunting seat Zwiefalten built in 1722. Until then Stonfels, Schotten, Nidda and Bingenheim had to host the royal hunters. Why had the Landgraf picked the "Kirschberg" near Eichelsachsen? The forest Eichelsachsen was his favorite hunting ground because the best stags and numerous herds were found in Breitenstein, Friedrichsberg, Auerberg, Kohlag, Reiperts, and Altenberg. The "Kirschberg" also lay next to a busy road between Frankfurt and Fulda, a scenic place. Caravans of riders and packwagons came from Darmstadt across Frankfurt and Nidda through Roteberg and Breitenstein to Zwiefalten. Housing all these hunting parties was not easy. They brought some provisions with them, but the countryside had to deliver animals for meat. Game, fish and poultry made up the rest.

This hunting drive was a heavy burden on all the surrounding territory. The various services required, such as finding foodstuffs, putting up people and horses, created great hardship. The damage caused by and to game was phenomenal. One can hardly imagine the wealth of wildlife that existed then. Mostly in the presence of his serene highness and Ludwig VIII, reigning landowner of Hesse, 16,188 animals and fowl were destroyed in 1750 alone—mass murder! The fields around the forests became desolate. People kept watch at night over their fields and chased the stags away by clapping. The forest was closed to everyone as long as this prince lived in Zwiefalten, the same forest that served as fodder for animals. Adding lanes, stalking walks, watering places, ponds and hunting lodges were all done by forced labor. Farmers drove; others did handwork. Above all this was the destruction of the forests, fields, and wildlife. No wonder the population became poverty stricken and many sought emigration. Poor as a churchmouse was the Vogelsberger in 1766.

The nailsmith Johannes Goetz of Eichelsdorf was staying in Buedingen to sell a sackfull of nails. He was about to give up but a shoemaker finally bought them, almost as a gift. "Hannes, money is just too tight!" Hannes brought home little enough money, but soon a rumor went through the village like wildfire that the empress of Russia would give a farm to anyone who settles in her country, as well as horses, cows, sheep, a wagon, plow and harrow as well as the seeds for planting. Also no taxes for thirty years, no need to join the military ever, free journey into Russia and money during the trip. Not bad! The narrow smithy was piled full of people from morning until night. "Hannes, how much is the stipend?" "Hannes, how many acres does each one get?" Hannes here, Hannes there. Hannes was the hero of the day—and Hannes is going to Russia, and more than thirty Eichelsdorfer with him with many others from almost all the places of the Vogelsberg. The Landgraf would never have given them permission so they went without permission, in the night and the fog. House and yard and the few acres were quickly sold under the table. The bundle for the trip was not very heavy. Away they went to the meeting place of Buedingen.

The commissar looked them over. The tallest was Hannes Goetz. He was a sturdy man, 26 years old, and very healthy. "Yes," comments the commissar, "The empress does not want single people. She wants couples and pays them a double stipend." Hannes scratches his head and thinks: "I could get double stipend. But where should I get a wife without stealing her? There is Lisbeth Koch from Feuerbach. She also heard what the commissar wanted. Lisbeth appealed to me more each time I brought her father shoenails. I will ask Lisbeth if she wants me." Hannes goes to Lisbeth and says, "Lisbeth, you heard what the commissar said. How is it, do you want me?" And Lisbeth only gives her hand to Hannes—she would have liked to kiss him, if only there were not so many people around, and says "Willingly, Hannes, I have loved you for a long time." And soon, on July 1, 1766, these two were married in the beautiful Buedingen church. Many others followed suit, and between 24th of February and the 8th of July, 375 pairs found one another.

In the beginning of August, 1766 they left Buedingen. Women and children rode on rack wagons, the men trudging beside them. How large the world is! Many lodgings were needed before the pilgrimage reached Luebeck. A sailboat accommodated the Vogelsbergers, and house after house was deserted, and the trek went to the east. "Dear homeland, good-bye." Weeks later the Vogelsbergers saw Petersburg. The empress stands among the colonists, and all are happy she can speak German. Now we go farther in small wagons deep into Russia. Forest, nothing but forest! Forests in the morning, at noon, and at night. Spruce, more spruce, birches, more birches, and alder, day after day! Suddenly dark clouds appear. Snow! The Vogelsbergers spend a long winter in Russian villages with cabbage soup, lice, and stench! "Hannes, if only we were home once again."

Even the Russian winter ends and once again Russian horses pull small wagons day after day. Once again it is August. The Cossack officer, who week after week led the wagontrain, raises his hand, and cries "Halt!" It is the 28th of August, 1767. "What does he want?" The men press forward. "What is the matter?" The Cossack points to the land around. "Here will be the colony!" "What? Where?" "Here a colony," repeats the Cossack. "Dear God," sobs Lisbeth, "We are to stay here? I see not even one house!" The colonists had left the forested region to the north days ago. The grass is dry and brown, and there is dust, nothing but dust. The men look at the Cossack in astonishment. "Build houses!" the Cossack commands, the Vogelsbergers stare at him in disbelief. "Wood?" they ask. The Russian points backwards. "Axes?" The Russian points south. "Saratov!"

A wagon goes to Saratov to get tools and after several days the Russian farmer returns. "Nothing!" And already the fall wind is blowing over the rolling landscape. The nights under the wagon cover are cool indeed. Soon it will be winter, and no roof over one's head. The Russian farmers begin to dig in the earth of a hill on the southern slope. They cover deep holes with boards which they are forced to take from their wagons and throw earth over it, allowing only a small opening. The Cossack lieutenant gives out the winter provisions they brought along, mounts his horse, and is followed by the Russian horses and wagons towards the forests in the northwest. The snow-flakes fall and fall. It is bearable in the earth hut but if only there were no wolves! The snowstorm above is dwindling, but the howling of wolves is felt through and through.

Finally May arrives and memories come of Eichelsdorf where the forest above the village is green. Potatoes are being planted, also oats and barley are sown. A warm wind begins to waft over the distant Volgaland in the south. Suddenly it is spring here as well. Rivulets of snowwater compel the colonists to leave their earth huts. Sadly the poorest of them sit on their bundles beside the gurgling earthhuts and stare at the endless steppes. With each step their feet sink into a morass of snow and slime. The nights are terrible without a roof over head. Children run fevers, cough and die. The women sob at small graves. The men grit their teeth. "Let us not get soft." The waters dissipate, the land dries and almost overnight the steppe is speckled green and red, yellow, blue and white. A lark sings in the deep blue sky. The dot in the east gets larger and larger...it's a rider and behind him are Russian horses with small wagons. A Cossack lieutenant brings new provisions, axes, saws, plows, harrows and seeds. The next morning, before sunup, the wagons roll northwest, to the forest. The men wave good-bye; women's eyes shine once more, after a long while. Wood is sawed. Building lumber! The Russian horses take weeks to drag the logs. The saw sounds happily, the axe is heard afar, deft Russian hands fit log upon log. The first log house! And near the house a small fir tree, just like at home. House upon house rises up, while the horses pull the plow. Seeds fly, the harrow goes over the earth softly and soon dark green shines among the bright wildflowers. Finally the last loghouse, the ninetieth, is built. The scythe sounds, the first scythe in German hands, in the new Fatherland. Yagodnaya Polyana—Berry Field—has arisen, the Vogelsberger village on the Volga.

Catherine the Great and the German Immigration Campaign
by Richard D. Scheuerman (1980)

In the German village of Nidda in the state of Hesse stands a small stone structure with a single entrance, its massive wooden door crowned by a plaque on which is inscribed: *Der Johanniterturm: Altestes und ehrwurdigstes Baudenkmal der Stadt...Im 30 jahrigen Krieg zerstort.* Built during medieval times as part of a larger chapel, it stands alone in the town as a silent reminder of an earlier time in German history when wars ravaged the region. From such villages in Hesse and Rhine Palatinate thousands of people came in the 1760s to seek a new life elsewhere and while many during this period migrated to the American colonies, others looked eastward to Russia.

Catherine II of Russia (1762-96) issued on July 22, 1763 a Manifesto of the Empress that succeeded in luring thousands of Germans to the vast southwest frontier of her empire. This was actually the result of a program originated by Tsarina Elisabeth Petrovna (1741-62) who as early as 1752 had considered peopling the Turkish border region with French Protestants at the suggestion of a French immigration official, de la Fonte. A committee was appointed to consider the project and an active program was formulated only to be tabled when the Seven Years' War broke out in Europe, without any French being settled in the area. The idea was perpetuated and given new vigor after Catherine II was crowned tsarina as she had long held grandiose plans for modernizing Russia. Even as a grand duchess married to the heir to the throne, she wrote "We need people. We must make our wide spaces teem with swarms of people if this be possible" (quoted in F. Koch, 1977, p. 5).

On ascending the throne Catherine declared that her chief task would be "to devote care and attention to the peace and prosperity of the Empire's wide expanses of territory, which God had entrusted to her, and to the increase of its inhabitants." An intelligent and clever woman, she mastered the Russian language and became devoted to Russia's growth and prosperity. A key element of her program involved the colonization of the fertile lower Volga region which for centuries had stood idle near the unstable Turkish border, virtually a happy hunting ground for adventurers, vagrants, bands of marauders and river pirates. Both the eastern plains side *(Wiesenseite)* of the lower Volga and the hilly western side (*Bergseite*) were inhabited by a variety of nomadic peoples of Turkic and Mongolian descent including the Tatars, Bashkirs, Kirghiz, and Kalmyks.

19

Since a prerequisite to the continuation of her ambitious policies was the cooperation of the Russian aristocracy, Catherine found it both unwise and impractical to suggest that the institution of serfdom be altered in order to provide the Russian peasantry with the opportunity to colonize the frontiers. While not only challenging the order of the nobility on whose support she depended, Catherine realized that the peasants themselves were incapable of effective colonization. Writing to the new commission investigating the subject Catherine wrote:

> Russia not only does not have enough inhabitants but it also has such vast expanses of land which are neither populated or cultivated. So enough incentive cannot be found for the state population to increase.... To restore an Empire, denuded of inhabitants, it is useless to expect help from the children who in the future may be born. Such a hope is in any case untimely; people living in these open spaces of theirs have no zeal or incentive. Fields which could feed a whole people hardly provide enough food for one household.... (K. Esselborn, 1926, p. 84).

The logical solution to the dilemma was to summon capable foreign colonists to Russia in order that they "might by their acquired arts, handicrafts, industry, and various machinery as yet unknown in Russia, reveal to Russian citizens the easiest and most efficient ways of tilling the ground, breeding domestic animals, nurturing forests, making the fullest use of all products, establishing their own factories, and regulating the entire peasant economy." This philosophy was a part of the eighteenth century. Central to this concept was that agriculture was the basic form of productive labor, and that only through its ties to trade and industry could the national wealth increase. This policy was in contrast to mercantilistic conceptions of economic growth dominant in Western Europe and pursued previously by the Empress Elisabeth who sought to extend the financial base of the economy by employing new methods of manufacturing, principally through the silk and fur industries.

However, Catherine did in part resurrect the framework of Elisabeth's earlier scheme to bring French Protestants into Russia as she was particularly impressed with the manner in which the French farmers had transformed the "marshy, sandy, and infertile domains of the King of Prussia" into a region of great productivity. In a decree written personally by the empress and delivered to the Russian Senate on October 14, 1762, Catherine ordered immediate cooperation with the Foreign Office to facilitate the entry of all foreigners wishing to enter Russia. Her manifesto of December 4, 1762 gave the program further impetus and more active measures were taken to inform European peoples of settlement opportunities in Russia as the senate was ordered to publish the manifest "in all languages and in all foreign newspapers." A decree on December 29 directed the Russian Foreign Office to distribute hundreds of copies of the manifesto in various languages to their diplomatic representa-

Along Midde Gaza

tives. Furthermore, the Russian ambassadors and representatives were ordered to "not only make known the manifesto by publishing it in the usual trade periodicals, but also to make every effort to see that it has an effect." The appeal brought little response.

The conflict on the continent brought on by the Seven Years' War had still not been resolved and the general feeling of the Russian diplomats was that Catherine's pledge of "imperial kindness and benevolence" in the manifesto was hardly sufficient to attract a significant number of colonists. Writing from London to his uncle the Russian chancellor, Count Vorontsov stated that, "A mere promise to accept those who apply will not attract a large number of settlers, for in that case they will be leaving a situation where they have some hope of security in order to enter a completely unknown situation." After considering these observations, the Foreign Office submitted a report to the Senate recommending payment for each settler's travel expenses since it was assumed it was largely the poor who desired to emigrate and asked for clarification of such issues as which areas would be open to foreign colonist settlement, what benefits and facilities would be available to them and how their transport would be arranged once in Russia. In addition the Senate was reminded of Elisabeth's earlier scheme negotiated with de la Fonte and these proposals were attached in order to help resolve the question (G. Pissarevskii, 1909, pp. 45-48).

The program may well have succumbed to the same fate as other long pending legislation in the bureaucratic committee of the senate had not Catherine personally intervened in the matter. At her insistence, a list of privileges and conditions were drafted under the supervision of the procurator-general, A. I. Glebov, to form the July 22, 1763 Manifesto of the Empress Catherine II. As the foundation of Russia's new colonization policy, it became the instrument through which thousands of impoverished Europeans, primarily Germans, were enabled to begin a new life in Russia between 1763 and 1766. Variously termed a "masterpiece of immigration propaganda" and the "Magna Carta" of the German colonists in Russia, the manifesto enumerated the conditions of settlement which included travel to Russia at crown expense, immunity from taxes, exemption from military service, and free land. An attached register of vacant lands specified a vast area up and down the Volga River from Saratov in the province of Astrakhan. It was to this region in particular that the colonists were directed.

In July of 1763, on the same day that the manifesto was promulgated, a second decree established a special government department to administer the anticipated flood of foreign settlement. The Chancery for the Guardianship of Foreigners (the "Tutel-Kanzlei") was responsible only to the empress and given far-reaching authority. As the equivalent of a government ministry, its central functions were to supervise the Russian representatives of the program throughout Europe and arrange for colonist transportation and payments. Headed by the appointed president who was a personal favorite of the empress, Count Gregory Orlov supervised operations in what was destined to become a ponderous bureaucracy which often led to disastrous incidents during settlement. With an enormous annual budget of 200,000 rubles, the Tutel-Kanzlei consisted of several counselors appointed by the president, a "special secretary with a knowledge of foreign languages" to adjudicate diplomatic problems, lesser bureaucrats, translators and, later, immigrant agents in Europe.

Despite the favorable intentions of the Russian diplomats in Europe, it became increasingly difficult to execute their normal responsibilities while directing immigration activities and in 1764 only about 400 families arrived in Russia, most from Westphalia with others from Scandinavia. Mismanagement was widespread as scores of disreputable individuals received financial support initially, only to refuse to emigrate at the appointed time. It also became evident that opposition to the program was widespread throughout Europe and only in England, Holland, and southwestern Germany did the activities of the recruiting agents initially meet little opposition. These areas of Germany were particularly receptive to Catherine's invitation, due to the religious conflicts, abject poverty caused by the wars, and the corrupt rule of the princes. Centers for departure to Russia during this early stage were established in Regensburg, Freiburg, Roslau, Worms, and elsewhere.

Due to the great response in the two Hessian states of Cassel and Darmstadt and in the Rhineland, it was decided to concentrate a major effort of the colonization campaign there under the authority of the Russian ambassador to the Reichstag at Regensburg, Johann Simolin. In an effort to alleviate the deceptive practices of some prospective emigrants, the program underwent two important revisions in Germany at Simolin's recommendation. Since previous experience demonstrated the difficulties of transportation and regular payment of expenses during overland treks to Russia, the payment was systematized by selecting Luebeck in December, 1763, as the central gathering and dispersal point to Russia. A reliable merchant there, Heinrich Schmidt, was appointed special commissioner in May, 1764 to supervise the operations. From there Hanseatic or English vessels shipped the emigrants to Kronstadt near St. Petersburg (G. Bauer, 1907, pp. 18-22).

The Tutel-Kanzlei also found it advisable to offer proprietorships to individuals capable of organizing scores of emigrants for settlement in Russia. Several French immigration recruiters responded, most of whom acted with numerous independent agents through unscrupulous tactics to entice people to emigrate. The fraudulent methods they utilized to fill various transport quotas led to their designation in such terms as *Menschenfanger* (people catchers) and *Seelenverkaufer* (soul sellers). While they succeeded in attracting thousands to Russia, their approach was condemned by Simolin whose more orderly program involved, as much as possible, the sanction of local authorities. As the combined effect of these efforts grew, particularly in Germany, the ruling families realized that their labor force and tax base was steadily eroding and responded with legislation restricting emigration. In 1764 action was taken in the German states of Bavaria, Saxony, Hamburg, and Wurzburg to forbid further emigration to Russia and in the following year Frederick II of Prussia followed by taking steps to remove the foreign agents from his county.

By 1766 it had become clear to Simolin and the various French recruiters that concentrated work in areas of southern Germany where the ruinous effects of the Seven Years' War were still widespread would be advantageous. Simolin was assisted in his endeavors by two German special commissioners, Friedrich Meixner in Ulm and Johann Facius, headquartered in Frankfurt a.m., beneath whom functioned a number of German agents at various assembly points. Facius' achievements in Hesse became particularly noteworthy to Simolin while at the same time attracting the suspicions of the local magistrates.

In a letter to the government of Hesse-Darmstadt on February 7, 1766, the Councellor-President of Mainz, Friedrich Karl Joseph von Erthal, wrote, "According to reliable reports, emissaries...are busily recruiting many of our country's subjects to go to foreign colonies. They are successful by picturing untrue advantages, in gaining large crowds of colonists...who soon go to ruin....Since, however, the country is in danger because of this disadvantageous depopulation, we deem it necessary for the preservation of our country's welfare...that the harmful recruiters be prevented from carrying out their intentions as soon as possible."

The Hessian government concurred in a letter of reply on February 24, 1766, adding that it would "instruct each and every official to meet this evil with great care and diligently further recruitment." Accordingly, edicts forbidding emigration and threatening emigrants with the expropriation of the possessions were issued in Mainz on February 18, by the Prince of Nassau-Weilburg on April 12, and by the Mayor and Council of the Free City of Frankfurt a.M. on April 21. Concerted action was taken similarly by the princes of the Lower Rhine and in the province of the Palatinate and on April 28 by the Landgrave of Hesse (H. P. Williams, 1975, pp. 79-80).

In such pronouncements the activities of the agents for settlement in Russia were variously labelled *das verderbliche Unheil* (the pernicious disaster), *enter Menschen Handel* (a slave trade), and a trade dealing with people *wie mit dem Viehe* (as though they were cattle). In some cases advocating the arrest and execution of the offenders, Simolin sought to arbitrate the matter through the proper diplomatic channels while suggesting to Facius in Frankfurt that he "quietly and well ahead of time" find a more secure place to reside in the area.

Various court-appointed investigators made journeys throughout Hesse to ascertain the nature of the problem, finding much of the citizenry still resolved to emigrate due to the pressing economic situation, particularly distressing conditions prevailing from the Odenwald to Vogelsberg areas. Official recommendations to eliminate servile tributes, establish food repositories, and reduce interest rates on loans were destined by government officials who chose to advocate a less costly and inadequate solution of "honest work and diligence."

After considerable effort following his expulsion from Frankfurt, Facius succeeded in relocating his operations to Buedingen, the capital of the small Duchy of Isenburg located northeast of Frankfurt a.M. near the hilly Vogelsberg area. In his relatively isolated area Facius received an overwhelming response at a time when a Hamburg official of the Tutel-Kanzlei ordered him to "halt the sending of more colonists for the year entirely." Simolin immediately filed a vehement objection to Catherine II herself upon learning of Facius' embarrassing position in Buedingen where scores of Germans were preparing to leave and were living in the city on crown subsidies. The entire issue of curtailing the program at this point was contrary to Similin's personal plans to establish a continuing ordered flow of European colonists to develop the Russian's vast agricultural and industrial potential. However, bureaucratic difficulties in the Tutel-Kanzlei with the settlement program for the vast empire were becoming increasingly apparent and heavy foreign diplomatic pressure was now being exerted in St. Petersburg.

Though Simolin's intervention allowed Facius to continue his operations in Isenburg throughout the summer of 1766, the Russian government arranged for the publication of a decree in German newspapers in September, 1766, warning that "in the year following 1766, settlers would no longer be accepted" and they were exhorted not to be deceived into "making agreements with persons independently assembling settlers." A dispatch the previous June received by Simolin from the Russian vice-chancellor, Nikita Panin, directed him to "limit himself to sending only the settlers who have already been accepted and who cannot be decently discharged" (G. Pissarevskii, 1909, pp. 220-22).

When promised a subsidy for the use of his capital as Facius' new *Sammelplatz* for organizing emigrant caravans, the Duke of Isenburg in Buedingen reciprocated by promising to "afford every assistance" to him. A guarantee was secured against what often resulted in inflated prices under such conditions for food, provisions, wood, straw, and other supplies. Simolin was soon reporting that "Commissioner Facius, having now changed his place of residence from Frankfurt to Buedingen, cannot find words to adequately praise the goodwill and friendliness which the ruling family there has shown, both to him personally and in the matter of the settlers, on the recommendation of my letter." He further stated that in order to "accommodate the colonists, he was given the use of the local town-hall and another large public building, and if they found these too crowded, he was allowed to quarter the settlers in the house of any citizen. Bakers, butchers, and brewers were ordered to provide sufficient edible provisions and to sell these for a fair price." The general public was ordered not "to lend anything to a settler, and if he did, no complaints would be dealt with." According to Simolin, the "ruling Duke of Isenburg-Buedingen himself made it clear to the commissioner that if he experienced any difficulties, he was to apply directly to him" (G. Pissarevskii, 1909, pp. 148-49).

Facius sent the first group of settlers from Buedingen to Luebeck between February 25 and March 6, 1766. The Germans moved overland through Schlitz, Cassel, and Hildesheim to the port city of Luebeck, a journey involving approximately 500 people per trek. As the party moved through these towns, it was not uncommon to attract the interest of others who joined the groups of immigrants bound for the Volga region. In Luebeck they boarded ships and began their long arduous journey to their new home in Russia. Once on Russian soil, the Germans acquired wagons which they loaded with their goods and their families. Thus, they began their movement through and lives in their adopted country of Russia. A typical column departing Buedingen in the summer of 1766 consisted of eighty families from some thirty-seven villages in Vogelsberg and neighboring areas who would ultimately found the Volga colony of Yagodnaya Polyana (Berry Meadow) the following year.

The 900 mile voyage from Germany to Russia could normally be made in nine days although events often prolonged it to weeks and in one instance to nearly three months. For the most part the delays were unavoidable due to inclement weather or unfavorable winds, but often ship captains wanted to wait and sell their provisions at inflated prices as supplies diminished. According to one German passenger, "The majority of us had never been upon a ship; it was hard for people to stand up because of the natural swaying of the boat. They tumbled against each other; fear and trembling mastered every mind; one cried, another swore, the majority prayed, yet in such a varied mixture that out of it all arose a strange and woeful cry." Reports on food and accommodations vary, some offering only praise for their treatment while others stated the only food available was salt, moldy bread, and water (C. Zuege, 1802, p. 49).

After arrival in Kronstadt, the Russian naval port on an island in the Gulf of Finland, the colonists were taken to the city of Oranienbaum (Lomonosov) on the mainland, the site of one of Catherine's royal residences. The German pastor of the Lutheran Church there would often lead them in the oath of allegiance to the Russian Crown. Catherine herself sometimes went there personally to welcome the colonists in their native tongue. Many of them had intended to pursue their trades near St. Petersburg but most were compelled by Guardianship Chancery officials to join the others in developing the agricultural districts on the lower Volga. The colonists often remained in Oranienbaum from two to six weeks while preparations were made for their trek to the Volga which could take place over various routes.

The route taken by the families that would establish Yagodnaya Polyana was entirely overland from Oranienbaum, the men on foot escorting wagons loaded with women, children, and provisions as they traveled southeast through Novgorod, Waldai, and Tver. The road then continued through Moscow, Ryazan, Pensa, and Petrovsk to the Saratov area. Guided by Russian officers, the caravans traveled deep into the interior on the primitive roads that became nearly impassable in the fall and spring while the heavy Russian snows prevented travel by both river and land during the harsh winter months. While the advertisements had indicated such an excursion from St. Petersburg to Saratov could be accomplished in two to three weeks by land or from five to six weeks *zu Wasser auf dem Wolga,* in actuality it often took from nine to eighteen months for the settlers to complete the entire trip.

During the coldest winter months the immigrants were quartered in the homes of Russian peasants in such villages as Torschok and Kostroma. Under such circumstances it became necessary for them to adapt to the peasant diet consisting largely of cabbage soup, millet porridge, and kvass. Great distances remained to be covered after travel recommenced in the spring and many colonists finally reached their destinations on the Volga too late to plant their crops and many were compelled to eat the seed grain to avoid starvation. The first contingent of German colonists arrived in the Volga settlement area to establish the village of Dobrinka, located near Kamyshin, on June 29, 1764. By the fall of the year additional expeditions founded Beideck, Shilling, Galka, and Anton. The steady stream of German settlers peaked in 1767 when sixty-eight colonies were founded including the village of Yagodnaya Polyana (G. Kromm, 1910, p. 2).

Immigrant Registers to Yagodnaya Polyana (1767) and Pobotschnaya (1772) by Georg Kromm (1912)

Family	Age	German Origin
1. Johann Reinhard Baum, widower,		
mayor	42	Lombach/Wurt
Children: Son: Hieronymus	16	Mohnbach
Daughter: Elisabeth Dorothea	18	Hanau/Frankfurt
2. Christoph Konschuh	29	Ortenberg
Wife: Katharina	30	
Son: Johann Daniel	3	
Foster son: Johann Peter		
Schneidmuller, son of deceased		
Johannes Schneidmuller	7	Simroth
3. Johann Heinrich Jungmann,		
widower, educated	56	Wallernhausen
Children: Son: Johann Heinrich	35	
Son: Johann Konrad	7	
Daughter: Elisabeth	10	
4. Johann Daniel Konschuh	25	Ortenburg
Wife: Dorothea		28
His father: Konrad Wilhelm		
Konschuh		60
5. Johann Benner	25	Lissburg (or
		Limburg)
Wife: Anna Katharina	25	
6. Johann Christoph Baer or Ber	48	Isenburg
Wife: Ana Katharina	48	

29

7. Johann George Repp	27	Schotten
Wife: Anna Dorothea	22	
Daughter: Katharina Marie	1 mo.	
8. Bernhard Stang	50	Wallernhausen
Son: Johann Heinrich	23	
9. Nikolaus Daubert	27	Nidda
Wife: Katharina Elisabeth	25	Glasshutten
Nephew: Adam Schneider	24	Ortenberg/Limburg
10. Konrad Assmus, widower	57	Wallernausen
Daughter: Anna Elisabeth	19	
11. Johann Kaspar Rausch	26	Ulrichstein
Wife: Anna Marie	25	Helpershain
12. Johann Peter Assmus	25	Wallernausen
Wife: Anna Elisabeth	23	
Maid: Helene Margaretha Muller	26	Nidda
13. Johann Peter Appel	50	Nidda
14. Johann Heinrich Appel	22	Nidda
Wife: Katharina	19	
15. Johann Adam Appel	43	Nidda
Wife: Anna Marie	22	
Son: Simon	11	
16. Daniel Fischer	26	Schotten or
Wife: Katharina	32	Eichelsachsen
Son: Johann Georg	6	
Son: Johann Adam	2	
17. Johann Heinrich Kles	48	Ulfa
Wife: Anna Gertrude	46	
Step Children:		
From first wife: Johannes Luft	20	Nidda
Anna Marie Luft	18	
From second wife: Johannes Koch	14	Nidda

18. Johannes Koch	25	Nidda or Feuerbach
Wife: Elisabeth	23	
Brother: Johann Peter Koch	23	
19. Johannes Weitz	39	Nidda or
Wife: Eva Katharina	30	Eichelsdorf
Son: Johann Heinrich	5	
20. Anna Margarethe Kromm, widow	42	Schotten
Son: Christian Kromm	20	
Son: Johann George Kromm	16	
Daughter: Katharina Kromm	12	
21. Johann Philipp Diesing	25	Schotten
Wife: Anna Marie	20	
22. Konrad Hofmann	31	Schotten
Wife: Christine Wilhelmine	32	
Daughter: Marie Katharina	2 1/2	
23. Johann Adam Schreiber	25	Schmalkaden
or Maiber		
Wife: Anna Katharina	60	
24. Konrad Beutel	29	Nidda/Wallernhausen
Wife: Elisabeth	25	
25. Johannes Beutel	22	Nidda/Wallernhausen
Wife: Anna Elisabeth	28	
26. Hartmann Scheuermann	48	Nidda
Wife: Elisabeth	40	Ober Lais
Son: Konrad	21	
Son: Johann Jost	18	
Son: Johann Heinrich	15	
Son: Hans Heinrich	12	
Son: Johann Heinrich	6	
Daughter: Elisabeth	8	
27. Wilhelm Leinweber	45	Kreuznach/Offenbach
Wife: Anna Margaretha	40	
Son: Ludwig	20	
Son: Wilhelm	18	
Son: Johann Peter	16	
Daughter: Anna Marillis	13	

28. Johann Seifeld or Seibel, widower 50   Schotten
    Son: Valentin   8
    Daughter: Anna Marie   20
    Daughter: Katharina   18

29. Johann Kaiser   40   Nidda/Burkhards
    Wife: Juliana   35
    Son: Johann Peter   14
    Daughter: Elisabeth   16
    Daughter: Katharina   8
    Daughter: Anna Elisabeth   5

30. Konrad Dippel   24   Schotten
    Wife: Anna Elisabeth

31. Philip Kromm   55   Schotten
    Wife: Anna Elisabeth   50
    Son: Konrad   16
    Daughter: Anna Marie   13

32. Konrad Wilhelm Hergert   25   Niederseemen
    Wife: Marie Elisabeth   25
    Daughter: Juliana   6 mos.
    His brother: Johann   8
    His sister: Anna Kunigunde   14

33. Johann Heinrich Kraft   32   Ristedt
        (moved to Straub)
    Wife: Eva Marie   35

34. Johann Peter Stuckart   38   Bobenhausen
    Wife: Anna Marie
    Stepdaughter from present wife
        from her first marriage:
    Anna Marie Kokon or Kochin   6

35. Johann George Ruhl   34   Nidda/Ober Lais
    Wife: Anna Elisabeth   39
    Son: Johann Heinrich   8

36. Matthaus Macheleit   37   Rudolstadt
    Wife: Anna Rosina   32
    Servant: Martin Ludwig   20

37. Johann Heinrich Schneider	43	Ortenberg
Wife: Susanna	50	
38. Johann Peter Schneidmueller	25	Simroth (Siemerode)
Wife: Anna Veronika	22	
39. Johannes Becher	20	Nidda
Wife: Katharina	20	
40. Johann Heinrich Volker	29	Erbach
Wife: Anna	27	
41. Andreas Pfaffenroth	31	Nidda/Berstadt
Wife: Anna Lisa	34	
Children from her first marriage:		
Son: Johann Konrad	8	
Daughter: Katharina	13	
Daughter: Anna Marie	11	
42. Michael Lahnert	23	Erbach
Wife: Juliana	22	
43. Konrad Kniss	22	Simroth (Siemerode)
Wife: Anna Elisabeth	18	
His brother: Nicolaus Kniss	19	
44. Johann Adam Hollstein	41	Erbach
Wife: Marie Barbara	27	
Son of First Wife: Johann Adam	12	
Daughter of First Wife:		
Anna Barbara	16	
" " " " Eva Marie	14	
" " " "		
Lisa Margarethe	9	
Son of second wife: Johannes	2	
45. Martin Schmidt	30	Ulmstadt
Wife: Anna Katharina	26	
Son: Heinrich Wilhelm	2 mos.	
46. Christoph Zurgiebel	25	Erbach
Wife: Grete Elisabeth	29	

The Village Spring

| 47. | Adam Blumenschein | 22 | Erbach |
| | Wife: Dorothea | 26 | |

48. Anna Margaretha,
      widow of Valentin Werth or Wirtz 30   Nidda

49.	Andreas Fischer	28	Nidda
	Wife: Anna Marie	22	
	Foster Children from deceased		
	Johann George Muller		
	Son: Johann Heinrich Mueller	14	Nidda
	Daughter: Anna Marie	10	Schwickartshausen

50.	Konrad Goerlitz	24	Nidda/Wallernhausen
	Wife: Anna Katharina	27	
	Son: Johann Heinrich	9 mos.	

51.	Johann Heinrich Beutel	26	Nidda
	Wife: Marie Elisabeth	22	
	Her father: Johann Heinrich Gorlitz	57	Wallernhausen

52.	Johann Konrad Ruhl	22	Nidda/Ober Lais
	Wife: Anna Elisabeth	30	
	Children from her first marriage:		
	Son: Johann Adam Befus	13	Sterndorf
	Son: Justin Befus	11	(Storndorf)??
	Daughter: Juliana Befus	16	Storndorf

53.	Johann Peter Ruhl	26	Nidda/Ober Lais
	Wife: Marie Margaretha	23	
	Son: Simon	4	
	Daughter: Eva Katharina	1 1/2	

| 54. | Johann Adam Feller | 30 | Nidda/ |
| | Wife: Anna Marie | 24 | Streithain |

55.	Anna Marie, widow of Johann		
	George Werz or Wurtz	39	Nidda
	Son: Johannes	14	
	Son: Johann Peter	11	
	Son: Johann Georg	6	

| 56. | Emilian Schuckart | 40 | Nidda/Atzenhain |
| | Wife: Elisabeth | 38 | |

Children from first wife:
Son: Konrad   19
Son: Johann Konrad   16
Son: Johann Martin   8
Daughter: Ana Lise   12
From her first marriage:
Daughter: Marie Magdalena   11

57. Johann Peter Lieder, single   30   Fulda

58. Nikolaus Gorr   23   Nidda/Lissberg
    Wife: Anna Margaretha   24

59. Sebastian Litzenberger   53   Offenbach
    Wife: Anna Lise   49
    Sons: Johann Philipp   18
          Johann Georg   11
    Daughter: Elisabeth 21

60. Simon Block   23   Nidda/Streithain
    Wife: Anna Juliana   38

62. Johann Konrad Mohr   28   Stolberg/Munzenberg
    Wife: Hanette Christine   23

63. Anna Marie Goetz, widow   Eichelsdorf/Nidda

64. Johannes Lautenschlager   27   Erbach
    Wife: Margarethe Elisabeth   28
    Son: Johann Nikolaus   1 1/2

65. Elisabeth Schaefer, widow of
        deceased Johann Georg Schafer   39   Kumbach
    Son: Johann Nikolaus Schafer   7
    Daughter: Elisabeth Schafer   1 1/2

66. Johann Georg Stapper   31   Hanau
    Wife: Anna Margarethe   19   Hollbach

67. Philipp Lust   41   Ulmstadt
    Wife: Susanna   43
    Sons: Johann Heinrich   18
          Johann Georg   12
          Johann Nikolaus   4

Daughters: Eva Marie	15	
Marie Katharina	9	
68. Johann Georg Morasch	25	Bruinberg or
Wife: Veronika	21	Breuberg
Daughter: Anna Margarethe	8 days	
69. Nikolaus Langlitz	34	Nidda/Eichelsdorf
Wife: Anna Margarethe	36	
Son: Johann Heinrich	6	
70. Johannes Goetz	35	Nidda
Wife: Anna Marie	46	
Son: Johann Peter	8	
Daughter: Anna Marie	4	
His father: Johann Konrad Goetz	64	
71. Nikolaus Goetz	26	Nidda/Eichelsdorf
Wife: Anna Marie	20	
72. Anna Marie Goetz, widow of		
deceased Johann Georg Goetz	55	Nidda/Eichelsdorf
Son: Johann Andreas	18	
Daughter: Anna Elisabeth	21	
Daughter: Anna Marie	16	
73. Johann Heinrich Goetz	28	Nidda/Eichelsdorf
Wife: Elisabeth	30	
74. Johannes Goetz	31	Nidda/Eichelsdorf
Wife: Katharina	38	
Daughter: Anna Barbara	6	
75. Johannes Mueller	30	Nidda/
Wife: Anna Margarethe	31	Schwickarschausen
76. Ludwig Dietz	57	Nidda/Eichelsdorf
Wife: Anna Elisabeth	48	
Son: Johann Christian	19	
77. Johann Konrad Schneider	44	Limburger/or
Wife: Anna Margarethe		Ortenberg
Son: Johann Christian		Schwickartshausen

78. Konrad Baer or Ber	48	Nidda/Rainrod
Wife: Anna Katharina	48	
79. Johann Heinrich Rohn	22	Nidda/Sellnrod
Wife: Anna Elisabeth	20	
80. Johann Schaefer	31	Nidda/Ober Lais
Wife: Anna Margarethe	25	
81. Children from deceased Nikolaus Fuchs		
Johann Nikolaus Fuchs	12	Mesen
Johan Philipp Fuchs	10	Mesen
Anna Eva Fuchs	17	Mesen
Marie Katharina Fuchs	5	

Each family received besides many other benefits, as living provisions, two horses, one cow and of hard money, fifteen rubles. So states one copied document of the early record books of Saratov. Yagodnaya Polyana was established on 16 September 1767 by 80 families of which 417 were male and 172 female, in total 269 souls. During the passage of 144 1/2 years in time and calculated to the present day, the colony Yagodnaya Polyana increased in population from 269 to some 16,134 souls which the following presentation reveals.

1. Yagodnaya Polyana 9061—souls in the present population figure.

2. Schonthal 3169—these migrated from Yagodnaya to the Province Samara.

3. New-Yagodnaya 2284—these resettled to here from Yagodnaya Polyana.

4. North America 1620—these emigrated from Yagodnaya to North America.

Total 16,134—This colossal figure would constitute a huge parish.

Stepnaya, Prov. Samara, Nowo Usensk District, 11/24 April 1912, School-master Georg Kromm.

In addition to the above stated listings of the 80 families, other families followed in later transports:

1. Arndt, from Klausthal at Hanover.
2. Barth, no place of origin listed.
3. Bolander, no record.
4. Bolinger, from the neighboring village, Neu Skatowka
5. Braeuning, from village Bomara, Lothringen (Lorraine), sent here 1812 Prisoner of War.
6. Brecht, village Redmur, Duchy Braunschweig (Brunswick) 1812 Prisoner of War.
7. Brunn, from Norka, 90 versts from here.
8. Diel, from Krasnojar on the *Wiesenseite* (none here, all emigrated to America.)
9. Geier, from Buedingen.
10. Gross, born on the transport enroute to Russia.
11. Hahnemann or Hannemann, from Schenkendorf, Saalfeld.
12. Helm, place of origin not listed.
13. Kaemmerer, from Ober-Ulm at Mainz, 1812 Prisoner of War.
14. Klevona, from Swedish Pomerania, the town of Truppen.
15. Kreibel, from Schwetzingen near Mannheim in Baden, he came here later.
16. Nebert, from Berlin.
17. Nagler, from the town Zeulenroda in the Earldom Reuss, came here later.
18. Nix, from Nidda.
19. Piek, from Allerbach at Birkenfeld in the Zweibrucken area.
20. Schaadt, from Ranstadt. Stollberg.
21. Schmuck, from Buedingen, Earldom Isenburg.
22. Schorschelius, no record of origin.
23. Schneider, Nidda and Hutten (Glasshutten?)
24. Schuhmacher, from Tomsk district at Langensalz near Hamburg.
25. Schweizer, from the Canton Aaran in Switzerland, 1812 sent here as Prisoner of War.
26. Schwindt, from Norka, 90 versts from here.
27. Streif, from Hollbach, Mosel District, Province Lorraine, 1812 Prisoner of War.
28. Walter, from Danram? (The place of origin poorly written, difficult to read.)
29. Weigandt, no record of origin listed.
30. Zentner, from the Canton Zug, Switzerland, came as Prisoner of War 1812.

The 1772 Immigrant Register to Pobotschnaya, Russia, from Germany
(from the Russian State Archive of Ancient Acts, Moscow)

Family	Age

1. Johann Schaefer
   Wife: Anna Wilhelmina

2. Joachim Christian Wittig
   Wife: Eva Maria [Oshewald]
   Daughters: Maria   3 1/2
            Juliana   3/4

3. Samuel Schneider
   Wife: Maria Katerina Kalkoph
   Sons: Johann Paul   8
         Johann   6

4. Johann Heinrich Wagner
   Wife: Maria Katerina
   [Gerkhered]

5. Johann Phillip Brach
   Wife: Anna Maria Neidling
   Son: Johann Heinrich   11
   Daughter: Christina   9

6. Georg Ernst Schneider
   Wife: Anna Maria Schneider
   Sons: Jost Heinrich   8
         Wilhelm   6

7. Georg Schneider
   Wife: Susannah Gerhart

8. Johann Peter Schneider
   Wife: Gertrude Gerlach

9. Johann Kaspar Schumacher
   Wife: Anna Elizabetha Schukart
   Daughter: Anna Elizabetha   6 mo.

10. Johann Peter Thiel
    Wife: Anna Katerina [Popp]
    Daughter: Anna Gertrude   3
    Wife's sister: Anna
    Margaretha [Popp]   20

11. Samuel Rothe
    Wife: Johanna [Welle?]
    Sons: Johann Georg   16
          Johann   14
          Jacob   12 1/2
          Konrad   7
    Daughter: Katerina   20

12. Johann Heinrich Schmit
    Wife: Anna Katerina
        [Simmel?]
    Daughter: Anna Katerina   6

13. Johann [Knak?]
    Wife: Magdalena Sietz
    Sons: Johann Friedrich   4 1/4
          Johann   2 1/4

14. Anton Wagner

15. Franz Schlegel, Sr.
    Wife: Anna Dorothea Keller
    Sons: Johann   23
          Friedrich   21
          Konrad   15
          Johann Georg   11
    Daughters: Anna Maria   11 1/4
           Elizabetha   10
           Katarina   6

16. Franz Schlegel, Jr.
    Wife: Juliana [Laib?]
    Son: Konrad   5
    Daughters: Anna Margareta   6 1/2
           Anna Maria   1

17. Heinrich Schneider
    Wife: Susann [Evgel?]
    Sons: Johann Heinrich   27
          Georg Heinrich   20
    Daughters: Elizabetha   25
               Anna Margareta   22

18. Johann Nikolaus [Lahm?]
    Wife: Anna Katherina Schneider

19. Peter Winsel
    Wife: Anna Maria
          [Vengertner]
    Son: Johann Konrad   10
    Daughter: Anna Elizabetha   4

20. Johann Heinrich [Strub?]
    Wife: Katerina Elizabetha
          [Winsel]
    Son: Heinrich Phillip   7
    Daughters: Susanna Maria   10 1/4
               Maria Elizabetha   1 3/4
    Her father: Konrad Winsel

21. Ernst [Apel?]
    Wife: Katerina Helmut
    Sons: Ernst Heinrich   3
          Johann Heinrich   3/4
    Her sister: Elizabeth Helmut

22. Johann Heinrich Wagner

23. Phillip Kromm

24. Johann Heinrich [Popp?]

25. Johann Georg Ott

26. Johann Heinrich Keller
    Wife: Anna Katerina [Emrich]
    Son: Hohann Georg   1 1/2
    Daughter: Anna Katerina   4

27. Georg Christof Stein

42

28. David Heinrich [Niesper?]

29. Christof Falk
30. Wilhelmina [Dilman?], maiden
    Sister: Rozina   35

31. Peter Wilhelm
    Wife: Margareta [Zavina]

Sons:	Johann Georg	20
	Johann Konrad	16
	Johannes	13
	Andreas	12
	Phillip	6
	Peter	3
Daughter:	Anna Eleonora	18

32. Karl Miller

VOLGA BERGSEITE AND JERUSLAN: THE RUSSIAN EXPERIENCE

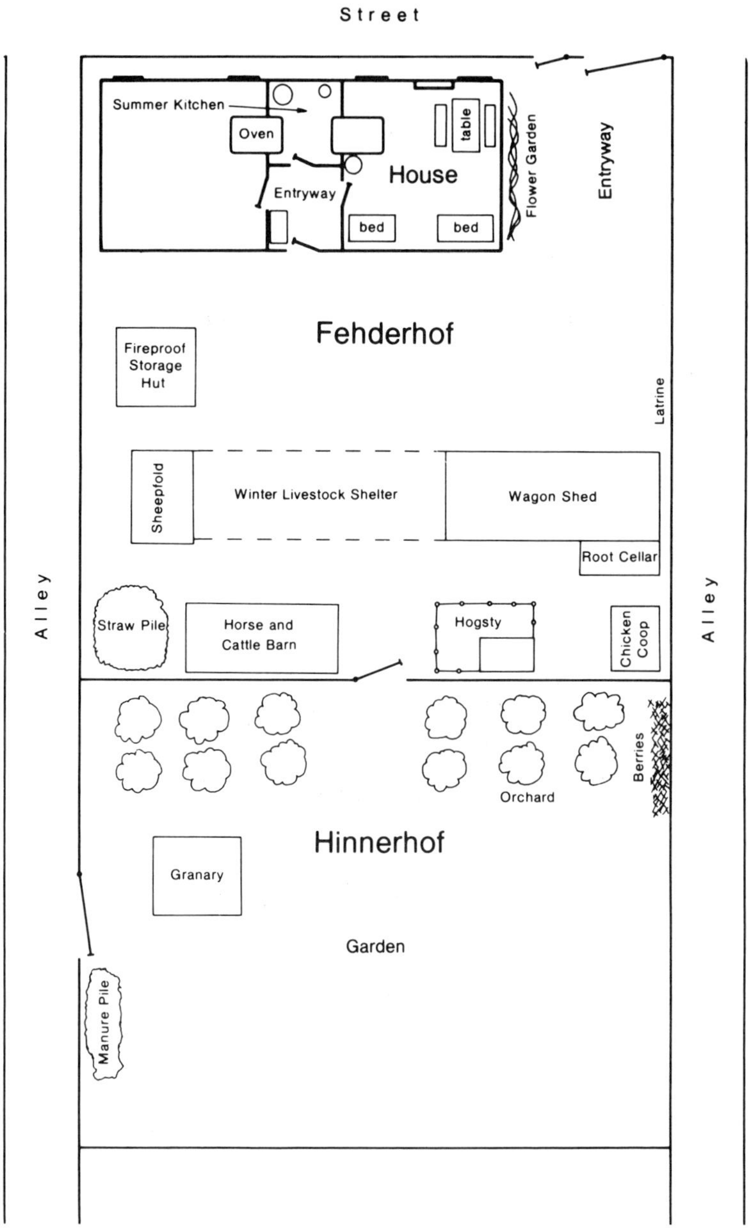

Street

Summer Kitchen

Oven

Entryway

House

table

Flower Garden

Entryway

bed

bed

Fehderhof

Fireproof
Storage
Hut

Latrine

Sheepfold

Winter Livestock Shelter

Wagon Shed

Root Cellar

Alley

Alley

Straw Pile

Horse and
Cattle Barn

Hogsty

Chicken
Coop

Berries

Orchard

Hinnerhof

Granary

Garden

Manure Pile

Volga German Farmyard

An Inspection of the Colony Yagodnaya Polyana
by G. Popov (1798)

The colony of Yagodnaya Polyana (Berry Glade) is populated by foreigners who were chosen in accordance with the opinion of the representatives of the government, the landowners, and the prominent people (of Russia).

This settlement is located sixty versts (thirty-nine miles) from the district city of Saratov, and five versts from the Big Moscow Road and the Chardym River. The greater part borders the lands of Artillery Captain Abrazantsov and the lands of the late Prince Alexander Alexeevich Vyazemsky, who was the Real Secret Chancellor and Bearer. Those lands belonged to the government. By the offer of General Lieutenant and the Bearer Potemkin, who was the governor of the Saratov Province, these lands were given to Abrazantsov and Vyazemsky. Part of their lands was marked off as a payment in quick treasure by the Saratov Treasury Chamber. This settlement land also included the County Peschancky, the Ukranian County (Sokura's lands), Russian County (Ozerka's lands), and the lands of settlement Pobotschnaya.

Inhabitants of this settlement live here because of prescriptions mentioned above. Their number equals to 412 males, 410 females, 822 in total, which consists of 97 families. They have a church, which was built recently, where they have two meetings every Sunday. The people do not have their own pastor, so at the present time their needs are fulfilled by inviting pastors from other Lutheran parishes. The closet parish to this settlement is located over 100 versts away. They cannot have their own pastor because they cannot afford one. And in this particular settlement we can find only Lutherans.

They have chosen the person who teachers their young children about reading, writing, and the law. They have established a special school only for that purpose. This settlement divides land into 2160 dessiatines [1 dessiatine = 2.7 acres] of convenient productive lands; 464 dessiatines meadow lands; 1947 dessiatines of wood; which equals a total of 4571 dessiatines. An additional 188 dessiatines of productive land and 70 dessiatines meadow-land have been taken as a loan for period of ten years. Those lands are located five versts from the place of their settlement. The lands are included in the articles by Saratov's Treasury Chamber in 787. Inhabitants till the soil on 1000 dessiatines. Their farmsteads contain 100 dessiatines and 30 dessiatines under the roads.

The rest of the land is not convenient because of its quality. Those circumstances lead to decreasing rent amounts and productive lands. Cattle and other grazing animals pasture themselves in this area. They do not have any special lands for the pasturing of horses, so they are renting some lands in the neighboring Ozerka's country. According to them, they have 300 dessiatines of grasslands. This is not enough to feed the cattle. All those shortages of land could be compensated by giving to them Captain Abrazantsov's lands and government lands of the Counties Peschchanky and Ozerka. Then it would be enough for them to live on. Those shortages could not be fixed any other way because the inhabitants need 3669 dessiatines of land, the counties of Ozerka's and Peschchanky are only 600 dessiatines of land, which are not sufficient for them. In the new location there are plenty of woods. All of the inhabitants live in average conditions. They have houses which are built from their own woodlands. It is not possible to say that the houses are good, nevertheless they are fairly good. But it seems that they do not last for a long period of time because of the quality of the wood. The trees are thin and not appropriate for building houses. There are not any houses built from stone or mud.

There are not enough stones which are appropriate for building. The farms consists of cottages with passages [doors], granaries, stables and fenced houses. There are vegetable gardens behind the farmsteads and by the Chardym River. The local inhabitants do not have any orchards. Many of them have bee-gardens. They also have two public mills. The mills thrash the grain which belongs to the people from this settlement and the neighboring counties. Productive land has been divided on three fields for over twenty years because it is the only way of using it. People plow the land above the required quantity of dessiatines, therefore they have enough land for the new settlements. One part of productive land lies close to the settlement, but the rest of it is in the distance of six versts away from the settlement.

Most of the time inhabitants sow rye and oats because the harvest of those cereal crops is the best. There is also plenty in the harvest of millet and peas but the people sow little of it because they do not have much of the productive land. Other kinds of cereal crops are absent. The above specified harvests are put into stacks, like the Russian farmers do. After the field work is done, they take the harvest to the neighboring threshing-floors where they are ground by the use of chains. There is a very good public grocery store which was built at a convenient place. The harvest is collected from the year of 1783 to 1794 because of the order of the Expedition Director of the Saratov Treasury Chamber. All the collected harvest was sold for the purpose of building the Church. It was done because of the local inhabitants' request and the Expedition's order. After that event the Expedition does not have any more information about the quantity of the collected harvest. At the present time the government representative has to do the registration of all the collected harvest. This kind of information has to be written down in the notebook continuously.

The people work diligently and they do not have any shortages of stock. They earn their living only by agriculture and raising the cattle. There are only three people capable of doing handicrafts. Two of them are shoemakers and the other one is a blacksmith. The people are selling bread and other surplus to Saratov. The prices differ because of the seasonal markets during the year. During the present summer they sold rye flour for 32 and 33 kopecks, flour for 50 and 55 kopecks per pood, oats for 30 and 50 kopecks, millet for 2 rubles, peas for 3 rubles, potatoes for 1 ruble and 60 kopecks or 2 rubles and 25 kopecks.

Attested the signature of the government representative and the society, written by the court's adviser, Popov.

The Village of Yagodnaya Polyana, Saratov District
by G. Gonyaskinsky (1894)

The village of Yagodnaya Polyana numbers about 8000 Germans of both sexes. It lies about sixty versts (40 miles) from Saratov and thirty-five versts (23 miles) from the nearest railway station. It is spread out with streets laid out exactly and equally on the slope of a mountain, at the foot of which flows the small Chardym River with many small mills, located here and there. On the other side of the river a row of mountains also rises up. Encircled by mountains and overgrown with forest it is not called Yagodnaya Polyana (Berry Meadow) for nothing, for in the glades of its forests in the summertime are many berries: garden strawberries, wild strawberries, cranberries, raspberries, cherries, boneberries and also many mushrooms: white, brown, butter mushrooms, field mushrooms, nightshade mushrooms, and honey meadow mushrooms (agaric) which the Germans do not make use of in food, and so leave their growth to the mercy of fate.

With its outward appearance of regular, evenly spaced buildings—a considerable number with sheetmetal roofs—and its inner life which preserves "Old Holy German" traditions, Yagodnaya Polyana seems to be a typical German town without the addition of anything Russian. It, as if hiding in the mountains from the rest of the world, lives its own characteristically casual life. The well-established life is incredible. Spending a day in one family is the same as in all 1000. The day begins with the sound of the church bell. Everybody from little to big prays and asks God to bless him and his things. After that everybody starts to work, the host with his routine chores of the farm code of life, the hostess firing up the specially built stove. The winter stove is attached in a special manner to the front side. The fireplace is located in the middle secondary living room; a stone stove with a boiler juts out into the living room, because it transmits the heat better. The food is prepared in the same room where the heat is produced, that is, from the cold pantry. The stove heats without a ventilation pipe. Smoke comes back from out of the stoking hole to the roof where there is a large opening built for its escape. The stove is lit twice a day for the preparation of food, lime leaf tea with sausage and bread. This stove is adapted just to this type of food which the Russians are accustomed to: pancakes, fried potatoes, cabbage soup without anything added, and potato pancakes, and so forth. In general, the type of food is only tasty in its fresh form. A woman who is unaccustomed to this sort of stove could not get used to it, since she would have to bend down into a doubled-up position, because the stoking hole is built just a little higher than the floor.

In the winter it is terribly cold in this house, and from the fire there is intense heat. One can only be amazed at the skill and endurance of the hostesses of Yagodnaya Polyana. With such an arrangement, the winter kitchens are separated from the living quarters, and this is why there is never any carbon monoxide poisoning or intoxication of fumes. The summer kitchen built primarily from the [half-timbers] and coated with clay and adobe most resembles the construction of Russian buildings which are located in a different area. This is done as a preventative measure against fires, and this is why the latter are rare in these colonies. This is also done for the comfort of the dwelling houses. In general, the Germans can boast to the Russians about the comfort of their domestic life. The floor is wooden and clean, usually scrubbed and washed. It is warm in the hut, but free from fumes. In the summer it is cool because the shutters are closed; that is why there are no flies in the room. Due to the cleanliness and neatness of the hostesses, there are neither bedbugs nor cockroaches.

The awakening of outdoor life is the same day after day. It begins with the incessant thunder of barrels on their journey from one spring to another for water. The German women all dress alike in their striped woolen skirts, black kerchiefs, short quilted jackets, and handmade shoes. With a quick and cheerful step, all are headed there with their buckets. Students with bags on their shoulders go to Russian and German schools. The clamor of public life is noticeable only in the morning. Then a quietness ensues which is only disturbed by the ringing of church bells announcing either a death or the movement of a funeral procession. Thus a working day for the inhabitants of Yagodnaya Polyana passes and ends again with the appeal summoning prayers of thanksgiving for all the generosity which God has sent down.

Yagodnaya Polyana in comparison with other villages has a considerable income, from eight to ten thousand rubles a year from the mills, and the taverns and so on. The village has a volost [district administrative office], a village governmental office, two schools, a church, a pastor, a postal station, a medical station, a bazaar, and several shops. The bazaar and shops are distinguished by an exceptional characteristic particular to the Germans, that is, to not have more than necessary. They have primarily only those goods which the Germans use: tea, sugar, matches, tobacco, pretzels, various snacks, textiles, leather, nails, and so forth. There are no perishable groceries, neither are they mentioned nor talked about. The shops do not have the decorated appearance on the outside which the Russian shops do. The goods are located in a dimly lit room and in the shops there are far fewer goods than there are in the general stock, so you will not find any external appeal here at all. The people buy and sell at fixed prices without the Russian type of bargaining. There is nothing of the nasty practice of asking as much as you can, that is of bargaining which is in the Russian village.

Everything here in the private life as well as in public life is measured, calculated, and totally excludes the Russian concept of chance. Life proceeds with a rational, well-thought-out step. Life is looked at seriously, as in the partaking of a sacrament, and the people could not even imagine life as a toy, or that they could give it up for a penny. Life consists of the fulfillment of only the most vital, rational necessities, that is, not be indebted one to another, to be fed, clothed and shod, to live in cleanliness, and to be thankful only to one God for everything. This is done by offering Him prayers daily at home and in church on the holidays. There are no heated arguments, no Russian boldness; even the weddings proceed primarily with the feasting of guest and with dances which resemble the quadrille and polka combined. The only impetuous part of this important event in a family is a ride in the troika in the cold frost with a bride dressed in summer garb and nothing on her head except flowers. (Weddings occur only in the winter after the new year.) Although they drink vodka at weddings, no drunk is ever on the streets. This breach of manners is frowned upon by public opinion and on the street a drunk is an abnormal occurrence in Yagodnaya. A German, if he feels he has had a little too much to drink, tries to become sober and not to get terribly drunk. That is why here there are no fatal incidents from vodka. Also it is not the German custom to have choral singing on the street.

In the winter the youth amuse themselves by gathering in a hut and in turn dancing to the music of self-taught musicians. The instruments they use are the violin, cymbals, and the accordian. The youth divide into two groups; the younger dance and sing to the music and the more adult group gather separately. Here the girls sit weaving, and the fellows usually disturb them, which presents general merriment, accompanying laughter, witticism and jokes. Usually these parties which start in the autumn have the result of the fellows dressing as grooms, their peaked caps decorated with peacock feathers and beads, and the brides with flowers on their heads and accompanying bouquets on their breasts. The groom goes to the church with young girls and the bride with young boys, and their happy married life and then their healthy life flows just as it did with their ancestors. The woman in the family is trusted and treasured. Neither she nor her mother-in-law is forced to overwork. After giving birth, every German woman has the rights of a patient. She lies in bed for nine days. Her close relatives take constant care of her. Up until six weeks she is forbidden to do any kind of heavy housework. Because of this the German women are healthy and cheerful at forty and fifty years of age. How could one not be healthy when life is lived properly, the climatic conditions are wonderful, the air is clean, and the water is from springs. One could not wish for anything better.

By the way, about the springs: located in the mountains, Yagodnaya Polyana abounds with springs. What is remarkable about the arrangement of Yagodnaya Polyana is its two springs. The first is located in the center of Yagodnaya Polyana. The other is on the edge of Yagodnaya Polyana. The first

Traditional Window Casework

is located on a square, not far from the church, the volost office, the village office, the school, the bazaar, and the post office. On the slope of the square under a steep cliff and in a deep basin, like in a pressure point, the springs gush out. For the collection of water from them, there is built a wooden reservoir which is covered from above with a wooden lid. When the water rises to the level of three openings in the reservoir, it flows along small troughs from which water is taken for drinking. For the horses and cattle, wooden boxes are built which are always full of water. For washing clothes, the water comes from other springs. Washing is located across the boxes for the cattle, with shallow basins divided into several squares. The constant change of water does not allow dirt to linger in the wash. Thus men use the very best cleanest water, the cattle after that, then for dirty uses, special springs are set apart.

It would be difficult to invent anything smarter than what the inhabitants of Yagodnaya Polyana have done. Thus during a cholera epidemic the inhabitants of Yagodnaya Polyana did not have to search for clean water, because it is difficult to find cleaner water than that which comes from mountain springs, in which not a single speck of dust is fallen. In addition, no season of the year, neither the hot summer nor the dirty spring nor fall, nor the frost of winter produces a change, either in the composition of the water or in the quantity. In general, the inhabitants of Yagodnaya Polyana in their ability to organize their life in a humane way can serve only as a good example to be followed by others.

The German Settlers on the Volga
by Georg Kromm (1910)

As is commonly known, less than two centuries ago, during the middle 1760s, many families from Schotten and its vicinity followed the manifesto of the Russian Empress Catherine II, and settled along the banks of the Volga River because they had found themselves in poverty and misery due to war and various types of suppression. A descendant of one of these families, consisting of a widow and two children who were probably also quite oppressed, namely the teacher George Kromm in Yagodnaya (which means "strawberry-meadow" in [Russian]), described conditions in Germany and in particular the situation of early settlers as well as his own, who came from the vicinity of Schotten, in a detailed and very interesting report covering thirty-six closely written pages. Excerpts from this report follow. Last year his son visited the homeland of his ancestors as a participant in a Protestant Mission School held in Mitzehnhausen. Perhaps these excerpts will provide clues to some families from Oberhessen as to the discovery of living relatives among the settlers on the Volga.

Catherine II's first manifesto was issued December 4, 1762, but was unsuccessful in attracting colonists because it did not contain special privileges attractive to immigrants. However, her second manifesto issued July 22, 1763, contained many such benevolent privileges and attracted thousands of immigrants, happy to leave their German homeland, for the distant lands of Russia. The conditions contained in this manifesto were, in short, as follows: That every foreigner willing to leave his country to move to Russia and settle there in uninhabited territories would be welcomed with joy. In addition, important privileges, advantages and financial support were offered to the prospective settlers. The Russian government promised the immigrants the necessary funds to cover their travel and food from the time of their departure to the day of arrival at their destination, in order to give even the poorest and most miserable the opportunity to find refuge in Russia.

The second manifesto, dated July 22, 1763, was effective especially in Germany where vast regions had been devastated by the Seven Years' War and fires that accompanied it. More than 800,000 soldiers had given their lives for absolutely nothing. It had plunged the nations of Europe into tremendous misery and deprived the people of shelter. There was no shortage of poor and unhappy people of all classes, and they could lose nothing by emigrating, but only gain by it.

Catherine's manifesto could not have been released at a more appropriate time. Hosts of volunteers from Wuerttemberg, Prussia, Baden, Hessen-

Darmstadt, Saxony, Bavaria, Mecklenburg, even from Switzerland, the Netherlands and France gathered around the Russian commisars in order to be led to a new homeland. Roslau on the Elbe River was designated as the best place to meet. The first emigrants arrived in this town on April 8, 1766. From here they were transported to the harbor of Luebeck on big ships and landed, after a happy voyage of nine days on the Baltic Sea, in the Port of Kronstadt, not far from St. Petersburg. Another group was not so fortunate. They reached the shores of Russia only after a very cumbersome and dangerous voyage of three months. One ship was lost during this voyage, but all the passengers were rescued. The sufferings the emigrants on this transport had to endure supposedly was indescribable. Due to the total lack of medical help and medication, many of the emigrants died on the high seas and their bodies were buried at sea.

Arriving in Russia, the colonists were taken to Oranienbaum, today a county seat, on the Gulf of Finland. Catherine II was then residing there in her country palace. She personally and graciously received the immigrants and assured them of her protection and continuing care and affection. In Oranienbaum, the immigrants were split up into three groups, each group set out for the trip to Saratov, their destination. One group went by the direct route via Novgorod, Tver, Moscow, Ryasan and Pensa to the county seat of Petrovsk. There they were camped during the winter. Another group went via the water route on the Neva, Lake Ladoga, and then to the tributaries that led to the Volga. Many of them, however, had stopped in Torzhok and Tver to spend the winter, while others got as far as Kostroma on barges. The third group finally stayed in Kolomna and, in the spring, continued their trip on the Oka and Volga Rivers to Saratov.

On June 24, St. John the Baptist's Day, the first immigrants arrived on the spot where Katharinenstadt stands today. They found nothing but sky and steppes, trees and water. Yet they immediately began to work erecting mud huts and tents which, for the time being, seemed necessary. They began to build their little houses on grounds that appeared especially favorable, some in Katharinenstadt proper (which, of course, was named after the great Empress Catherine II), and some in the regions adjacent to it. The others who had arrived at the same time, continued down the Volga to Saratov, where the government agents directed them, and founded their colonies on the hilly side and in the valley.

Besides Katharinenstadt and other colonies, the following were founded during the same year in the valley: Podstepnaja, Rosenheim, Volskaya (Kukkus), Privalnaya (Warenburg); on the west side of the Volga there were Talowka (Beideck), Sosnowka (Schilling) Norka, Ustkulalinka (Galka), Golobowka (Doennhof), and sixty verst north-west of Saratov, Yagodnaya Polyana was established. Somewhat later on, in 1772, the colony of Pobotschnaya was founded seven verst south of Yagodnaya Polyana, in 1802, the colony Neu-Skatowka (Neu-Straub) was established. These colonists had come over from Alt-Straub in the valley. Neu Straub was a daughter colony. Now these three colonies formed a parish. The last mentioned colony lies twelve miles south of Yagodnaya Polyana.

In 1768 the last colonists came to the Volga region and established colonies so there were now one hundred and two colonies on both sides of the Volga. They had a population of eight hundred families consisting of about 27,000 persons of both sexes. The call for settlers and the establishment of the colonies cost the Crown 5,199,813 rubles and 23 kopecks. It cost the Crown 1,025,402 rubles and 97 1/2 kopecks for the erection of houses and churches; 17,914 rubles and 25 kopecks were spent for medical help given to the sick. The government allowed 136,470 rubles 23 and 3/4 kopecks for families, who during the first years, were taken prisoners by the Kirghiz.

During the journey by water as well as on land, each colonist received subsistence pay or allowances promptly, which were sufficient to purchase the necessary food. The Crown also helped the colonists with their farming needs. Each family received two Kalmyk horses, one cow, one Russian plow, a harrow, an ax, a spade, a drill and an ordinary Russian farm wagon, which was designed to be pulled by one horse. The Crown was also willing to lend money to the colonists for purposes of buying seeds. There were all sorts of craftsmen, businessmen, artists, scientists, persons of status, and even a Count Doennhof from Berlin among the first settlers. Count Doennhof had been in the colony Doennhof, which was named after him. Count Doennhof was the first of the colonists who understood the Russian language fairly well. People still talk about a very capable Pastor Doennhof in Doennhof, who was perhaps a descendant of the count. Pastor Doennhof died about 1864. Less than half of the immigrants were farmers. They had to become the teachers in the new homeland. One has to admit that most of the immigrants were poor, many completely without means. However, there were a few who did have money when they arrived in Russia, and others later on came into considerable inheritances from foreign countries.

Since my oldest son Theophil Kromm sent the *Story of the German Settlers on the Volga from the Time of Their Immigration to Russia to the Introduction of Compulsory Military Service* (1766-1874), written by Gottlieb Bauer, to our dear relative Mr. Heinrich Arcularius in Schotten, I shall limit myself to the relevant data from Yagodnaya Polyana and its environment, as well as to our dear esteemed kinfolk in Schotten and vicinity. Many of our people here, in any event, did not originate from Schotten proper, as I had thought previously, but most came from the area of Nidda and the vicinity of Schotten, i.e., the Hessen-Darmstadt area. There is a family register of all families living here, which I will append to this genealogy, and this should clarify it. I will also include in this genealogy our relatives in Jeruslan, Government of Samara, as well as our relatives in North America, although not all of this information may belong here.

Evidently our Yagodnaya Polyana kin traveled with the first group of settlers via the direct route via Novgorod, Tver, Moscow, Ryasan and Pensa to the county seat Petrovsk, named after Peter the Great, where they spent the winter. Yet, this does not mean that they stayed in Petrovsk proper; they could have spent the winter in any of the above mentioned villages. In fact, one can assume that they stayed in one of the villages farther north since they arrived here in Yagodnaya Polyana only on August 28, 1767. Petrovsk is situated only forty verst north of here. Also traveling at that time was very slow, step by step, or pace by pace. They should have been able to make the trip in one day.

There is a good, wide road from Moscow to Pensa, Petrovsk and on to Saratov. Upon leaving Petrovsk, once they reached the village of Ozerki on this particular route, which is only seven verst from here, they should have arrived within three to four hours. Most likely the virgin forest here was an unsurmountable obstacle. Therefore, they had to continue on a road leading south until they reached the treeless steppes covered with grass, where they had to turn north to get here. There were roads leading in this direction. Following the main road, they arrived approximately two to three verst south of here in a beautiful, wide canyon, surrounded by forest, where there was also a well-traveled road. They rested at one of the springs in this canyon. Although the spring water was fresh and clear, they did not consider staying here. The group consisted of eighty families and they feared the spring would not supply enough water for all of them. Therefore, they decided to look for a better and larger water source and a better place, if one could be found. Some of the brave men, armed with weapons, went north exploring. After they had walked two or three verst, they heard roaring water, like a huge waterfall, in another, almost impenetrable canyon. The men worked their way through the wilderness, overcame innumerable obstacles, until they reached their goal. It was no small matter to undertake this venture as they could have been attacked by wild animals or robbers. However, all their anxieties disappeared when they discovered this huge spring and many smaller ones around it. They decided to establish their colony on this ground.

A few years later a grist mill was established. It was a two-gear mill, but as the years went by, it was torn down because the spring gave up less and less water. The millers had used larger and larger water wheels which caused the water level to rise over a period of sixty years by at least two fathoms, so that the water became muddy. Three years ago the well was repaired; modern means were used, which means a lot of cement was used. The total cost came to about 3,000 rubles. In olden times, this spring was in the midst of a virgin forest, but even in later years trees till surrounded it, as well as shrubbery and underbrush. I still remember that our own farm was full of tree stumps which had remained from the wilderness. It must have been difficult for our ancestors in the beginning, because they were exposed to robber bands and wild animals. All of our people are on friendly terms with the other colonists, as though we were one big family. There are already a few mixed marriages. However, these mixed marriages are among families who have not been living here for years.

August 28, 1909, was the 142nd anniversary of the founding of Yagodnaya Polyana. August 28, even to this day, is called "Arrival Day." For many years this day was celebrated with a church ceremony. Eventually, this was discontinued, but the day is still looked upon as a holiday. I remember from my boyhood that, although no church services were held, no work was performed on "Arrival Day."

The climate during the summer is very healthy, so many people who become ill during winter recover quickly during summer. During the past few years many people have moved away to Siberia. They are still moving there now, especially to the regions of Omsk and Akmolinsk. In fact, several hundred families moved away. Some have returned because they did not like it there, mainly due to the complete lack of spring water. They also missed other conveniences available here in abundance. It seems that the desire to move and to emigrate to other countries and regions is contagious, like a fever—the moving and emigration fever. During these periods people foolishly emigrate without thinking and every piece of well-intended advice is being ignored. They rush blindly and with great haste to their doom.

On August 5, 1774, our people were attacked by the horrible Pugachev and his robber gang who came through our colony on their way from Petrovsk to Saratov. He committed no special crimes, except that he took three of our men with him. It was said that they were later whipped to death. One still shows the mountain and gorge where he camped. It is also said that the rebel Pugachev pillaged the German colonies along the Volga, on the hilly side (west of the Volga) as well as those in the valley, east of the river, between August 9th and 13th, 1774. He supposedly had a great resemblance to Peter III, whom he claimed to be. In 1830, the last bear was killed by colonist Johannes Koch. A deep gorge with manifold rock formations is still called "Bear Gorge." Fossilized bones and deer antlers were found there.

The first church was built in 1783. I still well remember this church. It could have stood for many more years as the wood was good and hard, but it became too small and had to be torn down because it did not provide enough space. In 1857, the second church, which is much too small now and has been for some time, was built. An organ with eight registers and an organ stop was put in the church in 1873. No one knows when the first parsonage was built; probably in 1804, because from that time on the parish had its own pastor, namely Rambach, who served from 1804 until 1820. During prior years, from 1767-1804, the parishes were served by various vicars. The present parsonage seems to be the third one. A previous one burned down, and probably our oldest books and records were destroyed in this fire as the oldest and most important documents are missing. This parsonage also had a fire on May 23, 1873; yet the frame of the building remained fairly well-preserved so that the parish decided to rebuild it from the old, half-charred structure. To make it especially strong, they decided to cover the outside walls with slate. Unfortunately, it turned out that this was not a good idea. The repair costs were higher;

there always seems to be something wrong with it; and even now there is needed repair costing several hundred rubles. This parsonage was rebuilt in 1874. Many important books and documents of later years were probably destroyed in the second fire, as they also are missing. The parish of Yagodnaya Polyana, with the exception of two vicars, had the following pastors: Rambach, Hermann, Allendorf, Flittner, Hellmann, David, Holm, Hegele, Deirne, Kahn, Schilling, Coulin, and Woikus. Between each pastor there was a temporary vicar. The last two pastors had also been vicars, but were later elected and confirmed as pastors.

The first local government buildings were erected in 1869. Previously the best buildings in the colony had been rented for the officials. I am not certain when the first schools were built, but assume that it was very soon after the establishment of the colony. At that time schools seemed to be more important than they are today. As there was no shortage of lumber, schools were probably built very quickly, especially since they were also used for church services at that time. I do remember that an old school house burned down during the winter of 1852. This same year the people built the present two-story school house, which is covered with slate. This building now houses the parish school. Soon thereafter a big, completely slate covered school building was erected. It was divided into three classrooms, and the language of instruction was Russian. My oldest son, Theophil, is teaching there, while I myself, and my second son, Emanuel, are teaching in the parish school. We are German teachers, that is, our language of instruction is German. Lately German has been taught in the Russian school, although the main language of instruction is Russian. German subjects are considered unimportant there. The opposite is true in our parish school, where teaching in the German language is obligatory. There is a special Russian teacher in our parish school. He teaches the Russian language. In 1878, a very much appreciated postal service was established for the German population here, which comprises three parishes. We have had daily delivery and pick-up of mail lately.

Yagodnaya Polyana is a Russian word meaning "Berry Field." Large quantities of berries used to grow here, and in some years they still do nowadays. There are strawberries, which are plentiful this summer because we had rain all through May and up to June 20th, stoneberries, blackberries, raspberries, red currants, gooseberies, etc. The first four mentioned above are still growing in the wilderness. The latter kinds are now being grown mainly in gardens. One never, or rarely, finds them in the woods today. During my boyhood years I was delighted when I was told: "Let us go berry-picking in the woods." It did not take long, and we all brought home a jug full of various kinds of berries. Sometimes we went to pick only strawberries, another time only stoneberries, etc. Times were much better then. One waited until berries were ripe. Today, if one waits that long, he finds everything trampled down, crushed and destroyed, and not enough berries left to satisfy a person's appetite. In olden times whole families went berry-picking. They went out with jugs and pails; some even went in wagons. In addition, the woods today serve mainly as grazing land for animals. How can anything grow under these conditions? Also, there is much too much lumber theft. There are hardly any forests left, or none at all, where this stealing does not go on. If the thieves are caught, they are punished, but all this does not help. The "forest guards," as they are known, are chosen from the parish, and are probably at fault. They are afraid any thieves they might apprehend would later cause them harm. There is a need for better conservation methods if our descendants are not to be left without a forest at all. It is regrettable how cruelly our forests are being gradually destroyed. Yes, "destroyed," that is the right word. It will probably happen. Vandalism has become an everyday occurrence.

Yagodnaya Polyana was originally named "Reinhard" after the first mayor. However, this name did not exist for a long time. Soon the present name was permanently adopted. Pobotschnaja is also a Russian word meaning "Side Village" in German. The same pertains to Neu Statowka (also called New Skatovka). These colonists had originally settled in Skatovka, in the valley, and later on came over to join us. Skatovka in Russian also means "Slope Village" because there are several sloping mountains near the colony. All names have true justification; they fit well. The people who named the colonies gave careful thought.

Yagodnaya Polyana lies by a stream, actually a brook, called Chardym, which originates west of here, approximately four verst from the colony. Another brook flows into it, four verst north of here into the center of the colony. The word "Chardym" is said to be of Tatar origin. On the way to Sokur, which lies twelve verst northeast, there the two little streams are being fed by many other small streams, including two which flow through Pobotschnaya and Neu Skatovka, so that our Chardym can really be called a river by the time it reaches Sokur, and from there the waters flow into the mighty Volga.

Now Yagodnaya Polyana has a population of 1,300 families with about 10,000 persons. During the years 1857 and 1858, there was much moving within the Samara district. Many left here and settled in two new colonies. Schoenthal and New Yagodnaya, and seventeen years ago many started to leave for North America. These emigrants settled in Kansas, Colorado, Pine Island, New York; Baltimore, Oklahoma, Oshkosh, Wisconsin, and in the state of Washington. They also settled in western Canada in and around the city of Calgary.

The Volga German Farm Year
by Richard Scheuerman (1980)

The vast majority of colonists in Yagodnaya Polyana as in other Volga German villages during the nineteenth century were farmers. The first decade of despairing crop yields ended in 1775 when the cycle of rainfall ended the period of drought and adequate rains fell throughout the region. In addition the virgin acreage could be brought under greater cultivation as colonial smiths replaced the crude Russian *sokhi* iron-tipped wooden plows. The settlers introduced German moldboard plowshares which, when used singly or joined in pairs, could penetrate deeper and turn larger tracts of the heavy sod. Cultivation improved with iron harrow teeth and other implements and many colonists became adept at breeding quality draft horses to pull tillage equipment.

The settlers found it impractical to farm intensively since large areas were opened for them to cultivate. Commercial fertilizing techniques were unknown but they did practice three and four-year crop rotation. A typical field cycle might rotate from rye one year to sunflowers and potatoes the next. This land was summer-fallowed during the third year until sown back to rye. Several vast fields were maintained surrounding each colony to insure that adequate supplies of each commodity would be produced annually.

Farm work began every spring as the melting snows revealed a lush growth of winter rye covering at least one of the large colony fields. As the Volga Germans consumed rye flour heavily, it became the most important cereal grain raised in the colonies. It was generally planted in late August following summer rains while crops more susceptible to winter kill—sunflowers, spring grains, and potatoes—were planted in late March and April. Both soft and hard varieties of spring wheat were raised although hard wheat grew in demand, due to its high protein and gluten content, and was commonly raised as a cash export crop. Millet, the third major grain raised in the colonies, was also sown in the spring and was used in making *Hirsche,* a coarse porridge. Oats and barley, both used chiefly as animal fodder, were also spring crops (C. Blumenschein, 1980).

Care was taken in the preparation of seed grain to insure that it was free of weed seed and uncracked. This was accomplished by running the bulk grain from the previous harvest through both a fanning mill and a special sieve. The seedbed was often prepared by breaking the previously plowed ground with a crude triangular-shaped cultivator pulled by a team of horses. This was followed by pulling a ten to fifteen foot long roller which crushed the clods and packed the ground to conserve moisture. Sowing was by hand broadcast which was sometimes followed by a light harrowing. Sunflowers were planted by hand in alternate furrows during spring plowing, the successive rounds with the single or double share plow covering the preceding planting. Potatoes were planted in the same manner. It was exhausting labor that demanded skillful handling of the draft horses and careful measuring of the distance between seeds by those planting throughout the long day. At the same time others planted the large communal melon and cabbage gardens while women planted their other vegetables in the *Hinnerhof*.

In late spring the settlers turned their attention to the manufacture of *Mistholz* (manure wood), an economical fuel developed by the Volga Germans which prevented the destruction of their dwindling woodlands. Barnyards were usually cleaned weekly and the refuse deposited in one corner of the yard or, more commonly, at one of several places on the outskirts of the colony near a stream. Families gathered to prepare the *Mistholz* by adding water and straw to a layer of manure which was spread out over a hard flat surface. Horses were then led around several times to mix the mass. It was allowed to dry in the hot sun in large rectangular molds or cut into blocks with a spade and piled for use in winter as an odorless slow burning fuel. In May the colonists busied themselves by repairing their homes, mills, and farmyard buildings. Most houses received an annual coat of whitewash mixed from chalky soil near the village. This was also the time to cut the wild grasses which grew in the communal meadows in order to augment the winter hay supply. Following this it was necessary to hoe the vegetable crops in the fields and gardens while the livestock was turned out to graze on the volunteer grain growing in the fallow fields. In June spring plowing commenced on lands that would remain idle until sown to rye (H. Litzenberger, 1980).

It was not unusual for the colonists to find that their stores of rye were entirely depleted by early summer. It was often necessary, therefore, to cut a few bundles of rye ripening in the fields late in June or early in July. These bundles were allowed to dry for at least two weeks and then flailed to get several bushels of the grain. Rye was the first grain to mature and was usually ready for harvesting in mid-July. Prior to the introduction of mechanical binders early in the twentieth century, the rye was cut with sickles which the government had distributed in the colonies soon after their settlement. However, pioneer ingenuity led them to fashion larger scythes equipped with cradles in order to cut and windrow in one movement. Great dexterity was demonstrated by the women who followed the men to gather the cuttings into bundles which were tied together with several lengths of skillfully twisted and knotted rye stalks. The bundles were then collected into shocks for aeration which were carefully arranged into long rows. A pattern of thousands of shocks (*Kopitzen*) was soon visible on the hills dotting the landscape around the colony. At the same time the vast expanse of bright yellow sunflowers came into full bloom as they followed the sun's path during the warm daylight hours.

The next stage of the harvesting process involved the preparation of a threshing floor (*Den* or *Tenne*). This was usually located near the outskirts of the town at a designated area where each family was given a small area to stack their bundles for threshing. A team of horses was led around an area about fifty feet in diameter to flatten the surface. The area was then watered down and sprinkled with straw to form a hard surface. After two to three weeks of drying, the bundles were hauled to the threshing site by wagon. Several bundles at a time were then arranged side by side in a short row where a group of four or six adults stood on both sides to flail them. In large scale operations, dozens of bundles were spread out in a circular pattern to be threshed in a manner similar to that done with wheat later in the summer (F. Koch, 1977, p. 77).

Rhythmic folk songs were often sung by the workers as they set a tempo for swinging the long wooden flails. A narrow leather strap bolted on the end of the flail handle connected to a cylindrical piece of wood about a foot long. The bundles were then turned over and struck several times again and then opened for a final beating. Others lifted the stalks with wooden forks and stacked them for horse and cattle fodder. Until the middle of the nineteenth century, the colonists had to clean the threshings by tossing them into a crosswind by hand or with special wooden scoops to separate the slender brown kernels from the chaff in the ancient manner. This technique continued until about 1840 when fanning mills were introduced in the colonies. This made it more practical for the farmers to thresh the grain as it was needed, especially for those who did not have their own granaries. It was not uncommon to see families busy in winter flailing rye on a hard layer of ice in the *Fehderhof*. Families with granaries could store all their rye during the winter but, since these were built off the ground to prevent mice infestation and moisture damage, they also risked the loss of some grain by theft as holes could easily be drilled through the wooden flooring.

The first spring crops to mature, oats and barley, were usually harvested in late July. Both were cut and stacked in the barnyard for the animals. This was followed by the threshing of millet. The production of hemp and flax, gathered in late summer, had been introduced by the Tutel-Kanzlei to fill the domestic needs of the colonists. After the heads were cut and beaten into a silken mass, they could be spun on a wheel into large balls which provided the women with material to fashion clothes during the long winter months. By August the wheat fields maintained by the colonists were sufficiently ripened under the hot sun of the Volga summer to begin their harvest. The grain had to be threshed as soon as possible to avoid hail or fire damage. The farmers also dreaded the withering effects of a *Hohenrauch,* a searing hot dry wind from the southeastern desert region which could drastically reduce yield by shriveling the kernels and parching the ground (F. Koch, 1977, p. 78).

The Lust Mill, est. 1912

All able-bodied members of the family took part in the harvest work which began as early as two o'clock in the morning with the move out to the fields in the countryside. Wheat was principally an export crop although some white flour was used in making delicious fruit pastries (kuchen) and other foods. Wheat was often raised on acreages distant from the village on lands rented from wealthy Russian landlords on a fifty percent commission basis. The family would sometimes remain *"in dem Khutor"* for the entire week, living in tents if houses were not built, and returning to the village only on Saturday evening to prepare for worship on Sunday when all but the most essential labor ceased (Mrs. C. P. Morasch, 1971).

A circular threshing floor was again prepared, though as wide as 150 feet, at a central location on the family's property. Again the brittle stalks were cut and bundled, but then brought directly by wagons to the threshing site. As many as two hundred bundles were then arranged into a circle along the perimeter of the *Den* and opened. A team of horses was led over the grain to "ride it out" of the heads. As with rye, the stalks were turned several times with wooden forks then vigorously shaken, raked aside, and stacked. Meanwhile, others would scrape the golden particles and chaff into a pile in the center of the ring. By late afternoon as many as 300 bushels of wheat had accumulated which were then winnowed and sacked in a process that often lasted until ten o'clock at night. Adequate supplies of grain were stored for seeding purposes and domestic use, and an amount proportional to the size of the family was deposited in the local *Grossambar*, a communal grain reserve, for emergency use. For this reason the Volga Germans were able to avoid famine until the Soviet period despite periodic crop failure (J. Schierman, 1977).

About the same time that winnowing mills were introduced to the colonies (c. 1840), "threshing stones" also came into use which were much more efficient than merely leading horses through the pilings. The stones were long sandstone rollers with canted grooves which revolved in a wooden frame as they were pulled by a team of horses. Mechanical reapers and binders were not introduced until late in the nineteenth century and the revolutionary steam-powered stationary threshing machines appeared about 1910. Harvesting operations in August were often interrupted by summer rains which enabled the farmers to plant their winter rye while the standing grain dried. Planting took place on lands that had been spring plowed. Broadcasting continued to be the principal method of seeding in the colonies until American-made mechanical drills were made available to them just before the First World War. The farmers also began to turn the stubble on the recently harvested rye fields since these would later rotate to support spring crops.

The sunflower harvest usually began in early September. The four-foot high stalks were cut two rows at a time before the plump seeds became too brittle and were arranged in long rows with all the heads lying in the same direction. They were allowed to dry for about two weeks, during which time fall plowing continued. The stalks were then carefully placed on both sides of a wagon drawn between the rows. For this work the farmers sought oddly shaped branches in the timber which could be fashioned into four-pronged wooden forks. These resembled pairs of open claws on the end so that the stalk piles could be speared and placed with the heads in the middle of the wagon. The wagons were then taken to the prepared threshing floor and the loads dumped so that the heads remained in the middle of the pile. It was extended into a row about a foot high and the heads either flailed or pounded with a wooden paddle. The stalks were turned three or four times, shaken and then raked away on both sides into a large stack. This was then hauled home and used as a secondary fuel source. Some stalks were saved for extracting a type of baking soda. The seeds were run through a fanning mill and the chaff and leaves saved to feed the sheep.

Sunflower seed generally commanded a high price on the Volga since it yielded a high quality cooking oil that was processed in the *Oehlemule* (oil mills) located throughout the region. Sold by weight, the farmer's crop could be docked if it was too damp. Orchard fruit was preserved simply by sun-drying although apples were sometimes pickled for consumption later in the year. Wild pear trees were common and wild strawberries and other berry varieties ripened as early as June while August showers sprouted succulent mushrooms. Licorice root was gathered in the fall to be used in making the preferred Volga German drink—hot *Steppetee*. Volga German dinners typically consisted of nutritious combinations such as *Schnitzel Suppe und Kartoffel Wurst* (fruit soup and potato sausage), *Kraut und Brei* (sauerkraut and pork ribs) or *Klees und Arbuza* (fried eggs and dough with watermelon) (Mrs. A. P. Morasch, 1980).

The large numbers of animals maintained by the colonists provided an adequate supply of fresh meat, milk products, and eggs. Grazing areas were set aside in close proximity to the village but wolves were a constant threat to the livestock. Separate herders (*Herten*) were often appointed to safeguard the villagers' cattle, sheep, and swine which fed on nearby fallow land in the spring. Milk cows were returned every evening to the edge of town by the herders where they were then taken home by their owners. When the fallow land was planted, the animals were moved to the forest where they foraged through the summer until fall when they were turned out to the recently harvested fields. The livestock wintered in the protected confines of the *Fehderhof* where large temporary shelters were often built for the cattle and horses. Grain straw and hay for winter feed was stored in the spacious lofts of these structures.

Several families often joined together for the annual butchering bee which took place in November or early December. Fruit tree cuttings were slowly burned to smoke sausage and other meat products made by the colonists. These were hung on racks placed in the summer kitchen chimney for smoking and then stored in the granary or other dry place. One of the last tasks undertaken by the farmers before the heavy snows curtailed outside activity was the gathering of old timber in the forests to supplement the winter fuel supply. With the long harvest season over, fall plantings completed, and produce sold or stored, the villagers gathered to celebrate their bounty in an exuberant festival, the *Kerb*. This event signaled an end to the field season as the people prepared for the long Russian winter. Isolated on the steppe, the Volga German villages quieted to self-sufficient passivity. Courtship began among young couples considering matrimony and this custom often culminated in a mass marriage ceremony conducted in the gaily decorated church at Christmastime (A. Reich, 1969 and H. Litzenberger, 1980).

Following the period of sharp population decline between 1765 and 1775, when the number of families decreased from an estimated 8,000 to 5,502, the population began to steadily increase, reaching 31,000 by 1788 and 39,193 in 1798. The crown's plan of family allotments became increasingly complicated with each new generation. This required reapportionment within the limits of the colony's boundaries and in 1797 a new government survey was mandated which yielded a reduced allocation the following year of about forty-two acres (15.5 dessiatines) per male. Colonist grievances evoked a promise from the government to increase the total to twenty dessiatines, as had been the case after the 1788 revision. This was not fully accomplished, however, until 1835 when any benefits were virtually canceled, since by then the prolific Germans' shares averaged only about fifteen acres (5.6 dessiatines). This diminished even further to a scant 10.3 acres (3.8 dessiatines) in 1850 and the population was still increasing, reaching 238,000 in 1865, a growth tenfold larger than the number that settled on the Volga a century earlier (A. A. Klaus, 1869, pp. 190-95).

Problems arising from land tenure plagued colonial administration and when the 1763 Manifesto's tax exemption period expired, the colonists came to adopt the native Russian institution of the *mir* as a means of equitably resolving these matters and for orderly self-government. On March 12, 1812 they were officially given identical tax status as landed Russian peasants which required a tax levied equally on all the male "souls" (*dushi*) but remitted collectively from the village *mir*. It became convenient, therefore, to adapt land distribution in accordance with the *mir* system of repartitional tenure (*obshchinnoe pol'zovanie*) in which the land was divided among the male population in regular revisions and could not be sold or mortgaged. By 1816 the system was in general use throughout the colonies and usually incorporated into the administration of the daughter colonies.

Great care was taken during the periodic revisions to insure an equitable distribution of land. At these times a specified number of males, usually about twenty and invariably related to one another, joined together to form an economic unit. Each of the main colony fields was surveyed, divided, and marked into lots that were to be farmed by the groups. The size of the lots was sometimes proportional to the fertility of the soil which was usually divided into three classifications: good (fertile lowlands), medial (or steep), and poor (sandy or rocky areas). This guaranteed that each family would be provided with the spring crops and rye on variable soils and would have to maintain some summer-fallow (C. Blumenschein, 1980).

A public lottery, attended by at least one representative from every unit, was then held to determine who would receive which land parcels. Each male within a unit was then delegated a specific number of shares in their lands. The procedure was as complicated as it was judicious since each individual held title to as many as sixteen or more small plots. In addition, the communal garden properties were similarly apportioned. The basic problem of inadequate land supply, however, was not alleviated and new difficulties involving changing lines of demarcation, family size, and composition and varying soil quality compounded matters for the growing Volga German populace.

The government's solution to the dilemma of a regressive land supply was simply to expand Volga German settlement to other crown domains and between 1848 and 1863, the colonists founded sixty-eight daughter colonies (*Tochter Kolonien*). Most were located on the *Wiesenseite* where approximately 675,000 acres were appropriated into the Novousensk district in 1840. Of these colonies, over one-third were located along the Jeruslan River where residents of Yagodnaya Polyana founded New Yagodnaya (1855) and Schoental (1857) while others from Pobotschnoye established Schoendorf (1855) and Schoenfeld (1858) (G. Eisenach, 1950, pp. 214-16).

The Garden of My Youth
by Catherine Luft

In the beautiful garden of nature is Yagodnaya Polyana, the place of my birth and youth. There stood my cradle and there I spent my childhood and a part of my youth. I can yet today remember the green hills north and west of the village, the high Steinberg close to the village and the stately birch trees which grow so abundantly everywhere and I can yet almost hear the many springs bubbling from the hills day and night in endless streams. But I was not destined to spend my later years in my homeland. When I was seventeen years old, my parents and I took leave from beloved relatives and friends and traveled to the New World. The hour of departure was difficult and sad and we looked back with tear-drenched eyes until the village disappeared in the distance. Since then sixty-two years have passed and I have learned to love the new country. I am totally satisfied. Now I am already eighty years old but the precious memories of the old home come back again and again. Often I let my thoughts wander freely over mountains, hills, and streets and alleys of the village. At such times many dear and lovely memories come to mind. I would like to fulfill the wish of my children and describe what remains unforgettable to me since the departure from the land of my birth.

The village was situated on level land along the hillside of the Volga. Sixty yards northwest in a wonderful beautiful vicinity with woods and hills all around. The climate was just ideal for growing all kinds of plants. The trees especially blossomed everywhere here in that great territory and often attained great height. I remember the four big forests close to the village. Yet today it seems like a miracle to me. One could think that people had planted and taken care of them. One of these woods consisted of nothing but birch, another of oak, and another of aspen trees. In the fourth one all of these trees were growing all mixed up. I cannot tell how many acres there were but there were great stretches of them. In scattered places one could also see the beautiful linden trees, hazelnut and birdberry trees. The latter bore red cherries which nourished the birds specially in the winter when no other food could be found. How often we would go to gather mushrooms or pick the sweet wild strawberries which practically covered the ground in the woods with the "overflow" of berries! That is where the name of this place comes from—"Yagodnaya Polyana" which in translation means "Strawberryland."

73

I'm just thinking of the aspen forest. Through this forest I often drove with my father with horses and wagon out into the country. At such times he kept me amused by telling me all kinds of enchanting things about the woods and nature. Here, certainly, began my lifelong love of nature. It was a delight for me to be in the forest in August to gather mushrooms. Beyond the woods now we see the beautiful hills that spread out like a chain north and west of the village. Some were in part rocky and steep, but most were hills covered with trees. The one chain which lay north along the village, finally turned in a northern direction. Farther to the west over a large field of black acreage, lay the other chain which stretched farther toward the west. The hills of this chain were mostly green and covered with trees and we could drive up there on some of them with horses and wagon.

The village was well known for the beauty of its surroundings, but perhaps more for the many springs that originated in the hills. These springs were flowing when we went to gather mushrooms. Then the weather was warm, rainy and foggy, and the mushrooms, so to say, would push themselves out of the earth overnight. We gathered many baskets full which my father later would exchange for sheep wool from the Russians who liked our mushrooms very much. We liked them also, fried in the pan with eggs over them. The woods resounded with birds singing, specially in summer, when the different birds nested and fed their young. Many species were represented there: cuckoo, black raven, grey raven, owl, magpie, hawk, lark, and the one I loved so much, the nightingale that sang the most beautifully in dark midnight. This last one also lived in our orchard.

But I must go on. I have lost myself entirely in forest and bird song! I wonder what it's like today. I said the village was located on even ground. But there was one exception. Middle in the village, there rose a not high hill from which flowed also crystal clear and always cold water. It never became less. This spring was an attraction for the village and was, in reality, a wonder of nature. I have never again tasted such refreshing water and for this water I experienced great homesickness when I came to America. Near this hill there stood big containers or cisterns. The water ran into these constantly and people from far away came and got the water in big containers. There were also here and there dug-out wells but the water was not so good as that from the spring. All the water one needed for home use was carried home on the shoulders by means of a board cut out to fit around the neck and pieces of rope attached to carry a pail of water on each side. In 1906 the congregation built a wall of brick around the spring and opened the flow of water still more. But this wasn't the only spring in the village. On the west end was a similar one, not as big a one but it also flowed continually. From this one we got our water, carried it on our shoulders also although we lived only a block and a half away.

Like all of the villages of the Volga colonies, Yagodnaya Polyana was built according to plans after German style. The longest street ran east to the village and the collected water swelled up a dam near the Steinberg. From this dam a ditch was made which we called the "mill ditch." Here were the mills where all the grain was ground. At that time there was only one mill that was run with oil. Fifteen blocks long went from east to west and the cross streets went from south to north, lying chiefly along the incline of the aforementioned hill. In the center of the village, in a diagonal block, I would like to go around and, in short, describe the buildings. On the east side of the block at the southeast corner there was the big structure of the church, the only church in the village. It was the Evangelical Lutheran one and all who lived here belonged to it. I cannot think of it without remembering the huge pipe organ way above on the balcony. Oh, how glorious and fiery was the sound of that organ music! And up there was the choir where I, as a young girl of fourteen sang also, until I left when I was seventeen.

As usual, the three-story high belfry tower was next to the church. In the highest story hung three different sized bells. On Sunday morning, a half-hour before the service, the smallest bell would ring then a half hour later, the second smallest bell. But when the service began, all three bells rang together. That resounded throughout the village like a heavenly invitation and the people hurried to the service. God was prayed to in earnest and with respect, and we went home with new strength and peace. Whenever it stormed unusually hard, or also if fire broke out, the smallest bell was only hit on one side in a warning signal. Right behind the church and near by the spring, was the shed of the fire brigade. This protected the fire-wagon and horses that were used when there was a fire. On this wagon lay large barrels of water and the horses were always hitched up. And here also were chosen fire fighters who would await the alarm. Fire danger was great. We had open fireplaces and many houses had straw roofs. At the southeast corner of the block, near the church, was the parsonage, where the pastor and his family and a servant girl lived. It was somewhat larger than the farm houses. The yard of the parsonage had a beautiful flower garden protected all around with bushes we called "pod" trees. During summer these bushes were always green and had small yellow flowers. Later, in autumn, there were pods on them. Now, around the corner and to the west, we cross a small bridge where the water of the spring flowed out and soon come to the southeast corner of the block. There, across the street, on the other corner, was the brandy shop and the drugstore. I never saw the inside of the brandy shop. There was a window at the side of the building through which they handed out the brandy.

Again, around the corner in northerly direction, we come to the German schoolhouse, perhaps half-way to the northwest corner of the block. It was also a big building. However, it had no classrooms but a big, open room. The settlers had, years before, held their church services in there before they had built the church. At such times, the congregation had also held church business meetings here. In the German school we had instruction from eight in the morning until twelve o'clock noon. Here we learned to read and write and draw; lots of religious instruction—Bible stories, the Lutheran catechism, songs from the Volga Songbook and all that was necessary for Confirmation. Much of it we had to learn by heart which was good for us for our adult life. It says in the Bible, "Just as a youth learns when he is young, he will not depart from it when he is old." I had a good teacher named Johann Georg Kromm. What he made me learn by heart, I still know it mostly all by heart.

Just across the streets of the German schoolhouse, there was a store where one could buy yarn, cotton materials and thread and other things necessary for clothing and household items for bedding and clothing. Not far away was the fellowship hall on the same side of the street. Here the church council met, also the police and other officers of the church. For a time my father was secretary of the church and worked there. These officers were elected for two years. All business of the village was entrusted to them. Here the people came to pay taxes or "land money" as they called it sometimes. From this money the pastor was paid and all the officials. Other matters of business were carried out here for the village. Farther around the block toward the northwest side was another store which had all kinds of household articles for sale. Around this corner in northeast direction and again halfway in the block, was the long shed of the market. To this market came the ones who lived there and also neighboring farmers—every Friday to buy and to sell. Also Russian farmers from not too distant colonies came with their wares. I recall the small pears the Russian women brought to sell. They would dry the pears first. Then they boiled a sauce or broth made with honey or sugar, poured it over the pears. It was similar to prune juice here. Only the Russian women could make them and can them. German women just never understood how to do it like the Russian women.

Farther past the marketplace at the northeast corner of the block was the District House or Court. Here sat the head officer (judge), the secretary and other officials who also served in villages in that area. The head official was to serve three years. To this district belonged two other German villages, Pobotschnaja and Straub and some Russian villages. Here, for example, orphan children's inheritance was held and saved. This was guarded by two guardians until the children became of age. Across from this corner was the post office where all mail came through. One had to go and get the mail oneself. Farther on to the north was the doctor house. Not all colonies had such a doctor house. We had only one doctor and it was impossible for him to care for all inhabitants but we just did not go to the doctor right away. Now we are going south again around the block and come to the Russian schoolhouse. It was not far from the church and pastor house. Some children of the village attended this school from one o'clock till four o'clock afternoons. Here each class or grade had its own room. The instruction was in Russian only and here a big mistake was made. In the German school we learned the Russian as long as we sat in school. But when we went home, we did not say a Russian word and what we learned was soon forgotten. I am sorry about it now more than ever before.

Diagonally across the street from the Russian school was the store which sold iron. It had all that a farmer needed from nails to tin which was used for the roofs of the houses. Although the people were able to buy different wares here, they had to see to getting life's necessities all by themselves. As said, all the mentioned buildings were in the center of the village and, from there in all directions lay the farmers' houses. Although the people could purchase all kinds of wares in the store, they had to see to buying life's necessities by themselves. They built their homes, fabricated things needed in them also farm tools and with hard labor made their clothing, food and drink. No time for laziness. Even children to help work early in life. The need and their diligence aroused the power of invention and self-supporting which typifies the German colonist. There the old saying was fulfilled, "Necessity makes invention."

In time, many persons by their skill in trades and other special skills, founded all kinds of small businesses. My father was a shoemaker and shoe-repairer. And my mother made a special shoe for which she was known in the whole region. It was somewhat like a houseshoe. The top part was knitted and had a leather sole and a half-inch heel. It really looked cute and pretty and was worn by men and women alike at home or on the street. My mother used only the scantiest of tools to make this shoe—scissors, an awl, needle and thread. I remember one spring before Pentecost. Before this festival mother received orders for forty pairs of these shoes. Everyone wanted their shoes for the festival. The picture of my mother bending over these "knitted shoes" remains always in my mind! Several persons were busy in the men's tailor shop and also women who made women's and children's clothing. Just now comes to mind the Russian sheepskin which was worn a lot. The Germans could never learn how to use this pelt properly. So Russian tailors went from village to village to make them properly.

Almost every family also had a spinning wheel. So they spun fine and coarse yarn (thread) which was used for knitted stockings, mittens and houseshoes. The maker of spinning wheels lived in our neighborhood. One family was busy with clothing and colored all kinds of woolen yarn in black, blue, red, green, and dark blue colors. From this wool, also dresses were woven often with bright colored stripes. Some people also wove cotton for clothes. The maker of spinning wheels and his family also braided straw for strawhuts and the same man made woodwork for farm wagons before sending them to the blacksmith for the iron work. Another domestic job was weaving. Not all people wove their own clothing and other things they needed but we had a loom in the house. This work was done specially in winter when the field work became less.

Linen cloth was one of the main cloths that people used for different things. We had to begin with the raw stuff, because the cloth was made from hemp. The hemp seed was sown in spring. It came up quite soon and grew up into a high stalk and much bigger than a thick straw blade. When it ripened it was pulled out with the roots and thoroughly dried. After drying, the stems were put through an instrument which we called "the breaker." By this process, the outer peeling fell off and the linen thread lay there all open. Next, the thread went through a hackle and changed much more until there were all fine threads like long hair. These threads were then spun and woven into cloth. The cloth, however, was not yet ready for use. It had to be bleached and now boiled in lye water, homemade soap and wood ashes. After boiling, it was well washed in the brook and then spread out on the snow in open fields. There it lay for days in the sun and nights in the frost until it was bleached enough. Now finally it was ready for use. The number one cloth was used for tablecloths and bedspreads. On the bedspreads there was wide lace crocheted around the edges. These covers were highly treasured. The number two cloth was used for men's work pants, the coarsest cloth for tents, wagon covers and fruit sacks. That was a lot of trouble and work connected with this, but one saw the reward of work and was happy over the experience.

I do not want to forget the tinsmith and blacksmith whose specialties had made life so much more comfortable. The tinsmith made many tools that could be used outside and took care of getting the tin for the house roofs. For the heavier iron-work on the farm tools one had to go to the blacksmith. He is the one who made the iron work on the wagons, after finishing the work on the wood part, and he made the wheel-rims, for the wheels of the wagons, for the German plowshares, and shoes for horses' hooves. His blacksmith shop was out of the village, near Steinberg.

Now I want to relate something in detail of the houses in the village. The houses and public buildings were modeled a la German architecture. Our forbears, of course, were strangers in a foreign land, and they held fast to homeland ways. Now and then they had to seek advice from their Russian neighbors, but they were not immediately inclined to adopt Russian customs. As much as possible they were striving to remain content in what they could do for themselves and be self-sufficient as much as possible. In contrast to German houses, the Russians had more simple ones, but were of the same building material. I still remember that the houses of the Russians had smaller rooms and the German ones had larger and lighter windows.

The building material of the houses was mostly wood blocks. However, some people gathered stones off rocky cliffs of which there were a great plenty. They were smeared with clay and, when dried, they were whitened with white earth similar to lime. This earth, as used in our village was dug up in huge lumps in a deep ditch not far from Yagodnaya Polyana. The lumps were carried by hand to a chosen place and water was poured on them. (I carried these clumps as a young girl!) Horses were used then to help mix earth and water until the mixture reached a suitable color. There was so to say, the white color, that was used so much in the village. There was danger of getting killed in digging out this dirt. It happened when I was still in Russia, that the ditch or mine had collapsed and a man was killed. But, the work was not in vain. The whitened walls were clean and beautiful. The floors consisted usually of broad boards, and if they with a were painted with a light brown paint, it had a really a nice shine. In the inside furnishings of the houses, also the similarity of the German way became visible. Our home was a typical one of our time.

In the main part of the home stood our beds, a somewhat smaller resting bed, dining table, chairs and a long bench next to the wall. This furniture for the most part, was made by hand. My grandfather and father were carpenters and did a lot of carpenter work in the village. I must digress a bit here and tell about the carpenter work that my family, especially my grandfather and my father did. I still think of the planer's bench where all furniture was finished. Beds, boxes, benches, dining tables were made on this bench. When someone died, the casket and the wooden cross with the name carved on it, was made. We used the crosses instead of gravestones. Not only was the whole building in our place, all their own work but also many houses in the village were the work of my grandfather and father.

Now, again back to the main room of the house. In this same room was the big stove built of bricks. With this stove the house was heated throughout the winter and our baking was done in it. I can not forget the bread that tasted so good baked on those bricks. On Saturdays, baking day filled the whole house with the odor of fresh baked bread. In the kitchen was the cook stove where all the cooking utensils hung. Here, also in a corner was the iron kettle in which clothing was boiled in soap and wood ash and lye. The same kettle was used also for boiling soap. From the kitchen the house was heated by the kitchen stove.

Once more back to the washing. All of it was rubbed by hand, then boiled in the aforementioned lye. Next, one would go to the spring dip, the pieces in and then thoroughly rinse out everything, piece by piece thus we washed in summer or winter, cold or warm. In the back yard behind the house, was the bakery, with another larger brick-oven. In it we baked fifteen loaves of rye bread at one time. I was told that in earlier times our family consisted of twenty-one members. Then several generations lived together and worked together. Several other buildings were behind the house—the stable for horses, barn for the cows, pigsty, the chickens found their protection here, also there was a wagon shed and another one for stove-wood, lots of heating material for the long cold winter. Here also the grain was stored and tools needed for work as well as heating material for the winter.

In the yard was also the ice cellar or "snow-cellar" as it was called. It was dug out of the earth and packed with ice and snow. In spring, before snow and ice started to melt, all perishables were stored in there. Behind the house and yard, every house plot had a vegetable garden. We had taken all the land for an orchard. Here stood thirty-six different kinds of apple trees. I don't know if it was the climate, but we have never found such apples in this land. They were absolutely tops in taste and smell! In the orchard were early and late

Mrs. Tanova's Chickens

cherries and two bushes of gooseberries. Also raspberries were not missing. Strawberries were not planted as they grew wild and everyone could go and pick all he wished. We did not have sugar to can them or any fresh fruit. Strawberries had to be used as soon as possible. We used them in cooking and baking as long as they stayed fresh. The apples that we did not eat were cut into pieces and dried. We called them "Schnitzel."

The dried apples could be stored all winter. One kind of apples we also canned. We took a big container, put apple leaves at the bottom of the container and then apples, then again leaves until the container was full. Then a tea was brewed with liquorice and anise. When the tea was ready, and cooled, it was poured over the apples. These kept over the winter and tasted very good during the long cold months. From here we go to the west end of the village. To our bee garden where Grandfather and his friend had a bee farm. The garden was surrounded by woods, but the bee hives stood in an open place. I can still see the one-hundred beehives that the bees served. The hives were thick tree stumps, hollowed out and they placed honey-comb in them and the bees moved in! Grandfather also lived also most of the summer in the bee garden. Often I had to take his dinner to him and got quite a few bee stings. Sometimes a bee swarm had just come out and was hanging there up in a tree! If I got in the way, I had to feel it! For me beekeeping is very interesting.

In autumn the honey had to be removed from the hives and only enough left that when they awaken from their winter sleep in spring so they would have nourishment until they could fly out again. Also in autumn, when all tears or cracks in the hives were repaired and sealed, the bees sleep again until spring. In spring and through summer, till September, people had been very busy on the land. All healthy people, young as well as old, were very busy on the land, even those who could do but little, had a part to do. We were people of the land; the land was our livelihood and had to be cared for. But I can say, even if the work was hard sometimes and endless, we did have a rich payment in the harvest.

Our land lay forty verst or about eleven miles, from the village. How much it yielded I no longer can say. I only know that since my father had no sons, he got less land than those who had sons. His sons all died as little children, some before I was born and several after my birth. Finally, I was the only surviving one of twelve children. So, I took, so to say, the place of a son, in order to better help my father with the field work. Whenever we drove out to the place where our acreage was, when I was a child and young girl, I sat behind him in the wagon when my father drove the horses through the aspen forest and then past other people's farms. I can see them stretching out black and fruitful, or in other times, green with growing fruits, and in harvest, gold with waving, ripening harvest. As far as I know, the land in our region was all black, usable earth. This required no fertilizer. When the rain came at the right time, the seeds sprouted and one could just see them grow. We were told there was red earth but it was too far away from our village and so I had never seen it.

We sowed different early and late fruits. In spring we sowed hemp, oats, millet, and buckwheat and also planted the much-used potatoes, lentils, beans, cabbage (we called it "Kraut"), watermelons, sweet melons, cucumbers, as well as pumpkins. Some land lay fallow until later in summer when rye and wheat were sown on it. Then when the weather was warm and the rain came, this seed soon came up and the fields became green quickly. When the first fruits were in the earth, we had a short respite from field work and went into the woods to gather firewood for the long winter. All who lived in the village had part in the woods. Everyone could fell as many trees as was needed. But care had to be taken so that the firewood was thrown on heaps and dried yet a bit over the summer.

As long as I am telling about firewood I would like to mention the so-called "Mistholz" (dungwood). I have said above that our land did not need any dung because it was rich enough by itself. So the dung was heaped up on a place outside the village. There it lay in huge heaps through the winter until spring when it had fermented. At this time then water was poured over it and straw added. Horses then were used to stomp all of this down until it was well mixed. Next the dung was packed into a wooden form which formed it like bricks. The dung-wood bricks lay then for days until they dried. They burned well and warmed us throughout the cold winter. Now back to the land. The fruits were making the fields green, so we had to start to hoe. For us there were large stretches of potatoes and sunflowers. But we could not think of the size; the weeds had to be hoed out, otherwise the young plants would have been overgrown! This work was monotonous! We often had backaches until it was done. We lived almost the whole summer in tents out in the field. Not only did I help with the field work but I also had to cook and wash the dishes. My mother did not often go into the fields. She stayed home and took care of the children and the house.

Much work was connected with the sunflowers, but because they were not only a valuable thing to sell but also useful in the marketplace, we did not mind the work. In September when they ripened, we cut off the heads with a hand-sickle and put them in small heaps to dry. When they were dry, a threshing flail helped to get the kernels out of the heads of the plants. The kernels were in great demand at the marketplace in the City of Saratov. The money that it gave us was used for other things, things like sugar and sweetwood that we did not grow. Sweetwood made very good nourishing tea which was drunk a lot. One could also buy oil-presses and make it at home. The sunflower kernels were put between two big rocks and as horses pulled the rocks round and around, the kernels were crushed and the oil pressed out. In my time it was not done anymore. People rather bought it. This was used for cooking—chiefly because we ate less meat. Bigger farmers had more meat.

After all the hoeing came rye, wheat, barley, and oats harvest. Some of these were mowed with the scythe; others with hand-sickle, and then tied in sheafs. The sheafs, except the ones of wheat, were driven in wagons to a certain threshing place to be threshed with threshing flail. The wheat kernels were driven out by horses or horses and wagons. So it went from one job to the other. Today it seems to me it was a lot of hard work. I must admit it was so, but one could be happy over the harvest blessing and forgot the hard work soon after. Here it can be said that people of that time were more cheerful than today. I am just thinking of the year 1909. After the fruit harvest was over, the land was plowed again and it lay until spring. At the end were the potatoes which were dug up. Then we went home. Then we still made the sauerkraut and a big supply for the winter. Sometimes winter began already in the month of October.

In the cold winter we stayed home most of the time. Then the days were more quiet and we busied ourselves with easy jobs. Busy hands were flying with knitting needles and were busy at the loom and spinning wheel. There was cloth to weave, yarn to spin and stockings and mittens to knit. My father sat for hours behind the loom and I remember with what skill he threw the shuttle back and forth. Sometimes when he would feel too confined in the house, he would dress warmly, take his gun and go into the forest. If he had good luck, he would bring home a rabbit and was all new and refreshed in spirit and began to weave again. So passed the winter months. In winter we prepared for summer and in summer for winter. Thus life was lived along the Volga River. Some farmers, who had more land than we, could help themselves better than we could. There were many wealthy farmers in the village.

In the month of May we celebrated Pentecost with a big festival in church and festival days were observed in different ways. As much as possible all heavy work came to an end when the harvest was abundant. How glad the people were! The rain came at the right time! As much as possible, all heavy work came to a standstill and all in the village was put in order. House, yard and street were swept and even the people tried to look their best! As customary on such festival days, visits were made and everyone was prepared with cooking and baking to receive guests.

On Pentecost Sunday for the morning service, the first class of the year, the children of the confirmation class were confirmed. For this day the church was decorated most beautifully and the children made a lovely picture as they sat there up front in the church. Every child was dressed, usually wearing a new dress for this occasion! The decoration of the church was done by the children themselves. On Saturday already they went into the woods to get flowers to make wreaths with birchtree twigs to beautify the church. The sweet odor of the flowers and tree branches filled the church. I myself belonged to the autumn confirmation class and we decorated the church with artificial wreaths and flowers. I just remembered, I wore a blue dress for my confirmation.

Also on Pentecost Sunday there was the big, general "Lay Brothers' Conference" which was held every year in Yagodnaya Polyana. These brethren experienced personally their conversion to God and believed He demanded a God-fearing life from them. They remained members of the church and supported it, but they held their own prayer meetings and explanation of the Bible. They also sang beautifully! If only I could hear them singing again! Our family belonged to the Brotherhood and I can say we had many blessed hours with the "Brothers."

When Pentecost Sunday came closer we were expecting the visiting brothers who were coming to the conference. They came from far and near with horses and wagons. but some also came on foot. Those from far away left their villages on Friday; many who lived near, started from home Saturday and some early Sunday morning. Whole families came and we welcomed them always with great joy. Wherever they stopped they were offered night lodging and immediately invited to stay for the whole visit. Sometimes they were invited to come and eat with another family. At such times many a table was full and I remember the very elevating and enlivening discussion at the table. Also for the night's rest we gave our beds to the guests and it still makes me smile when I think back how often as a child I wrapped myself in a quilt and lay down on the floor to sleep! We did that gladly. The brethren in reality carried out Holy Scripture where it is written—Romans 12:13: "Share your belongings with your needy fellow Christians and open your home to strangers." These customs were carried on in their new home.

We need not entertain our guests. They edified one another in the fellowship of their faith. Often, after a meal, the brothers had talked on something in the Bible or they sang and prayed until it was time to go and open the conference. All this made a great impression on me as a child. The first prayer meeting of the conference was held already on Saturday evening, but then early on Sunday morning, when the sun rose, the brethren gathered on a not so high hill and conducted services under the open sky. With my spiritual eye I still see the beauty of nature. All was alive; trees and bushes were the greenest, the song of birds resounded throughout wood and meadow, and the smell of the wildflowers hovered in the air. We felt God's presence and sang and prayed to him with overflowing hearts. In the stillness of the morning the song resounded as if it were by a huge choir, until they heard it down in the village. The beautiful hymns from the Volga hymn book and the *Gemeindschaft Liederbuch* were never more beautiful and caused many tears. The visiting brothers sometimes brought new songs and we learned them by ear. We learned most of them that way. I always had a good ear for music and learned them quite fast. Then I was called on to start the singing. And I just learned them by heart. I still know them to this day. I remember many I learned by heart and I still have many yet in my mind and still sing them yet to this day.

In the meeting on the hill the Pentecost story was read and several brothers preached about it. After that we sang again and in the morning hours we fell on our knees and prayed with great earnestness and zeal to God. When it was time, we all went down to the service in the church. The mode of the brethren was that they never left the organized church, but they felt they had to express their personal belief this way. Everywhere they lived, the brethren held prayer meetings. They came together to sing, pray, encourage one another, and they assembled where they could find room: in houses, schoolhouse, also out in the open. What blessed hours were spent in these meetings and I cannot tell you how precious God's Word was to our glowing hearts. Nothing could keep us apart; that is how serious we were in our belief. When I left Yagodnaya Polyana we had nine prayer meetings in the village.

The brethren visited one another's village to village and, as said, met several times per year from far and near to hold conferences. I am thinking of the Ascension Day Conference in Yagodnaya Polyana when all nine prayer meetings in the village met on the mountain. The young people ran up the mountain and the older ones drove up with horses and wagons. The air was fresh and pure. The Ascension story was read; we sang and prayed to God. It was a lovely sight! That day remains unforgettable as a high point in my young life. The movement of the "Brotherhood" began by the work of missionaries of several Brotherhood churches, especially the Moravian Brethren from Herrnhut in Germany. These felt a call to work among the German colonists on the Volga. They came to the villages at a time when attending church had become routine or had fallen off entirely and when people were searching for a meaningful spiritual life. Of these times I personally do not know much, but it was told to me and I have read about it that a ripe mission field could be found along the shores of the Volga.

Through these weak times the church had some villages with no pastors and they had to depend on the schoolteacher to read the sermon. Pastors hesitated to go to such places and those who did go were not always ordained men. The consequence was the deterioration of spirit in many Volga churches. By the work of the missionaries, many people turned to God and lived again in hope and faith. It was the source of brotherhood in Russia. The story of the brotherhood in Russia is written down in the book by George J. Eisenach, titled *The Religious Life of the Russian Germans in Russia and America.* Dr. Eisenach writes that the Brotherhood was organized in 1871 and there was in 1872 a great awakening on the Volga when many people converted to God and joined the Brotherhood.

My personal conversion to God took place in the time of the second great Awakening Movement of the Brotherhood that began in 1904. As a child of ten years I went with my uncle to a prayer meeting in a neighboring village and there I gave my heart and soul forever to the Lord Jesus Christ. My decision, so earnestly reached in my young heart, has lasted seventy years already and I am convinced it will always lead me to eternity. When the Brotherhood first began in our village, I cannot say but I was told that a young single man from the neighboring village of Pobotschnaya by the name of Heinrich Langlitz brought the message of the brothers to our village for the first time. The message was plain: The people should personally turn to God and lead a pious and religious life. So serious and zealous in prayer and recognition of God's grace was the young man who won many for God that the "Awakening Celebration" kept burning on. Everywhere Brotherhood Movment took root, church attendance increased, and there was new life in the churches.

The Brotherhood Church on the Volga elected two traveling evangelists who preached the Gospel from village to village. It was my honor to meet one of these earnest pastors when he visited Yagodnaya Polyana. His name was Heinrich Peter Ehlers. He was a holy man and many stories of his God-fearing life were told. As a young girl I hung on his every word that he preached and I convinced myself never to miss hearing him when he came. One day we heard that Brother Ehlers was coming to our village but we were to work in our field. I begged my father to let me stay home. But he said we had to take care of our fruits and that I had to go along. We worked for several days in the field and when the day came closer when Brother Ehler would come to our village and I looked for a reason to return to the village. Then finally it happened that my uncle and I had to return to our village, each with a load of fruit. We drove all night, I with my wagon and he with his. Real early the next morning we arrived and at six o'clock I sat in the church totally absorbed in Brother Ehlers' sermon.

As said before, much was related about him. In worldly goods he was poor, but in spiritual things he was the richest man. It was said he never hesitated to share his last piece of bread with someone in need. Because he often made mission trips, he was seldom home. It happened once that his wife and children were without food. When he came home, his wife complained: "You are always gone and I have to suffer hunger with the family. There is hardly any food left to live on." These words hurt him so much he kneeled down under a cherry tree and prayed a long time about this situation. Then he went back into the house and went to bed. At midnight someone tapped on the window and asked for Pastor Ehlers. The man said he was sent by a brother to bring flour and meat for him and his family. Then Brother Ehlers said, "Dear God, I knew that you would help, but I did not know you would do it so quickly!"

Another time in winter a brother had taken him by sled to the next meeting where he was to preach. As they were driving, a blind man was walking along who was going to the meeting also. Brother Ehlers stopped the horses and helped the blind man onto the sled. The brother said to him, "Brother Ehlers, the Lord will repay you a hundredfold." Not long after, a money order came from America for $100 but Brother Ehlers got only ninety-six dollars. He said, "That is a mistake. It should be one hundred dollars." When they checked on it, they learned that it really was $100 but due to the rules of the country they lost $4.00 due to the money exchange between U.S. and Russia.

Brother Ehlers preached with a soft voice but what he said was very serious and important. He warned that serious times were going to come to the German colonists and that a great affliction would be coming over them. And so it happened. During the Bolshevik Revolution in 1917 and later after World War I, the people on the Volga were driven from their homes and scattered, and they suffered death, hunger and imprisonment. It makes me sad when I think of it. How grateful I am to my Heavenly Father that He brought our family out in time. I am also certain that God chose Brother Ehlers to pass the news on to the people along the Volga and that thereby many were saved from death by his warnings and also from eternal destruction.

Before I continue, I want to say that not all people and pastors had an understanding for those of the Brotherhood. Their ways seemed fanatic with excessive zeal and at the time they were persecuted. The evangelist Ehlers, however, always urged the brothers not to leave the church. Many did not take it as a warning of the church but only as serious and believing members that they really were. One of the pastors, Pastor Wilhelm Staerkel from the village Norka, helped the brothers to organize. He became converted in one of the revival meetings. One can read more about him in Dr. Eisenach's book. I heard Pastor Staerkel preach once in Saratov.

In closing I want to say that the Brotherhood resisted temptation and endured difficult times. Where they immigrated to they kept their customs in their new homes. Today, however, there are no longer so many Brethren from Russia still living and in America, where once many prayer meetings and conferences were held, there are now only smaller groups or no prayer meetings to be found. And conferences are much less than before. The old brothers find it hard to keep up the old customs of a lifetime and, if they can, they uplift their spirits with God's Word and sing again the beloved songs often with quivering or fading voices. The older brothers die but the flame of Brotherhood which was lit so long ago, cannot be extinguished and its light leads future generations closer to God. Eternity alone will evaluate the Brotherhood correctly.

When I was ten years old, I received a blow that verified my decision to belong to God. It was in April and we went out into the field. But my little brother Adam, six years old, was sick and I was uneasy leaving him at home. He also ran after me as if he did not want to lose sight of me. We loved each other very much. The land lay perhaps forty verst away from the village. On the second day my uncle, who had run the forty verst, said that Adam was very sick. Because we did not have our own horses this time, we began to run back to the village. We ran thirty verst before anyone came and drove us the last distance home. Adam was really deathly sick and after two days died in Mother's lap as she held him in her arms. Words cannot describe my pain. I died with Adam—and also for this world. My hope is to see him again in the New World.

Late in 1912, my parents decided to leave Russia. They had thought of this for a long time and I often heard them talking about it and also with friends. But now the time was ripe to get their things in order and get on the way to America. When they told me their plans, I broke into tears as I did not want to leave Yagodnaya Polyana, my dear home. How could I? How could I leave the rich church life and my dear friends? No, I did not want to leave Yagodnaya Polyana my dear home. How could I leave behind me my dear friends? How could I leave the church and its loving fellowship? No, I wanted to stay in Russia!

Although I had no desire to accept my parent's decision, I knew they had reason enough to strengthen their decision. My father was a man without sons and a man without sons was not entitled to get more land according to the government rules. His two sons died as children and now I was his only child alive, son or daughter. But other people also lacked land even if they were blessed with sons. Because of the growth of population there was not enough land in the colonies. In order to help this shortage of land in Yagodnaya Polyana, earlier many families had been moved to New Yagodnaya and Schoental, daughter colonies quite a distance away from Yagodnaya.

The church went again and bought land also from a nobleman fifty miles away from the village. From time to time the people experienced also the whim of nature in dry spells, failure of crops, plagues of grasshoppers and caterpillars. They ate even the fruits and leaves of the trees until everything looked black. Through times like this, people lacked food and sought and got it in the schoolhouse kitchen that was installed and run for such times. I remember in 1903 when I was eight years old and there was a crop failure in Yagodnaya Polyana. Some of our neighbor children were sent to the soup kitchen. They said I should go with them and, although Mother had forbidden it, because of childish curiosity I went and ate kraut soup and blackbread with them. Still other changes came about at that time.

Little by little the government took away many rights of the colonists. Where once they had been excused from military duty, no more! Young men avoided this by a hasty exist from Russia. Such was the case of my future husband who left Russia one day before his pass became invalid. As said, the indifference of the Russian government about the land and hard times, caused people to find better conditions, not only those in Yagodnaya Polyana but also in other villages along the shores of the Volga.

During this time, there came time after time news from relatives in North America that the conditions were much better across the ocean. That convinced my parents more and more. My father's two brothers and three sisters were already living in the state of Wisconsin of the United States. Also some sisters of my mother had already earlier come to the United States. But our destination was the city of Calgary in Canada. The day of our departure was set for nine o'clock a.m., January 3, 1913. Everything we could not carry or pack, had to be given away to friends and relatives. I am still sorry that so many of our treasured things were left behind. I'm thinking of the books, art works, personal things, our livestock farm tools, and household furniture to be auctioned off.

These friends and relatives, all of us, wanted to delay our leaving as long as they could. With us that morning were eleven other families who were leaving the village. The sleds with horses hitched, were loaded already with boxes and bundles in the village and were awaiting our arrival. We had to walk a ways from our house through the village to the sleds and on the way other friends joined us. I remember how extremely cold it was. The snow crackled under us as we walked. That morning I froze so badly that my feet were cold for two years after that. Conversation was scarce among us. Our hearts were too full. When we arrived where the sleds were, quite a large group was assembled. Now we had to hurry to take our leave. We cried and kissed one another for the last time. Someone wrapped us up very warmly in the sled and covered us against the bitter cold. That is the way the long trip out of Russia began. The whole day we drove toward the city Petrovsk, about forty verst from the village and arrived at four o'clock in the afternoon at the train station. Here we had to wait until four o'clock the next morning for the train to the city Verspablova at the border of Poland. Then we went over the Russian border to Edyukuden, at the German border. We went through inspection and entered Germany, land of our forefathers. Here we were just considered to be Russians.

By train we went on to Bremen harbor in Germany. Here we waited again, almost a week before we could go across the English Channel. It was evening when we left Bremen. The way over was stormy and many became seasick. As we came to the English city of Hull, it was morning. After the landing we went with buses pulled by horses to the harbor city Liverpool. Again we were there a week before we finally on January 31 went on the ship *Corsican.* It was seven o'clock in the evening when we left Liverpool. When the ship began to move, the first food was served us and that was enough for me. I became seasick, as did my father and after that I could not eat and very seldom got up. The ocean really became stormy with high and foamy waves. Europe and Russia lay behind us forever as we set out by the grace of God to fashion a new life in America.

The Volga German Mama and her Epicure
by Anna Weitz (1980)

For certain, the Volga German Mama must have been uniquely endued by the Maker to have withstood the skimpiness of life and still have emerged as an individual in her own right. How else did she maintain the physical ability and the unfailing moral and spiritual stamina needed through her difficult role as wife and mother in her German colony in Russia and later in America?

Her status in the Old Country was clearly defined. As soon as she was married, she moved into the house of her husband's parents. In that house, the groom's mother was the matriarch and his sisters were second in rank. The wife's role was to refrain from any self-expression, to breast feed and teach her children, to assist with the household tasks of cooking, cleaning, bread baking, carrying water from the town's well to the house, as directed. She also took her turn working in the fields—hand planting, hoeing, harvesting the grain, sunflowers, hops, potatoes and other crops. In winter, she helped spin, weave, dye, knit, and sew the big family's clothing.

Lucky was the young wife who came into a family with gentle, kind female relatives, but unfortunately, hers frequently became a Cinderella mean sister type of existence. Living together in such close quarters was of course the core of most dissention. Imagine working, eating, sleeping, bearing children, all in the same rooms with two or even three generations of relatives! Imagine, too, that some homes had an attached lean-to that housed a cow and other domestic animals. No wonder that in the early 1900's so many young couples were drawn to the prospect of leaving it all behind to begin a new life in America. No wonder that the thought of having their own premises with more privacies and freedoms and the hope of a better future spurred them on over every obstacle enroute to their destination, and sustained them in those early difficult years in this new land.

It was here, in America, that the Volga German Mama came to be. For starters, she replaced her cumbersome clothing—the coarse undergarments, the many petticoats, the long itchy wool skirts and knee-high heavy felt boots ("Shtivvel")—with light leather footwear, store-bought cottons that covered her body. She did keep her tightly-drawn long hair style and the triangle head scarf. She continued to knit her family's sox and sweaters and her own shawls. In their small family unit now, her husband was "boss." Ya! Ya! But this was certainly more tolerable to her than it had been. She assumed her role as wife, homemaker, teacher of their children, all under privation and with limited facilities and finances. She attempted to learn the English language, to shop, to supplement the family income by doing richer people's washing. She was clean and God-fearing and industrious. She gave strength and encouragement and great love to her own. She was a good neighbor and sometimes a midwife. She encouraged Papa to get his American citizenship papers as soon as possible.

While some aspects of the Volga German-born Mama's life did not and will not entirely change, it can be said that she herself, in her own good time, brought about an unobtrusive "liberation" for herself. At last, at long last. With the years came the mellowing of Papa, too. While he may not have included her as a complete equal or in any big decision-making, he did discuss plans and share ideas with her. He even became tolerant of some of her whimsies. The whole family verbally conceded that Papa was the head master of the home, but during two and three generations of Volga Germans living in America, families have in times of stress or the need for understanding actually sought maternal contact. They learned to appreciate the quiet stability, the unselfishness and staunch-heartedness of Mama—their own one-of-a-kind Volga-German Mama. Lucky are those few who still have one!

The Volga German Mama was legendary for her culinary skills. Cooking measurements, in earlier days, were approximate ("ungafir," was the term). It was a "knipsi" (pinch) of this, a "gapsha" (handful) of that, a "klaschizzelchaful" (little bowlful). I have converted these into current measurements. Most of these dishes can be created out of such basic ingredients as flour and potatoes, plus varied flavorings. So equip yourself with a good-sized cooking kettle and a cast-iron fry pan with a tight-fitting lid and proceed to let the tantalizing odors of this kind of German cookery emanate from your kitchen.

Now I do not say that these recipes do not vary according to personal or family preferences, but I have sought to set down the very tastiest ones from our best Volga German cooks and as I have prepared many of them through the years.

****

Basic Klees Dough

Since Klees were the "convenience foods" of our parents and grandparents and most of us grew up on them, let's start with their basic dough recipe.

Mix 2 cups of flour, a pinch of salt and a level teaspoon of baking powder. Now gradually add enough water to make a soft, pliable dough. With more flour, roll and knead, shaping mass into two rolls. With a scissors or sharp knife, cut off little oblong portions about the size of half of your little finger, in half a large kettleful of rapidly-boiling water, salted. Boil 20 minutes, pour into colander and drain. You are now ready to garnish them in one of several ways.

Fry Klees in generous amount of butter or margarine until golden brown. Or add a slightly beaten egg or two and fry until eggs are well set. Some folks cook chunks of potatoes and onion with the klees and then butter-fry all after drained. We like to serve cold watermelon with fried Klees or sour watermelon chunks.

If it is _Gashmeltta Klees_ you desire, slightly brown bits of bacon and onion. Drain off excessive fat, pour milk or thin cream in pan, then the entire liquid over the cooked Klees. Serve hot in bowls. Sauerkraut cooked with a bit of onion and diced bacon until well-done, can be used as a delicious topping of these Klees—juice and all. Potatoes form the base of the next two Klees recipes.

Shtop (or Klitch) Klees

1 cup cold mashed potatoes
1 tablespoon flour
1/4 teaspoon salt

Roll spoonful portions in medium hot bacon drippings and fry until lightly crusted all around.

Gatofel Klees

2 cups cold mashed potatoes
3/4 cup flour
2 beaten eggs
1/2 teaspoon salt
1/2 teaspoon baking powder

Mix well. Form into little balls and boil in salted water about 5 minutes. Drain and garnish with heated sweet cream and butter-browned bread crumbs.

The aristocrats of the Klees family are the filled ones—_abens, madda, kirsha_ (strawberry, cottage-cheese, and cherry, respectively). To encase these fillings, we use a soft noodle dough. Here is how.

Mix 2 1/2 cups of unsifted flour, 3 eggs (slightly beaten) then gradually add enough water (about 3/4 cup) to bind, for a not too firm slightly sticky dough. Knead dough on floured board. Roll out to about 1/8 inch thick. Cut into about 4 inch squares, then put a heaping tablespoon of filling in each square. Bring

Village Farmyard Scene

opposite corners to center top, pinch shut and pinch-close the 4 seams very securely. Drop into salted, boiling water and cook slowly until done—about 25 minutes. Lift out Klees into a deep earthenware or heat-proof bowl and pour seasoned, warmed light cream over them.

To prepare the fillings:

Strawberry—diced, sugared fresh berries, drained and a bit of flour added to absorb moisture.
Cherry—semi-sweets or sweet varieties are good, sugared and floured. I find the best brands of canned cherry pie-fillings just right.
Cottage-cheese—1 1/2 cups dry cottage cheese (if too soft, add a few dry bread crumbs.) 1/4 teaspoon salt, 1 tablespoon of grated onion, 1 egg. Mix well and follow filling and cooking procedures already given.

All filled Klees should be topped with butter-browned bread cubes; and to the cottage cheese ones, fried, crisp bacon, crumpled over, further improves them.

Homemade German Noodles

Use the ingredients given for a soft noodle dough, but work in more flour as you knead dough on board. Knead it well. Divide into 3 pieces, shape each into a pat, and roll each paper-thin. Place sheets on a lint-free cloth or towels and let dry until the consistency of a chamois cloth, turning sheets to dry both sides. Roll like jelly-roll and cut very thin. (Watch out for your fingernails until you have mastered this art.) They are ready to use when cut. When very dry, they can be frozen or stored in jars for future use.

To serve, boil in salted water. Strain. Add about 1/2 pound butter or margarine. Toss lightly. Top with browned-ahead-in-butter bread crumbs.

****

Pleena are the quick and easy German pancakes.

Gatofel Pleena

For each person to eat them, grate 1 medium large potato and 1 small onion. Add 1/4 teaspoon salt and 1 slightly beaten egg. Mix. Spoon 2 tablespoons of mixture (including liquid) on a generously greased, medium hot fry pan, flattening into pancakes. When edges show browning, turn cakes and finish on other side. Serve hot! Will keep hot if you'll put them into a 250 degree oven after each baking.

Sees Pleena

Into a bowl of 4 well-beaten eggs add 1/2 teaspoon salt, 1 tablespoon of sugar, 1 cup of flour and about 2 cups of milk. Spoon-mix, then beat smooth with an egg beater. Batter should be very thin. Place about 1/2 cup of it into well-greased skillet, tipping pan as needed to spread mixture over entire pan surface. When edges show browning, turn with broad turner and finish. A firm, but very thin, lacey pancake should emerge. Good served with potato soup.

****

With the exception of potatoes and cabbage, vegetable eaters our people were not. Could be that is the reason they excelled so in the preparation of these. Possibly top on the list were the following specialties.

Gahocktus

Grind 6 cups of raw potatoes, 1 large onion and about 2 cups of hamburger (some like a bit of pork in it, others use ground leftover cooked meat, entirely.) Add salt and pepper to taste, 3 or 4 tablespoons of cooking oil or bacon grease, 2 cups of water. Mix well and bake in well-greased pan for about an hour at 350 degrees.

Salaud Sopa (Wilted Lettuce)

Shred 2 medium heads of lettuce or equal amount of leaf lettuce. Grate a tablespoon of onion over it. In a fry-pan, crisp 4 slices of bacon, diced. Remove bacon and set aside. Into the bacon grease put 2 1/2 cups water, 1/4 cup vinegar, pinch of salt. Bring to boil and remove from stove. At once add 3 slightly-beaten eggs and stir with fork until eggs are firm. Mix into lettuce and let lettuce simmer a little to wilt. Finally, add 1 1/2 cups sour cream and top with the bacon pieces. Ladle over boiled potatoes to serve.

****

Gatofel Wurst (Potato Sausage)

1 lb. hamburger
1 lb. fresh ground sausage
2 lb. ground potatoes
1 onion ground
1 cup warm water
1 tablespoon salt
a dash each of pepper and garlic salt

96

Mix well and stuff into casings (about 1/4 lb. purchased from your butcher.) Tie ends. Place in well-greased pan. Puncture big bubbles with a darning needle so casing will not split during baking. Bake in 350 degree oven for 1 hour.

****

Rye Bread *(Proot)* was the everyday "staff of life" in the old country, while *Kucha*, made with white flour, was the holiday bread.

Crusty Rye Bread
(2 loaves)

Cook a medium-sized potato in water until soft. Sieve potato back into its own liquid and add enough water to make 2 cups. Cool to lukewarm. Add 1 package of dry yeast (first dissolved in 1/4 cup of warm water), 1/4 cup sugar, 1 teaspoon salt and 2 cups of white flour. Mix well and let rise until spongy. Stir down and let rise again. Now add 1 1/2 cups of rye flour and enough white flour to make a stiff dough. Knead well. Cover with a cloth and let rise in a warm place until double its size (about 1 hour). Shape into round, flat loaves and set out in heavily greased and floured pie pans. Brush tops with melted shortening. Let rise 20 to 25 minutes. Bake in 350 degree oven for 1 hour. Remove from oven, wipe tops with a wet cloth, set on racks and cover with a dishtowel until cool.

Of late, I have used Pillsbury Hot Roll Mix for the base of all *Kucha* and raised doughnuts with excellent results. However, I pass along the "from scratch" recipe also.

Make a sponge with 1 package yeast, 1 cup of warm potato water and 1 cup of warm milk, 1/2 cup sugar and 1 cup flour. Let set in a warm place until doubled in size. Now add 2 beaten eggs, 1/4 cup cooking oil, 1 teaspoon salt and enough flour to make a soft dough. Let rise an hour and it is ready to be rolled out on a floured board and cut into the usual round doughnuts or into little squares, knife-slit twice and then deep-fried in hot oil for *Krebble* (German Raised Doughnuts). Or, the dough becomes *Kucha* when rolled out, put into greased pans for baking, after topping with well-drained, sugared and lightly-floured fruits, with *Reevel* or a mixture of cottage cheese, sour cream, and grated onion; or shaped into rolls or loaves or twists.

To make *Reevel Kucha*, prepare a topping made with 1 cup flour, 1/2 cup sugar, 1 cube of melted butter. Roll back and forth gently between hands until coarse, crumbly, balls are formed. Sprinkle on dough just before baking.

Kraut Kucha transcend all preferred delicacies, according to informal polling. Simmer in a bit of butter and a little water until limp: 1 head of shredded cabbage, 1 finely-chopped onion, salt and pepper to taste. Cool and place by tablespoonfuls in the center of 5 inch squares, cut from *Kucha* dough rolled on floured board. Bring opposite corners to top and pinch. Then pinch-seal all 4 seams, dip other side in generously greased pan and turn to bake with seams down, in 400 oven for about 20-25 minutes.

Apple Kucha are made the same way, substituting sugar and a little cinnamon for the onion and seasoning while steaming.

****

Today's soup devotees will enjoy our Volga German soups. They were actually complete meals in themselves—thick and hearty.

The good smoky taste of ham hocks makes Split Pea, Lentil, or Bean Soup so flavorsome. Here is how we make each today:

2 cups of whichever legume you choose
2 quarts of water
1 sizable ham hock
1/2 cup each of chopped celery, carrots, and onion.

Place all ingredients into a large kettle and boil gently for about 2 hours. Remove hock, chop up meat and return to soup, plus salt and pepper to taste. Just before serving try a tablespoon of sour cream in each bowlful.

A meaty soup-bone cooked in water until tender, with a small diced onion and salt to taste, makes a tasty base for several soups. For *Gashta Sopa,* 1 cup of pearl barley cooked in the broth until tender, then a bit of sweet or sour cream added just before serving, is excellent. For *Sauerkraut Sopa* add a small can of kraut, a large potato diced and the meat from the bone. Cook until potatoes are done. Dice and fry 3 slices of bacon til crisp. Remove from pan. Into remaining grease add a tablespoon of flour and brown lightly. Dip a cup of the soup broth in this, stir well and return it all to the soup.

Milk soups were thought beneficial for quelling upset stomachs—even for curing colds. Into 2 quarts of heated-to-boil milk, add 3 fistfuls of noodles and bring to a full boil and cook about 3 minutes. Remove from stove and season to taste.

Reevel Sopa also had a milk base. Reevel are made by combining 1 cup of flour and an egg. With your hands roll-mix until tiny balls are formed. Drop these into the milk (or into a good beef or chicken broth if you prefer). And cook just a few minutes till done. Chicken broth and noodles make a tasty soup, also.

Gatofel Sopa

Boil 4 medium potatoes, diced and diced onion in salted water until soft. Partly crush the potatoes with a potato masher, add rich milk or a cup of sour cream and a dash of pepper and serve. Sees Pleena are a good accompaniment here.

Schnitzel Sopa (Fruit Soup)

How many of you remember neighbors bringing in "Gatotish Assa" (Schnitzel Sopa and Krebble) when your mother was in childbed—at home of course? I do—all 7 times! Simmer-cook 1 package of mixed dried fruit, 1 cup dark raisins, 1 slice of lemon, in water to cover, for about 2 hours or until fruit is soft, but not mushy. While fruit is boiling, mix 2 tablespoons flour, 1/2 cup light Karo syrup, 1 tablespoon hot water. Add this to finished fruit and continue cooking a few minutes longer. At serving time, add a bit of sweet cream (optional).

****

In most of our homes, Papa said grace before we ate, followed by each of us kids mumbling in fast turn, "Abba, lieber Fatter, Amen." In some families, sometimes Father had his little pre-meal "schnapps", which was called "Autzanei" (remedial medicine). Then usually Mother prayed before eating— always lapsing into the high German "segne diese Speise" type thanks. Certainly, we were blessed with a great heritage for which to be grateful.

Enduring the Soviet Experience: One Family's Story
by Olga Litzenberger (1992)

Today the Germans in Russia are going through an uneasy time. Thousands of German families are leaving Russia, the land of their ancestors for generations. During World War II Russian Germans went through the hell of national genocide. Having not been allowed to take part on the front line of the battle, they "forged a victory" in the Labor Army or concentration camps. Eight hundred thousand out of two million Germans were behind barbed wire. Among those people were my Grandfather Litzenberger, Phillip Yacovlevich, my grandmother Elizabetha Yacovlevna; their brothers and sisters, and my aunt who was three years old in 1941.

The first Litzenberger—his name was Sebastian—came to the Volga with his family in 1767. He came after the invitational manifesto of Catherine II. The manifesto invited foreigners to Russia and promised them a number of incredibly tempting privileges. Many of them, however, were not given. Sometimes, after periods of good harvest came times of drought and famine. Nevertheless, the German colonists not only could survive, keeping their culture and customs, on that new land but also could have a prosperous life despite the severe climate and transform those nomadic steppes into a fertile land.

Descendants of the first Litzenberger lived in the village of Yagodnaya Polyana. In 1859 four colonies separated from this mother colony: Schoenfeld, Schoental, Schoendorf, and Rosental. There were twelve people with the last name Litzenberger just in Schoenfeld (now Michailovka) in 1892. My grandfather and grandmother lived there until the decree of 1941 which changed the lives of the Russian Germans. My grandfather, Phillip Yacovlevich, was born on March 30, 1914. There were two more sons in his family: older brother Andrei and younger Jacob (Yacov) born in 1921. After the Revolution of October 1918 the decree "About Proclamation of the Autonomous Labor Commune of Germans from the Volga" was signed by V. I. Lenin. On January 6, 1924 this commune had been renamed the "Autonomic Soviet Socialist Republic of Volga Germans," and by that time its population was 526,000 people.

The Litzenberger family lived in this republic. My grandfather married Elizabeth Beitel, and Berta, their first daughter, was born on January 30, 1938. They lived very happily and had their own house. At first my grandfather worked as a smith's apprentice at a machine-tractor station, and then he became a remarkable smith. This kind of profession was very respected at that time. According to my grandfather harvests were very good on his collective farm. The German Autonomous Republic had 219,900 cattle, a gigantic meat factory, bacon factory, and 89 dairies. The supply of meat, poultry, milk, and grain into Russia was quite substantial. The first immense cultural and scientific contributions were made to our country by the Soviet Germans.

However, the way of life for hundreds of thousands of people established over generations was destroyed within a few days. All economic structures were annihilated by decree on August 28, 1941. Stalin's system made the Soviet Germans its own victims, broke their lives, threw them across the world, and shattered families—wives from husbands, children from parents, brothers and sisters. The life of my grandparents and hundreds of thousands of other people were destroyed by just one government decree. They had lost the rights to live and work at the place of their ancestors whose graves they were forced to leave. According to the August, 1941 Decree of Presidium of the Supreme Soviet, they had to relocate to another strange and unknown place. The decree of September 3 liquidated the Autonomous Republic and its fifteen regions were added to the Saratov province, and another seven to Stalingrad. Within two weeks more than 40,000 families were removed from the liquidated republic.

The text of the decree reveals the falsification of the charges. It read, in part, that "...According to true data, which was received by military authorities, there are thousands and tens of thousands of saboteurs and spies among the German population that lives in the Volga region and they are going to make insurrection in the region after a signal received from Germany. No one from the German population living on the Volga has made a report to Soviet authorities about such numerous saboteurs and spies — consequently the German population of the Volga are keeping among themselves enemies of Soviet people....In order to avoid undesirable consequences and to prevent a serious bloodshed the Presidium of the Supreme Soviet USSR have found it necessary to remove the German population at Povolzhie to another place. To all of them have to be given land and state aid in the new regions...."

My great uncle and father told me about the relocation. It began on a Saturday, in the middle of September, when a platoon of soldiers suddenly came to their village. They explained to the people about the impending move. One week was given for preparation. Those seven days were very sad, the last days on their own native land from which they would be apart for the rest of their lives without hope of returning. They would never come back to their land to see the lovely land of their childhood and graves of their relatives. Those seven days people tried to do a thousand and one things at once. They were not allowed to leave the collective farm's fields during harvest, working in the fields together with Russians who believed the Presidium of Supreme Soviet's decree about "fascist spies" and were in a hurry to expropriate their property. The Germans did not actually know which thing they really needed to take and which to leave behind. My grandmother was puzzled by thousands of questions: Whether or not to take winter clothing; where they would be sent and for how long; what to do with little Berta and how to protect her through this hard trip; how to put all things that were allowed in one suitcase. They gave all their cattle and grain to the collective farm and received only a receipt which was not valid for money but worthless proof of that action. The furniture and other possessions were given to friends and neighbors. A big part of their belongings were left in their abandoned homes.

Early the following Saturday morning, with eyes full of tears, they left their native villages which had been their blessed home for 170 years. Using horses and wagons they came to the train station Mockrous. It was a bitter separation from their home and the start of a new and tragic experience. They awaited the unknown. Men in military uniforms surrounded and squeezed them into boxcars of fifty persons each. Their departure was not well organized; the innocent and scared suffered needlessly. They remained two days at the train station fifteen kilometers from their home. There was no possibility of getting out from the car. Two days later the train finally departed. No one knew where they are going. Omsk? Novosibirsk? Barnaul? More and more deep into Siberia they lumbered. On their way people were starving and dying because of cold and hunger. My grandmother's friend delivered a boy during that trip and unable to survive, the infant died.

After arriving at their destination two weeks later all tired, hungry, and frozen, people were delivered to different villages. They were in Kazakhstan. My grandparents came to a collective farm named Kizil-Kagam ("Red Flag" in Kazakh), about fourteen kilometers from the city of Kokchatav. My grandfather's oldest brother Andrei's family were sent to the Tselinograd district, his younger brother Jacob to the Novosibirsk area, and his wife's brother Jacob went to the Pavlodar district. The overwhelming majority of Kizil-Kagam's population was Kazakh so communication was practically impossible. Not one German knew their language. To survive from hunger all possessions were traded for food. All Germans underwent registration in a special commandant's office. Soviet passports were taken away and instead of their citizenship papers the Germans received the so-called "wolf's ticket" which explained the conditions of their new life. According to this document they not only lost their rights to leave this new place but also to leave the village. Any person who would disobey this law could be punished by twenty years in prison. All Germans were forced to sign this document.

In January, 1942 the Labor Army was created which for all purposes was slave labor. People were kept behind barbed wire and working and living conditions were not humane. The economic policy toward Germans was directed to use their manual labor for "forging victory in the backwoods" of World War II. Because of the war, anything German was to be beaten for any reason and the innocent Volga Germans died by the thousands in the trenches of this Labor Army. In January, 1942 all males of 18 to 50 were taken into the Labor Army. They were separated from their families, wives, and children. Moreover, in fall of 1942 youths of sixteen to eighteen years old of both sexes were considered to be old enough for service. Young women whose children were over three years old also were made eligible.

My grandfather worked in that army at Balchashsk Copper Factory from 1942 to 1946. After four years of hard work he became seriously ill. He remembers that they went to their job in line and twice every day had to be counted by guards. My grandfather did not like to recall those turbulent times and said almost nothing about it to his children. In 1946 he eventually fled from the Labor Army because of the deplorable conditions there. His wife's brother told me this story that he could not tell anyone for fifty years. Deportation of the Soviet Germans was a forbidden topic for a long time in our country and only in August 29, 1964 did a decree rehabilitate the Germans in Russia. However, the text was not made public for years. In December, 1942 Jacob was sixteen years old and was taken for the Labor Army to Buguruslan, Bashkiria. Seven thousand workers were placed into eighty dugouts with a capacity in each of ninety men. The dugouts were underground and had no windows or doors. In the middle of it was snow. They worked from 7:00 a.m. and until 7:00 p.m., having just 600 grams of bread and soup from sauerkraut if they had made the daily norm of work. People died because of dysentery, typhus, cold, and hunger. There was a special team of sixteen men on duty every day to collect corpses, make graves, and bury them without coffins or clothing.

The years of slave labor could not break the young and robust Jacob, and today he lives with his wife, three children, and six grandchildren in the village of Podsinie located near the city of Chakasii. He is sixty-seven years old and still works as an electrician. His son Alexander and his family emigrated to Germany in April, 1992. After my grandfather's escape from the Labor Army, he returned to his wife and daughter in Kizil-Kagam. In August 6, 1947 their son Andrei was born; he is my father. In March 13, 1949 their daughter Emma was born. My grandfather had begun to work at his former trade again. He was a remarkable smith and this profession helped him keep out of the Labor Army. The Soviet authorities looked for him a long time after his escape. However, a local judge liked the products which were made by his golden hands. My grandfather had bought his own right to be with his family by selling a remarkable samovar he made himself. However, he lost his documents which were required for getting a pension. Of course there is no comparison between the two loses and life is more important. His golden hands saved him from inevitable death.

They had a hard life even after the war as the country was in ruins. Many cities, factories, and collective farms had been destroyed. This created difficulties in providing food for people. My grandfather maintained himself by selling goods that he made. In 1951 my grandfather's family moved to a village called Vasilkovka which was two kilometers away from Kizil-Kagam. That village was bigger than the collective-farm and there was a school. Eventually all Germans came out of the collective-farm to live in that village. Germans tried to keep their culture and religion but it was hard. German children studied the

104

Kazakh language! Basilkovka was a Ukrainian village. Ukrainian Kazakhs were also deported to this place by a tzar's decree after they committed some revolt. Germans were another population exiled just for being Germans during Stalin's time. My grandparents had lived together, shoulder by shoulder, with Germans, Kazakhs, Ukrainians, and Russians.

In 1953 my grandmother died from stomach cancer. Her children aged fifteen, six, and four were left without a mother. Before she died she asked her husband to marry again for the sake of the children. Sophia (Schneider) Ochs was a widow aged forty-four who had her own children and she and my grandfather were later married. In 1957 my grandfather retired. His years in the Labor Army had affected his health. He died in October 30, 1968 at the age of fifty-four. Sofia died in 1978. It has been difficult for all the Litzenbergers to reestablish their relationships since the 1941 deportation. Many perished in the tragic events of that time and some may have emigrated to the West in recent years. I would like to believe that the day will come when our families can reunite and that all the German families in Russia who were repressed for no reason will yet find justice.

Grandmother's Favorite Place

CHESAPEAKE TO PACIFIC:
LIFE IN THE NEW WORLD

The Plain and Prairie
by Richard Scheuerman (1980)

As early as 1840, Count Paul Kiselev, head of the Russian Ministry of Imperial Domains, was commissioned by Nicholus I to study the implication of a general emancipation of the serfs. His investigations led to little immediate change although this study of the rural populace revealed the conspicuous isolation of the German colonies. Kiselev's findings confirmed an earlier government report which related that "there are only a few of the colonists who enlighten themselves as much as they should concerning the Russian language, wherefore they do not know the Russian laws...and evidently take pains to avoid every intercourse with Russia." A major contributing factor to this situation was their special status as *colonisty* which guaranteed certain advantages not available to the general public. Accordingly, legislation altering their judicial and political systems was introduced in the 1860s. In 1861 Russia's twenty-five million serfs were freed from serfdom and in 1864 zemstvo reform established district and provincial assemblies among all classes through an indirect electoral process and within a decade these were functioning in the Volga, uniting both Germans and Russians in common assemblies. Local colonial autonomy was now replaced by the integrated zemstvos which had jurisdiction over education, public finances, and other matters (G. Bauer, 1907, p. 163).

Since in most areas of colonial settlement the Germans remained the predominant ethnic group, they generally acquiesced to these changes. It was not until 1871 that developments culminated in a decree perceived by thousands of Volga Germans as unacceptably threatening. By that time the flourishing colonies also attracted an element of suspicion due to their comparative prosperity as their farms were models of productivity to the native Russians (H. Schlommer, 1964, p. 60).

The Ukase of June 4, 1871 was promulgated by the Council of Ministers just as routinely as other policies of the day. It was to have, however, far-reaching effects on the Germans in Russia. The senate decree repealed all privileges originally granted "for eternal time" under the terms of Catherine's 1763 Manifesto including military exemption. Attempts by the tsar and his foreign minister, Prince Alexander Gorchakov, to modify the military exemption clause succeeded only in allowing a ten-year grace period in which colonists would have the option to legally emigrate although few of these landed people seemed eager to do so. Grievances expressed to the authorities brought no redress and even Alexander II remarked with reference to the sudden abrogation that "a hundred years is an eternity!"

A decisive preemption of the ordered transition toward assimilation with the Russian populace occurred with the unexpectedly early issuance of the law of universal military conscription and corresponding annulment of the grace period on January 1, 1874. The dread of serving in the Russian army was widespread among the males in the nation and especially the Germans, many of whom had a poor command of the Russian language and were often looked upon with disdain in the predominately native Russian regiments. Discipline was cruel with minimum chance for advancement and terms of service lasted up to six years. Wages were pitifully low and the eligible draft age began at twenty. Lotteries were held to fill the ranks of the standing army. The threat of conscription became the chief motivating factor for the initial emigration of Germans from Russia to North and South America and in 1874 over 6,000 Germans, predominately Mennonites, immigrated to the United States. A tragic drought struck the Volga region in 1878 along with cattle diseases as well as epidemics of typhus and smallpox among the people. The resulting economic decline prompted continued German emigration from Russia as did events during the reactionary reigns of Alexander II (1881-94) and Nicholas II (1894-1917) (A. Giesinger, 1974, p. 227).

In addition, antagonism was still being directed against the pietistic Brethren in many Volga colonies. By contrast, there was strong attraction to North America brought about by the early immigrants to the United States who reported to their friends and relatives in the Old World about the many opportunities of the New World. Promotional literature was sent to Europe expounding upon the wealth of the country and the rich soil that was yet to be turned.

In the spring of 1874, mass meetings were held to discuss the situation among Catholic colonists on the *Wiesenseite* at Herzog and in Balzer on the *Bergseite* by the Protestants. A prime mover in the drive to emigrate was Rev. Wilhelm Staerkel, the Reformed pastor in Norka who, having done mission work in Kansas and Missouri in the 1860s, extolled the virtues of that land and related the liberal provisions of the Homestead Act of 1862. Accordingly, a total of fourteen scouts were selected to explore potential areas of settlement in the United States during the summer of 1874 (F. Koch, 1977, p. 205).

Upon arrival in the United States, the party divided into several groups to explore areas in Nebraska, Kansas, Iowa, and possibly Arkansas. Prairie grass and a soil sample were retrieved to confirm that optimistic report upon their return to the Volga as was technical information regarding the various modes of transportation and settlement. In the fall and winter of 1874, a small group departed for Nebraska, Kansas, and Arkansas. One year later, on August 23, 1875 emigrants from Balzer, Dietel, and Mohr went to Red Oak, Iowa under the leadership of Heinrich Schwabauer. Part of this group followed Jacob

Bender to Sutton, Nebraska where they had heard Black Sea Germans had settled, while others went to Kansas. In November of that same year, Catholics from the Volga reached Topeka and Rush County, Kansas. Both Topeka and Lincoln became central distribution points for Volga German settlement in the region which began en mass in the summer of 1876.

Following the assassination of the reforming Tsar Alexander II in 1881, his reactionary son, Alexander III (1881-94), countered in a reign characterized by further attempts directed, in the words of Peter Durnovo, chief of the state police, "toward the complete liberation of Russia from the foreign element." Such sentiment at higher levels of government led to anti-German policy in both the foreign and domestic realm, continued under Nicholas I (1894-1917). A ukase issued on March 26, 1892, prohibited the private ownership of land by foreign residents in Russia—the status of the Volga Germans—and forbade the leasing of land by foreigners. Immunity from these stipulations was contingent upon application for naturalization and membership in the Russian Orthodox Church, an unlikely prospect to most Volga Germans.

Their school systems also came increasingly under the scrutiny of the authorities and in 1890 legislation was introduced requiring a Russian teacher in every German school, followed by a decree in 1897 requiring Russian as the principal language of instruction. In 1905 certain restrictions on the private ownership of land and use of German were rescinded, but the status of German ethnicity in Russia continued to be precarious. Finally, per capita land supply continued to regress with the growing population while tragic crop failures struck the Volga region in 1884, 1889, 1892, and 1897. The developments continued in great contrast to revelations of prosperity and security in America (G. Bonwetsch, 1919, p. 109).

In some aspects, Russia and the United States were undergoing similar changes in the late nineteenth century. Both were becoming more aware of their great natural wealth and had recently met the problems of servile emancipation while looking forward to growth in transportation and industry. Relations between the two countries were good and while William F. Cody supervised a spirited buffalo hunt on Grand Duke Alexis' United States tour in 1872, both nations' diplomats often referred to mutual "manifest destinies." However, the United States, though not always oblivious to ethnic distinctions, molded a new order in the nineteenth century through unprecedented achievements in transportation, agriculture, and education. Revision of the Homestead Act of 1862 led to grants of available land to foreigners who simply declared their intentions of becoming United States citizens through which they could secure a deed to a 160 acre tract after having cultivated a portion of it for five years. Preemptions could be obtained under the same qualifications but after only six months of residence at $1.25 per acre. Supplementary federal legislation such as the Timber Culture Act of 1873 and Desert Land Act of 1877 eventually succeeded in filling what Abraham

Lincoln had earlier termed a labor deficiency in agriculture (M. Hansen, 1940, pp. 72-73).

The completion of the first transcontinental railroad in May, 1869 was another event that sparked a new era of settlement in the American West. Not only were new areas now made readily accessible to settlers, but the scheme to subsidize the construction of over 1,000 miles of Union Pacific track was to grant lands adjacent to the lines, the sale of which would then become a profitable enterprise for the railroad. Through this arrangement Congress mandated grants totaling millions of acres to the Union Pacific as well as other railroad companies operating lines west of the Mississippi River. By 1872 the Kansas Pacific and the Atchison, Topeka and Santa Fe were given the claim to seven million acres in Kansas Territory alone, consisting of alternate sections along the right of way for twenty miles on both sides.

Carl B. Schmidt, a native of Saxony who had settled in Lawrence, Kansas was selected in 1873 to head the immigration office of the Atchison, Topeka and Santa Fe. His contacts with German ethnic groups throughout the country led him to seek communication with dissatisfied Germans in Russia in order to arrange their settlement in America. He supervised the inspection of property near Great Bend, Kansas by leaders of a contingent of Volga Germans, mostly Catholics from the *Wiesenseite*, who arrived in Baltimore on the *S. S. Ohio* on November 23, 1875 and went to Topeka, Kansas five days later.

Most of the group under the tutelage of Schmidt deemed the price of land near Great Bend, $5 per acre, too expensive and later formed Catholic communities in Ellis County. Here they either homesteaded or purchased lands offered there for less by the Kansas Pacific Railroad with the first families arriving in Hays and Victoria in February, 1876. A contemporary reporter's commentary described the scene of their arrival in the following terms:

> The whole outfit, wagons, horses, dogs, cows, women, and children of the men folks of the Russians, who had taken claims in this (Ellis) county, arrived last Wednesday night and a queer looking set they are. Most of them came fully supplied with stock, wagons, household furniture, etc....
>
> They are strong looking animals, and seem capable of any work, especially the women, who seem to perform as much menial labor as the children, which are numerous....

Subsequent statements also noted another interesting quality of Volga German life: "One of the pleasing features of the Russian presence in our town is their singing. All have good voices, and none have any hesitancy in displaying their vocal accomplishments" (*Hays City Sentinal*, August 16, 1876).

Among the few Protestants on board the November *S. S. Ohio* transport were the families of (most locating near Great Bend, Kansas): George Brach, Peter Ochs, Henry Scheuermann, and two Conrad Scheuermanns. They were soon joined in Kansas by the families of George H. Green, Henry Rothe, and

Conrad Aschenbrenner who had arrived in New York on January 6, 1876 on the *S. S. City of Montreal.*

Songs of lament grew in intensity on the Volga as more Germans tore the bonds of family and homeland to emigrate to America. The news of local *V' shteyeroongen* became more frequent as families auctioned off most household wares to pay travel expenses. They took little more than the physical necessities of food and clothing along with the *Wolga Gesangbuch* and family Bible which were all carefully packed in a large wooden-ribbed trunk. Travel from the Volga region was facilitated by the linking of Saratov in 1871 by railroad with southern and northern points. This also opened the region to foreign contact through visits by American railroad immigration agents with literature extolling the virtues of life in the Midwest (N. Saul, 1976, pp. 4-11).

The general pattern of travel began upon receipt of a passport from the provincial capitals of Saratov or Pokrovsk. Since the authorities often denied requests for permanent residence abroad, some applicants registered for temporary certification while intending to flee induction into the army. Railroad service from Saratov made connections for travel to Bremen, Hamburg, or other European port cities where enormous passenger vessels transported them across the Atlantic in a normal two-week journey to Baltimore, Philadelphia, or Castle Gardens, New York. Like so many other immigrants to the United States, many Russian Germans had their first experiences in dealing with the New World at one of these unpleasant receiving stations, particularly Castle Gardens which was the largest in all of North America prior to 1892. The principal passenger lines used by the Volga Germans included the Hamburg American Line, the Inman Line of Liverpool, and North German Lloyd (of Bremen).

Other Volga Germans who were among the first to settle in Kansas traveled aboard the *S. S. Mosel* which arrived in New York on October 24, 1876 carrying over 200 Volga Germans largely from the *Wiesenseite* where most had lived in the daughter colonies along the Jeruslan River of Neu Yagodnaya, Schontal, Schonfeld, and Schondorf. Villages there had been established in the 1850s principally by residents of Yagodnaya Polyana and Pobotschnoye on the *Bergseite* but unfavorable conditions along the Jeruslan prompted another move. Having relatives who had settled in Kansas in 1875 (those noted previously on the *S. S. Ohio* and *S. S. City of Montreal*), these Volga Germans also chose to emigrate and eventually formed the basis of the "Kansas Colony" that would be the first group of Russian Germans to move to the Pacific Northwest. They later settled in Portland, Oregon in 1881 and in Whitman County, Washington Territory the following year.

Families aboard the October transport of the *S. S. Mosel* included those of Conrad Appel; Mrs. Henry Brach; Christian, John, and Phillip Kleweno; Henry Litzenberger; Conrad, Henry, Phillip, John, John Phillip, and two Peter Ochses; Adam and Henry Repp; Adam Ruhl; John, Henry, Peter, and two George and Adam Schiermanns, and Henry Scheuermann. This group traveled to Lawrence, Kansas where they stayed for about a month in the fall of 1876 while it was determined where they would settle, eventually moving to Great Bend and Pawnee Rock where some established small businesses or worked for the railroad. Most, however, selected lands to farm and many settled in areas along the border of Barton and Rush County.

Intermarriage solidified relationships between the various pioneer families to form a close-knit ethnic group. They often lived in isolated areas where the bond of the groups of families was extremely important for their physical survival and their social well-being. Mrs. Henry Brack settled with her sons near Otis where they later became prominent in business and farming. Her son Peter's wife, Sophie (Kniss) was the sister-in-law of one of the Ochs cousins, John Peter, who remained in Great Bend, Kansas with others seeking employment on the Atchison, Topeka, and Santa Fe Railroad. They were all from the colony of Schonfeld. Many Volga Germans were compelled to live in old railroad cars due to their lack of finances and the lack of suitable housing in the area. One of the Schierman brothers, John, was a skilled carpenter and butcher, opening a small grocery store in Great Bend. John and Anna Marie's daughter, Mary, married one of the Ochs cousins, Peter. Henry Litzenberger and Henry Repp were brothers-in-law as their wives, Anna Elizabeth and Mary (Barth) respectively, were sisters and all of these people were from Neu Jagodnaja (Mrs. E. Repp, 1971).

Peter Brack wrote of these families' peregrinations in his autobiographical memoir, "Trips":

> My parents were Germans who had moved to Russia under the edict of Catherine, Czarina of Russia. When I was nine months of age we again moved,...this time 100 miles southeast from my birthplace. We traveled overland in two covered wagons drawn by single horses and on the second day of our journey were in Saratov....From there we went across the prairie sixty miles...to a treeless prairie where about twenty-six families established the new village in a large bend of the stream. They held an election to select officers of the village according to the Russian laws and thus organized the colony Schoenfeldt, which in English means Pleasant Field. My father was elected mayor and held this office until his death which occurred in his forty-eighth year when I was nine years of age. For his services as mayor he received one ruble a year. In the summer time he was a farmer and in the winter a shoemaker and weaver.
>
> ...We resided there until September 8, 1876, when we left with a large party of emigrants for the United States and landed in Castle Garden, New York on the 21st day of October, 1876, we came, (our whole party of over forty families) as far as Lawrence, Kansas, without delay and after

stopping there about four weeks my mother and our family with other families, making about 200 persons in all, came to Great Bend and Pawnee Rock and located in the western part of Barton County and eastern part of Rush where the most of we German-Russians are now prosperous farmers and dabbling some in other lines of investment but we always attend to our business (P. Brack, 1915, p. 3).

This outline reflects the pattern in which the immigrants came as a group of old acquaintances who started again in a country very reminiscent of their homeland, who carried on their traditions, spoke their native language, clung to their traditions and only gradually were assimilated into the American mainstream. For about ten years they farmed, went to church, brought in necessary supplies by wagon and team. Prior to 1886 Olney, Scheuerman, Belfield, and Schoental were recognized as post offices or community names. The nearest railroads had been at Larned, Great Bend, or Hays. Supplies were freighted in by teams in about a day's trip. At first there were no school or church buildings. These came after homes and fields of grain were established. People traveled by wagons drawn by horse or oxen, horseback or sometimes by buggy. There had been early Indian scares but Indians were no real menace after the first settlement. Old timers recalled uncomfortable things such as prairie fires, snakes, scarcity of rain, shortage of crops, lonesomeness, and blizzards. Good times were experienced in literaries, spelling bees, quilting bees, and church gatherings in schoolhouses or homes. The German Lutheran Church was organized in 1877 by forty-seven German families of the Schoental community. In later years the church divided into the Lutheran, Methodist, and Baptist churches in Otis and Bison with founding families including those named Kleweno, Hergert, Scheuerman, Rothe, Ochs, Wirtz, Hartman, Brack, and Moore.

The Volga Germans who migrated to the Great Plains did not experience the extreme forms of discrimination that other ethnic and religious groups experienced. This was due in part to the character of the Russian Germans. Besides being recognized as a hard-working industrious people, they were known for their willingness to learn the English language and to participate in the educational opportunities of the American frontier. Many Volga Germans deemed the American system of public education superior to the educational institutions of Russia. One Kansas newspaper, the Russel *Record,* noted in 1876 that "what pleases us the best is to see them [the Russian Germans] sending their children to public school. We will risk any people's becoming Americanized, who patronize free schools."

Booming grain production in the Midwest contributed to a 100% increase in the export of farm commodities from the United States between 1871 and 1874. This agricultural development was brought about by the advancement of American technology, and these new changes severely reduced Russia's traditional hold on the European market because its production declined during the same period. Many Germans from Russia first settled in the Midwest where agriculture was rapidly becoming an important national source of wealth and pride. Indeed, the word "bunchgrass" became synonymous with untapped soil fertility in America's Midwest, and one published account by a trading firm in Odessa, Russia ventured to suggest a significant development resulting from the expansion of American agriculture: "The mind is positively lost in painful thought when considering the quantity of corn [grain] America will soon be able to export. America will absolutely command the English market, and reduce prices to a minimum, with which it will e utterly impossible for us to compete" (*The London Times,* February 1, 1876).

The Kansas pioneers suffered considerably from the effects of the grass-hopper plagues in the late 1870s. Particularly from 1875 to 1877, massive hordes of these insects so infested the fields and air that the Germans were left with little seed to replant. A dismal gloom hung over the land as swarms of the pests darkened the midday sky. The subsequent drought also adversely affected them and some remarked of the terror felt during the frightening electrical storms. The Germans were not accustomed to such storms in Russia, and they dreaded the devastation of the plains tornadoes. One informant humorously related an Oz-like fantasy in which a cyclone was said to have taken a small lake and team of horses from a Rush County homestead which his father, after he came out of the root cellar, attempted to find. Enroute to town he found the road leading into a new lake and nearby the two horses stood—still harnessed and unharmed (D. Schierman, 1972)!

Because of these conditions on the plains, some disgruntled immigrant groups in the Midwest increasingly considered the possibility of settling in the Pacific Northwest. The settlers learned from some men who had worked in the Oregon Country on railway surveys that the land was fertile and beautiful. Their interest was further stimulated by the favorable descriptions provided by transportation companies from the Pacific Northwest. In order to encourage emmigration, these companies advertised the lush regions of the inland Northwest as the "Great Columbia Plain." Not only were transportation companies that owned land interested in selling acreage, but they also wanted to tap an unskilled labor source for the construction of their railroads. In order to fill this need, company officials turned to immigrants for a solution. Various railroad companies formed associations offering reduced rates to those who would travel westward to settle while guaranteeing employment until such arrangements were possible. The Union Pacific, Northern Pacific, Oregon Steamship Company, and others were particularly interested in encouraging the development of the West in order to profit not only from passenger service but the anticipated shipment of industrial and agricultural commodities that were to be developed by the transportation companies.

One man's name in particular became synonymous with the growth and development of the Northwest—Henry Villard—who by 1876 had shrewdly wrested control of Northwestern transportation systems from railroad magnate Ben Holladay of Overland Stage and Pony Express fame. In the centennial year, Villard assumed the presidency of several companies that were heavily in debt, including the Oregon and California Railroad and the Oregon Central Railroad, both of which were far from completion. In addition, Villard gained control of the Oregon Steamship Company which operated regularly between San Francisco and Portland. Within six years Henry Villard's position in Northwest transportation was clearly paramount as his holdings appeared secure and were among the largest of any individual in the entire nation. It was through the instrumentality of Villard's companies, principally the Oregon Railway and Navigation Company and the Northern Pacific Railroad, that the first Volga Germans settled in the Pacific Northwest.

The first Russian Germans in the American West, about seventeen families, arrived in Portland in 1881 after spending several years on the dry, grasshopper infested Kansas plains. Most were natives of the villages New Jagodnaja, Schoental, and Schoenfeld which were daughter colonies of Yagodnaya Polyana and Pobotschnoje. The group obtained special emigrant fares through the Union Pacific Railroad and Oregon Steam Navigation Company to travel to Portland where they had heard good farmland was available and included the families of George Green, John Kleweno, Henry Litzenberger, Henry Repp, Peter Ochs, and four Schierman brothers—Conrad, Henry, John, and George.

Realizing the vast untapped agricultural potential the Inland Pacific Northwest, Villard's Oregon improvement Company purchased 150,000 acres (the odd sections in fourteen townships) from the Northern Pacific in the center of present Whitman County. These lands were carefully selected and Villard intended to build his Palouse line directly through this district and populate it with dependable colonist farmers. The lands varied in price from $5 to $10 per acre and sold on a six-year installment plan at seven percent interest.

In March 1881, General Tannatt relocated his office to Walla Walla in order to be closer to the Oregon Improvement Company's operations in Eastern Washington. He made frequent trips to the company lands in the Palouse and began arranging for their settlement. Villard took a personal interest in this program of colonization which he outlined in the following 1881 stockholders' report:

> A regular land and emigration department has been organized, the lands fully surveyed and appraised, 5,000 acres are now being broken up. The plan is to divide the lands into farms not exceeding 160 acres, to fence and improve no more than 40 acres upon each quarter section, erecting thereon plain but substantial dwellings and the necessary outbuildings, so as to be able to offer farms ready for immediate occupancy at reasonable rates to incoming settlers. The Oregon Railway and Navigation Company is

extending its system of roads right through these lands, and there is every assurance that our land operations will be successful and will result in a large profit to the company. Villard's massive investment in the region resulted in the virtual economic transformation of the central Palouse from grazing to farming. In addition, the marketing potential of the entire region was enhanced, since the railroad allowed Palouse farmers to capitalize on growing European demands for Northwest grain exports. Exporting of Palouse wheat had begun as early as 1868, but had been limited to that which could be transported on the Oregon Steam Navigation Company down the Snake and Columbia Rivers. In 1879 only half the crop was shipped before navigation closed in December for the winter. Railroad transportation would thus insure a more dependable system of grain delivery throughout the year to both foreign and domestic markets.

The *Palouse Gazette* in November, 1881 observed that,

A few not engaged in agriculture will dislike to see so large an area of grazing country broken up; but this is a narrow consideration, compared with the standing it will give our farming lands and the stimulus it will bring to our country.

It was also reported that to begin populating the sparsely settled area with immigrants, the company had hired a number of writers "to go over every section of the country and give its true merits to the world, in newspapers, pamphlets, (and) magazines...."

The Trek to the Palouse

The Volga German "Kansas Colony" families in Portland inquired about the company's new lands in the Palouse in the spring of 1881 and an inspection tour was arranged for several representatives of the group—Phillip Green, Peter Ochs and the three Schierman brothers; Conrad, Henry, and John. The *Walla Walla Weekly Statesman* printed a letter received by R. W. Mitchell, a Colfax agent for the company's land department:

Five locating agents of the Kansas colony, composed of about 70 families, passed through here Thursday on their way to inspect lands of the O. I. Co. Col. Tustin is in charge of the party. They look like solid, progressive farmers, such as we are willing to welcome to our broad acres. One of them remarked, 'If the land is anything like what we have seen around Dayton, I guess we can be suited. We are surprised and delighted at what we have seen.' Mr. Mitchell of the O. I. Co. will meet this party in the Palouse Country next week.

Writing from Dayton to Villard's office, Tannatt relayed his intentions for dealing with the group in a note on May 10. "I want to sell them a township and will on Mr. Oakes' return if there is any trade with them." Indeed, the vanguard returned favorably impressed with the land's fertility and the hilly topography reminded them of the Volga *Bergseite*. Tannatt planned to meet them in Portland to arrange the sale but he found them reluctant to enter into such a massive deal on behalf of the others in Kansas. The village *mir* system in Russia had conditioned them to farm communally small fields, not entire townships, so after considering the possibilities, it was decided by several families to move to the Palouse the following year when the men could secure employment on Villard's Palouse line which was to be built through the Palouse. They would have time then to select company lands on which to establish a small colony.

During the same year, 1881, Villard's grandiose scheme for his railroad empire reached fruition. He had come to the realization that direct railway connections to the East were imperative if the Pacific Northwest was ever to be actively involved in the commerce of the nation and settlement of European immigrants. With this in mind, he had embarked secretly in December 1880, on collecting an unprecedented $8,000,000 "blind pool" from his financial supporters in order to purchase the controlling interest in Billing's stalemated Northern Pacific Railroad. In less than year his request was actually oversubscribed and on September 15, 1881, he was elected president of Northern Pacific. Work on both ends of the line again resumed and his dream of a northern transcontinental under his personal control rapidly approached reality.

General Tannatt continued to work in the Palouse and, on his return from a visit to "Endicott and Palouse lands" in April, 1882, he reported that both hillsides and level land were being plowed and seeded. Endicott, a company town platted on the Palouse line in January, 1881, was described by Tannatt as a "Boarding house, Company building, Smithshop, tool shed and three cottages." Other towns platted in 1882 as the Columbia and Palouse line progressed along Rebel Flat were Diamond and Plainsville (the present Whitman County Fairgrounds).

In the fall of 1882 the Volga Germans in Portland began their journey to the new Canaan. Their approach to the Palouse country was announced in the *Walla Walla Statesman* in September. Some were coming by wagon while Tannatt arranged for others to travel over the lines of the Oregon Railway and Navigation Company to its terminus at Texas Ferry on the Snake River. They arrived there in October and some of the men walked twenty miles to Endicott to procure wagons to transport their families and belongings to Endicott the following day. One of the spokesmen for the colony, Phillip Green, stated that "He had written home setting forth the fact that the land, climate and general outlook of this [Palouse] country, was all that could be desired." He also communicated to Tannatt that, "Three other Kansas colonies had sent inspectors or agents with the present party, who are to locate land for other coming immigrants. There is to be an exodus from Kansas this fall."

Some of the families lived in tents and company houses in Endicott while others who first settled on lands in the country fashioned crude earth pits similar to the *zemlyanki* dug by their ancestors on the Volga. In the following spring lumber was obtained from Colfax to build wooden houses. Many of the Volga Germans went to work extending the Columbia and Palouse line to Colfax which was reached the following year. In October, 1882, a local paper reported on the progress of the colony:

> Delegation for the Palouse Country—Calling at the office of O. I. Co. on Monday to introduce gentlemen from the East we found quite a delegation to whom Gen. Tannatt was explaining the Palouse Country and arranging for settlement. Some weeks since a portion of the Kansas Colony now here, with their own teams will be met by additional teams at Texas Ferry, to carry out household goods sent by train. Gen. Tannatt will meet them in Endicott, to complete contracts and outer houses built for their use. This organized method of handling immigrants is doing much for the Palouse Country, directly and indirectly for all of eastern Washington. The ample capital of O. I. Co. and their simple method of dealing promptly with new comers, upon an easily understood plan, is most proper—Mr. Greene who is with those who left on Saturday says twenty-four families are on the way hither and those now at Endicott are much pleased with the county and their reception (*Walla Walla Statesman,* October 21, 1882).

Adding new impetus to regional development was the long awaited completion of the Northern Pacific Railroad on September 8, 1883, when the final gap was closed on the transcontinental line at Gold Creek, Montana. More Volga Germans streamed into the area with other immigrant groups as the long, grueling wagon journeys were shortened to two weeks by relatively inexpensive rail transit.

In the New Land

The scenic rolling landscape reminded the Kansas Volga Germans of their homeland. They collectively purchased a quarter section of land five miles north of Endicott which was divided equally, reflecting the method of land tenure to which they had been accustomed in Russia. This "Palouse Colony" consisted of the families of Peter and Henry Ochs and those of Conrad, Henry, George, and John Schierman. They were joined by the John Schreiber and Phillip Aschenbrenner families and all worked together in the building of the first eight homes which were simple three-room structures. A small herd of livestock was maintained and they planted large gardens of potatoes, melons, corn, and sunflowers. They found that wheat and barley grew particularly well on the chestnut brown soil as well as oats, which were planted on the higher areas bordering the bluffs (D. Schierman, 1972).

It soon became apparent that with the abundance of prime farmland and mechanized methods of cultivation, an individual could acquire and manage larger estates in relative self-sufficiency unlike the small plots they had tended on the slopes in Russia. This led other early Volga Germans, immigrants like the Kammerzells, Fishers, Klewenos, Greens, Reps, and Litzenbergers, to settle in neighboring areas where they purchased their own farms. In the Palouse they learned by experience, as did other farmers, that contour farming was a necessity.

Some families chose to pursue business ventures in neighboring towns that served the interests of the agrarian populace. Early Volga German businesses in Endicott included H.P. Kleweno's general store, Youngman and Langlitz's harness shop, and saloons operated by Henry Litzenberger and P.H. Green. Still, the original Palouse Colony remained as a clearing house for newly arriving Volga Germans, serving as their temporary residence until they could locate nearby. By 1885 there were about a dozen Volga German families in the Palouse; all had come through Kansas. About 1890 the first large groups began arriving in the Palouse direct from the mother colony of Yagodnaya Polyana and lesser numbers from other villages. In that year first-generation Volga Germans in Whitman County numbered about 100, but this number grew to 327 in 1900.

Disposing of most of their possessions in Russia, the Volga German immigrants brought little more with them to the Palouse than their distinctive clothing (felt boots, Russian peasant shirts and beautifully embroidered head scarves), wooden soup spoons, and German Bibles and songbooks. In preparing the children for the long journey from Russia to the Northwest, Volga German parents would often tell them enchanting stories about their future homes on the other side of the world: "We are going to America, the land where milk and honey flows..." After their arrival in the area, the children could steal the wild honey from hollow trees along the Palouse River and herd the cows home each evening, their udders spurting out milk after grazing in the thick bunch grass pastures. Then the parents reminded them, "Look—see, you have the milk flowing from the cows and the honey flowing from the trees, just like we said it would be like here when we were in Russia" (C. G. Schmick, 1969).

There was little conflict between the Volga German colonist farmers and the American stockmen in the central Palouse. The small fenced fields of the farmers in the early 1880s were no threat to the stockmen, many of whom maintained enormous herds. Excluding small herds of less than fifteen head of cattle, Tannatt estimated in 1885 that within a radius of twelve miles of Endicott there were 3,562 cattle, 5,395 horses, 75,250 head of sheep but only 8,175 acres of land under cultivation. An additional 1,510 acres was in hay.

121

Traditional Duka Yoke

By the early 1890s, stockmen were increasingly turning to farming, along with the newly arriving Volga Germans who began expanding into the St. John, Dusty and Colfax areas. In the first decade of the twentieth century Volga German immigration to the Palouse continued despite the fact that most of the farmland had already been taken. Many new immigrants found employment at various Colfax businesses, as the town enjoyed an unprecedented period of prosperity. The major trade center and county seat for Whitman County, its population had risen from 1,649 in 1890 to 2,783 in 1910. At the same time the population of the county reached its highest point, 33,280 persons. The Volga Germans in Colfax congregated in the city's northeast section along First Street in what became known as "Russian Town" although they hated being labeled as "Russians." By 1910 the number of Russian-born Germans of the county reached 557 and this increased to 798 in 1920.

The Churches

The German Department of the Congregational Churches in America began in 1846 among German immigrants who had settled along the Iowa frontier and by the 1860s had grown into a leading German Protestant denomination in the United States. Its origins on the West Coast can be traced to the arrival of the Volga Germans in the Palouse country in 1882 since the Endicott Congregational Church was organized by some of these immigrants in 1883. Reverend Thomas W. Walters, resident pastor of Plymouth Congregational Church in Colfax first ministered to this group in 1883 until a traveling German from Ritzville, Reverend Fruicht, learned of their need. In a meeting held in Endicott in 1888, this congregation and others in Ritzville and Walla Walla were the first West Coast congregations formally accepted into the German Congregational Church. Other Russian German churches of this denomination were later established near Lacrosse (1895) and in Colfax (1897).

Volga German Lutherans in the Palouse country were without a minister until 1887 when the pioneer missionary, Reverend Henry Rieke of the Ohio Synod, located their colony on the Palouse River. He organized Trinity Lutheran Church in Endicott among some of these families in 1890 and the founding of other Volga German Churches followed in Farmington (Christ Lutheran, 1896) and Colfax (Peace Lutheran, 1902). The split within the Russian German religious community into Congregational and Lutheran churches was an outgrowth of the earlier dispute in Russia between the pietistic Lutherans and those who were more liturgically oriented.

With the outbreak of the First World War in 1914, Russian German emigration from Russia was severely curtailed and after the 1917 Bolshevik Revolution in Russia it virtually ended. Unfortunately for those who had immigrated to the Palouse, as elsewhere in America, the Russian Germans found themselves identified with two very unpopular European countries. It became common during World War I for many of them to begin church services in English although German services did continue among many first-generation Russian Germans in the Palouse until the 1960s.

The number of native-born Russian Germans in the Palouse began to decline after 1920, even though their birthrate remained high. By 1930 there were 1,879 first and second-generation Russian Germans in Palouse Country. These colonist farmers came at a critical time in the history of the region and were active participants in its transition into an area producing the highest yielding dryland crops in the world.

The Pine Island and Little York Story
by Susan M. Yungman (1972)

Somehow advertisements reached remote parts of Russia including Yagodnaya Polyana telling of the great opportunities in America. The loss of freedoms and exemptions which Catherine the Great had promised for an eternity to our people and the government's determination to Russianize the Germans caused the Volga-Germans to consider seriously the rumors about this foreign land—America. It is doubtful if the colonists ever felt really secure in Russia, but now their future appeared more uncertain than ever; their greatest fear—possible loss of religious freedom.

The choice had to be made—to become Russians or to emigrate a second time. They could migrate to Siberia where it was still possible to acquire cheap land, since the Russian government was encouraging settlement of this vast region; or, they could emigrate to the New World to the United States, Canada, or South America. Offers were being extended from the western hemisphere. In the U.S. the Homestead Act of 1862 was designed to encourage settlement. In Canada immigrants could obtain a homestead of 160 acres for just ten dollars! After three years they could claim ownership. Similar enticements were offered by countries in South America. Railroad companies to whom the American government had given large sections of land desired good farmers for their land and distributed pamphlets advertising same. Some of these pamphlets found their way to the Volga colonies. Emissaries were sent to the United States in search of suitable places to settle.

A number of young men who strongly objected to the prospect of being called into the service with the Russian army made their exodus. Gradually, under God's guidance, more Germans who refused to be made full-fledged Russians came to America in search of freedom and opportunities. This emigration began in 1872 and continued until the outbreak of World War I. According to the census of 1910, there were 243,351 Russian-Germans, first and second generations in the United States. By 1920 this number had increased to 303,532 with over 23,000 first generation and over 69,000 first and second generations in North Dakota alone. New York showed a total of 4,027 first generation and 8,560 first and second generations. By this time Germans from Russia had spread to every state in the Union. Between 1892 and 1912, 1,610 people came to America from Yagodnaya.

125

To travel from one country to another certain credentials were necessary. The passport papers cost about twelve rubles and the ship fare and journey to America about 400 rubles (or $200.00). Those planning to emigrate would sell most of their belongings. The necessities would be sewn into sacks and balls and a few choice possessions would be added—the Bible, Starck's Prayer Book and the *Wolga Gesangbuch* would usually be included. The pastor would supply the "family list" certifying a birth record for each member of the family. It was a sad occasion when farewells had to be said to friends, relatives, and especially to aging parents—probably forever. At Saratov they would board a train which took them to either Bremen or Hamburg, Germany where they would embark for America.

The first pioneers who found this to be a land of promise induced their relatives and friends to join them and sometimes even purchased the traveling tickets for them. This was somewhat the case with Father's family. Grandfather's sister Catherine and her husband John Schmick sent encouraging letters from a distant place called Washington in the United States. On this basis, in August of 1900, Grandfather, Grandmother, and their two sons, George 4th, "Yurich," fourteen years old, and Alexander, one year old, set out for the "New World."

They traveled from Russia to Germany by train and sailed from Hamburg on a ship named *Conrad the Great*. They were at sea for two weeks. On the trip abroad Father recalls that he wore a red embroidered shirt, the customary tightfitting trousers, elasticized boots made by his Uncle Henry, and a little black cap. He did not get seasick, possibly because he took full advantage of the "choice" foods available. Prunes and butter were a brand new taste treat and he says he had his share. At one time he was lost for several days and his parents finally located him in the kitchen peeling potatoes. They traveled second class. Father had mastered the Russian "Cossacksky," or Hopak, and he along with other boys entertained the upper class who would throw money down to them to keep them dancing. One other family that they knew made the journey at the same time. Their name was Leinweber.

They arrived at Ellis Island on September 3, 1900, where a Pastor Keyl met them and found a place for them to stay. Father's uncle was supposed to send them money to go west to the state of Washington. They waited for about three weeks and the money did not come. Pastor Keyl informed them that quite a few of their former friends had settled in a small community (later known as Little York) about sixty miles from New York City, raising vegetables, mostly onions. Consequently, they decided to go there. The money finally came from "Uncle John," but Grandfather turned it over to the Leinweber family—a loan for travel to Washington. They went to the area now called Endicott where the Schmicks had settled and some of their descendants are living today. One of these descendants and the author met quite by accident in North Carolina at a Marine Base where we were stationed during our term of service in World War II. Her name was Eileen Bafus Johnson, a great-granddaughter of John and Catherine Schmick.

Mother's people were talked into a deal by some opportunist. They left Russia in May of 1897 without a pass and crossed the Polish border by paying off this individual who took all their money, except enough for transportation to America. The only papers they had with them were a family list of church records. Grandma Youngman (Elizabeth Kromm Youngman) carried her daughter Anna ("Andya," who was seven years old at the time) on her back when they fled across the Polish border. Grandma lost her shoes while wading through the icy water, so when they arrived at the train station she had no shoes.

They took the train to Hamburg and from there sailed on the *Frederick the Great*, landing in New York on June 3, 1897. The whole journey took approximately a month from Russia to America—twelve days on the boat. Grandfather was very sea sick on the boat and thought he would die. His sons, August Jr. and John, also made this journey. (John was a twin—the other child had died.) When questioned about this trip, Mother's predominant memory was the heartbreak of leaving behind in Russia the baby she had so lovingly cared for.

Like so many immigrants they arrived at Ellis Island penniless. An old friend, Conrad Luft, who had migrated to America almost ten years earlier, met them when they arrived. Conrad made many trips to New York when friends from Russia were expected and he would do what he could to help them get settled in this new land. With Grandfather and his family there was the problem of no passport—they could have been shipped back but through the efforts of Pastor Keyl they somehow managed to stay and journeyed to the Orange County area.

Needless to say, the first years in this country were very difficult for these pioneers. However, considering the famines, the religious persecution and the 1941 deportation which our friends and relatives in Russia had to endure, we can only thank God that our grandparents came to the United States. In my own family, all communication with relatives in Russia came to a stop after 1917. What a thrill it must have been for the early immigrants to behold the Statue of Liberty as their ship sailed into the New York harbor.

And so they came: The Yungmans, Youngmans, Schmicks, Leinwebers, Schadts, Scheuermanns, Lufts, Lusts, Dauberts, Pfaffenroths, Gerlitz's, Ruhls, Rudys, Weitz's, Langlitz's, Mohrs; also the Schlagels, Eurichs, Wagners, Ochs, Otts, Millers, Wilhelms, Sircables, Klevenos, Kiels, some of these from the villages of Pobotschnaya and Neu-Straub. If there was one predominant factor which guided, sustained, and directed our people, it was their fervent Christian faith. They learned early in life to put their trust in God and He did protect them as they in their childlike faith set out for a new land, poorly equipped in money, education, and experience. When they finally did arrive in America, after reverses, discomforts, and inconveniences that we could not even comprehend, it was the religious missionaries who came to their aid and guided them to various areas where they might have an opportunity to root and grow again.

When the first Volga Germans arrived in New York at Castle Garden, the immigration station at that time, most of them had no idea just where they would settle in this new world. One such immigrant, Conrad Luft, with his wife and baby daughter, left Saratov in 1888. (Conrad's father, Adam Luft, was a brother to Daniel Luft, father of Mary C. Luft Yungman.) The Lufts were detained at Castle Garden until their future could be somewhat assured. Along came a Charles Donnelly searching for a good man among the immigrants to work on his farm in Orange County, New York. Conrad Luft got the job and consequently settled in what is now known as the hamlet of Little York located approximately sixty miles from New York City.

At that time Little York was mostly a forest bound on one side by a hill. At the foot of this hill the Luft family resided in a house owned by Mr. Donnelly (later Philip Ruhl home, next to the church). At that time there was only one other house in the Little York area and this house was inhabited by Negroes. The Luft family managed to make a living, and eventually wrote their friends and relatives in Russia telling them of this fine country and pleasant prospects. It did not take too much encouragement to influence his brother George to come over. George, as well as Conrad, had already served time in the Russian Army—among the first young men of the Volga Germans to be drafted, George in 1876, Conrad a year later. They both served five years. George was decorated for bravery by Grand Duke Paul, brother of the Czar, during the Russo-Turkish War. He was commissioned a second lieutenant on December 25, 1879.

On the basis of what he heard from his brother Conrad, George Luft brought his family and found work on the Durland farm (now Durlandville, N.Y.). This was in 1892, four years after Conrad had settled in the Little York area. (George Luft later settled in Goshen and became a prominent citizen. One of his sons, John, later became Mayor of Goshen, as well as president of the bank at Tuxedo, N.Y. His brother, George, also became a bank officer in Goshen.) On the same trip with George also came his sister Elizabeth and Henry Lust and family. These are the parents of Pauline Lust Paffenroth.

About a year after Conrad Luft settled in the Little York area, another daughter was born and named Katherine. She was the first baby born in the Little York area of the German-Russian settlers. A Negress was midwife when Katherine was born. Katherine was baptized by a Lutheran minister at Chester, N.Y. Conrad Luft later moved west to Oshkosh, Wisconsin—he was a pioneer in that area also. Katherine, however, returned to Little York to marry John Scheuermann. They raised a large family, and Katherine Luft Scheuermann is living today in the house built for her and John. Katherine is the paternal great-grandmother of Marlene A. Card, granddaughter of George Yungman 5th.

With the encouragement of Conrad Luft and the help of the early clergymen a number of the Volga-German immigrants found their way to the

Little York area—hence a new epoch in the life of our people. Two of these clergymen were Rev. C. J. Gustav Dreschsler, circuit pastor of the Newburgh, Florida, Chester area, and the Rev. Stephanus Keyl, who was Immigrant Missionary, from Staten Island, New York.

Upon clearing the timber from the swampland, the settlers found the soil around Little York to be rich, black (somewhat like the "chernosem" in Russia), fertile and most suitable for growing onions and other vegetables. They had no money with which to purchase land so they went to work wherever they could find it. Many worked for the railroad company, some for established farmers and land owners, and many were carpenters. After they saved enough money to make a down payment on some land, they bought virgin land, cleared the forests, made improvements, and after much struggle and hardships it did become a "land of milk and honey."

When Grandfather, George Yungman 3rd, arrived in the Little York area, his kindly friend Conrad Schmick gave them lodging until they could get a start. (The Schmick home was the same house where Conrad Luft first lived.) The first farmer for whom Grandfather worked was Ed Brown. This farm was located at least three miles from Little York and they would walk there every morning, including young George, my father, who was now old enough to work. His wages, he recalls, were 28 cents a day. They also worked for a farmer named John Drew (father of S. Roe Drew). The Drews showed them much kindness, which was unusual in those days, since the area residents generally were not receptive to these Volga Germans who were poor and spoke only German. Mr. Drew was also a dealer in horses—this was of great interest to Father.

Grandfather eventually was able to purchase a farm about one and one-half miles from Little York. They lived and farmed there several years before lime was discovered on the property. Grandfather could not afford to start a quarry so he sold the property in 1905. The Atlas Portland Company developed the quarry which was active for many years and finally shut down in 1943. Grandfather realized a good profit on the transaction and with it bought a house and about ten acres of land in Little York. This house is across the street from the church and was purchased from Philip Schlagel for $2200. The house had been built by an Irishman named Eber L. Pilgrim.

As the story goes, a quarry had developed about two miles up the road from this point on what is now called Mt. Adam—near Mt. Eve. One of the drunken quarry workers drifted into Little York and propositioned Mrs. Pilgrim—and consequently Mr. Pilgrim shot this man. He fell dead a few hundred feet from his house (by the Gerlitz barn). When the case came up in court in Goshen, Mrs. Conrad Luft was asked to testify in the matter since this man had also "made a pass" at her. "Ebe" was freed. After settling in his new home Grandfather rooted out the surrounding swamp land. This work was all done by hand as tractors were unheard of at this time and it was possible to clear only an acre or two per year. They raised mostly onions in the cultivated fertile muckland.

Mother's people—after Pastor Keyl took them under his wing—journeyed to the Orange County area and found work with a dairy farmer named Parkhurst. He resided on what is known as Spanktown Road across the road from the Spanktown School near Florida, N.Y. He permitted Grandfather, August Youngman Sr., and his family to live in a little house about 800 feet up the hill from the school house. It was a lonely unsettled area. "Nama" often related how she would wait patiently, fearfully, all by herself morning and night while the rest of the family were down at the barn milking the cows and doing their chores. She also recalled that Mr. Parkhurst had very little compassion for poor foreigners who were trying to get a foothold in this land. It was a struggle for survival and living was crude. They improvised the best they could; for example, using corn shucks to make beds to sleep on.

They worked very hard, and after saving their earnings bought land in Little York in May, 1898. This land was located directly across the road from where George Yungman 3rd finally settled and this is where George Yungman 4th got acquainted with Anna C. Youngman, "Nama." They had the same surname, although spelled differently by translation, and probably were related but were unable to trace relationships. At this time there were about a dozen homes in the Little York area. And how did Little York get its name? They say these early colonists joked about their village rivaling the metropolis and therefore called it "Little York." Later, when there was a rift in the church, a group of the settlers adopted Congregationalism and built another church not quite one-half mile away on the high road towards Pine Island; that hamlet was appropriately named Little Brooklyn.

Die Kirche (the Church) was always the focal point of the social and family life of our people. As early as February 17, 1895, Rev. C. J. Gustav Dreschsler conducted services in a private home (where "Aunt Gerlitz" later lived) with eighteen congregating. Konstantine Schneider, one of the more educated immigrants, conducted reading services when the pastor was absent and also conducted a school. The Rev. Dreschsler died in the fall of 1898 and the group succeeded in getting the Rev. S. Keyl, Lutheran Immigrant Missionary, to preach once a month. It was August and Elizabeth Youngman who would give up their own bed so the Pastor would have a place to sleep—most likely out of gratitude for al he had done for them but also because of the high regard they had for "der Pastor." In any case Pastor Stephanus Keyl was certainly worthy of such hospitality. He was the first Immigrant Missionary of the Lutheran Missouri Synod. Born in Niederfrohna, Saxony, Germany, in 1838, he came to America as an infant in 1839. He followed in the footsteps of his father and became a Lutheran minister. In 1867 he became the Immigrant Missionary to assist both bodily and spiritually the Lutheran immigrants at their arrival in New York City. As soon as they landed on American soil he was to greet them and endeavor to protect them against the many swindlers who swarmed the wharves where the immigrants landed. He also was to advise them regarding places and sections of our country where they might find work and especially where they might locate a Lutheran congregation and school.

Many times the immigrants did not have sufficient funds to pay the sometimes high traveling expenses and cost of food and Pastor Keyl had either to take the money from mission funds at his disposal or (as he often did) to take it from his own pockets. It was a work of love for Pastor Keyl which he started at Battery Place in New York City just opposite the well-known Castle Garden. It was also a big responsibility since he was the Immigrant Missionary of the entire Synod. One of the greatest obstacles for effective mission work was the lack of a hotel or boardinghouse where the immigrants could live for a short time until they were ready to travel elsewhere. Many boardinghouses were managed by unscrupulous and dishonest people whose only aim was to take as much money as possible out of the pockets of the immigrants. In 1885 a five-story building was purchased just opposite the Castle Garden. For twenty years Pastor Keyl did double duty as Immigrant Missionary and as caretaker of the "Lutherisches Pilgerhous" as the hotel was named. On March 31, 1905, the New Yorker Staatszeitung printed the following interesting statistics: "During the almost twenty years of its existence the Pilgerhous has sheltered 79,843 Germans and 5,342 Scandinavians."

Soon Castle Garden became too small for the many people who came from may countries in Europe. Congress decided to establish better and more spacious headquarters on Ellis Island, a small island not far from Bedloe Island where the Statue of Liberty was erected. Pastor Keyl was an "angel of mercy" to our people when they arrived in America. He was perhaps most instrumental in establishing our church and congregation in Little York. To this day the older members of the congregation remember Pastor Stephanus Keyl and the sacrifices he brought in preaching to them God's word every Sunday. As related by his son, Rev. Theo. S. Keyl, Pastor Keyl never took a vacation. He remained on the go every day. One of the few days he was compelled to remain home from work was during the great blizzard of 1888. "He was stockily built and of fine proportion. He had a fine black beard and had in the prime of his life a princely bearing."

In December of 1905 while he was on Ellis Island taking care of some immigrants, he suddenly collapsed and fell to the floor. He had suffered a stroke and passed away on December 15, 1905. Like a thunderbolt out of the clear sky the news of Pastor Keyl's death reached the many thousands with whom he came in contact during his labors as Immigrant Missionary. It was especially sad news to his charges in Little York. "Well done, thou good and faithful servant," Matt. 25:21, certainly is a fitting verse to be said for the Rev. Stephanus Keyl. A deed reflects that on February 11, 1898 land was purchased from John and Mary Wiegandt and George and Annie Luft by the German Evangelical Lutheran Church of Pine Island. Soon thereafter a church building was started in Little York. This was at the present location of St. Peter Evangelical Lutheran Church (St. Petri Kirche). By June 5, 1901, the congregation was incorporated and through the efforts of Pastor Keyl, they had a called pastor, the Rev. C. George Kaestner. Eventually the church was completed and a cemetery was added about one mile up the road towards Mt. Eve.

Many years later, Rev. Martin F. Kuegele requested Pastor Kaestner to give an accurate report of what had transpired during his ministry. The following is an excerpt of Pastor Kaestner's account: "In a meeting of the congregation at Little York, Orange Co., held July 7, 1901, a call was sent to the undersigned promising a yearly salary of $300.00. The signers of said call were Johannes Fuchs, August Youngman, Peter Miller, Conrad Schmick, Henry Lust. At the end of the following month I went to Pine Island. Arriving there I saw a man sitting on an antique carriage, the back seat of which was covered with a various colored bedspread. I approached the man and do not know why I said: (in German) 'Are you perhaps looking for the Pastor?' The man pulled his mustache and said, 'Yah, yah'. So I climbed into the carriage and we drove towards Little York. Little York! A God forsaken place it was, few houses, none painted, a church half-finished, weeds, weeds, and more weeds. I was brought to the driver's home, Mr. August Youngman Sr. Mrs. Youngman served meat, potatoes, and onions. After the meal I asked where the house was in which I was to live. Told it was next door, I looked for it but could not see it for the weeds—could barely see the roof". (This apparently was the house later owned by George Yungman 3rd).

Pastor Kaestner then tells about the problems they had in completing the church building, especially when there were already some unpaid bills. Then, when a number of the members decided to leave for Oshkosh, Wisconsin, the builder stopped work, fearing that he would not get paid. "It took a great deal of diplomacy to straighten out the mess, and the church was finished." The Pastor's father painted it and the congregation paid for the paint. Then they "...got some second-hand benches in Edenville, an old altar from Port Richmond (Staten Island), also a pulpit and vestry—came Dec. 21 about 6:00 P.M., worked until midnight building a platform, erecting altar, etc. About 1:00 A.M. Pastor Keyl came. They had a wreck on the Erie and he was on his way since the preceding afternoon." On December 22, 1901 the church was dedicated. Rev. S. Keyl preached German and Rev. C. G. Kaestner preached English for two English people who attended.

"Next came the school [in the] church basement (20x20x7) with no benches. With the help of three youths, Hans Scheuermann, Hans Youngman, Hans Pfaffenroth, got some boards from Sanford in Warwick and built benches. Main instruction were religion and German. Most difficulty was singing. Girls kept school clean and boys tended to the heating. Chimney was too low—not good. School started when the onions were all sold and ended when the seed onions were sown. Long before the service, everyone was near the church. Had no organ—one would start given song. Church was always filled to capacity and members were very attentive.

"Some unforgettable facts: If a child was born as late as Saturday it was brought to the church wrapped in numerous blankets on Sunday to be baptized. Weddings lasted for days—and as a rule too much 'spirit' and not the right kind. Funerals! The coffin was made by a carpenter, often the father of the child. One morning I missed the door on the stable. Upon inquiring learned that a father, whose child had died, made a coffin out of the door. There was no cemetery and could not bury in other surrounding cemeteries. A Mr. Parkhurst was willing to sell several acres of land. No money was paid. Mr. Parkhurst wrote in a few words that the land was for a cemetery for the church, that was all. Mr. Parkhurst died years later. The family found the note in an envelope. A number of the members then went to Judge Beattie's office and made a down payment on the property." While there, the judge was also persuaded to give citizenship papers to these men. At the end of his letter Pastor Kaestner states, "After many years, one often thinks of the wondrous things the Lord did, how He guided and led us, how He prospered us to this day."

The traditional Christmas Eve children's programs were real "productions" at that time, and "the event" of the year. Most of the program was in German, especially the singing of the German carols. The church would be decorated for this occasion and a beautiful large "Tannenbaum" was placed in front near the pulpit. Before electricity came into existence lighted candles were used on the trees. (After the program, each child received a bag containing hard candies, chocolate caps, assorted nuts, and an orange—a real treat!) This school was finally closed on April 30, 1933, when members were beginning to send their children to public schools, and the rest of the members were financially unable to carry on the burden of a private parochial school. Shortly after Father's people settled in Little York, he attended school one day in Edenville, N.Y. He did not care for it and, unfortunately, did not continue. He had attended school in Russia for about six years where he learned Latin and Russian.

"Nama" attended the Amity School for two years (1898-99) and afterward the church school under Pastor C. George Kaestner. (Her brother August Jr. attended Russian school for three years, Spanktown School in the fall of 1897 for about three months, two years at Amity School, and Sunday School classes under Konstantine Schneider. August Jr. and Adam Lust were the first ones confirmed in the original church basement by Pastor Keyl in 1900. The church was not yet complete. Father was confirmed on May 26, 1901.) Father had three brothers—Alexander, August "Happy," and Henry—and two sisters—Mary and Mathilda. The "German" immigrants gradually acquired American customs, became citizens, and the children grew and multiplied but since the Lutheran Reformation of 1517, our people have retained their Lutheran heritage to the present day.

German Colonist Log Home

In time Father started to court "Nama" but he ran into a problem since she already had a suitor, an extremely jealous one who at one point even pulled a loaded gun on Father because of it. This fellow's mother stopped him in time. Also, "Nama's" father was not in favor of his daughter going with their neighbor's son George who had a mischievous reputation. On many occasions Father had plagued "Old Augustya" with his pranks, such as stuffing old bags down the chimney and switching the wheels on the "buggy." (The buggy normally had high wheels on one end and low on the other and Father reversed them.) They were gentle, peace-loving people. He wanted no part of this mischief maker in the family. However, "Nama's" mother was in favor of the match and on January 12, 1908, they were married. It had just become law that a marriage license was required and they happened to have License Number One in the Town of Warwick. Someone once said "Nama" was the most beautiful bride they had ever seen.

They lived with Father's people while their own house was being built next door. Daughter Elizabeth was born in October of 1908, before they moved into their house, and then eight more children were born in that house— four more girls and four boys. And there they lived all the rest of their life together. The rest of their children were named as follows: Mary Catherine, George William (5th), Anna, Susan Marjorie (the author), Herman Clarence, Rose, Walter, Alfred, and Charles James. While the inside of their house was being painted, a German by the name of "Julius", an alcoholic, painted their dining room ceiling in oils. He had done work for others in the area but he told them that since he liked them so much he would give them his prize, which indeed it is and it is still in existence today.

"Aunt Ruhl," Mary Catherine Yungman Ruhl (1878-1968), sister to Grandfather, George 3rd, came from Baltimore just for the wedding of George and Anna and never returned to Baltimore. She and her husband Philip (who spoke Russian fluently since he had worked among Russians) originally arrived in Little York in 1902 with two children, the second of which, a girl, was born on the ship enroute. They moved to Colorado and then Baltimore, Maryland. In 1908 they settled in the house next to the church where they also lived the rest of their lives. Aunt Ruhl was usually the midwife when "Nama" had her children and, needless to say, was always very close to the family. She was probably "Nama's" best friend as Aunt Ruhl's was always her favorite place to visit. She was an excellent seamstress and made the lovely christening outfit in which all of us children were christened except Elizabeth, our oldest sister. Even some of the grandchildren were christened in it and at least one great-grandchild.

As a young couple, George 4th and Anna pursued onion farming just behind their home. Gradually trees were rooted out more and more and the forest receded. In time there was hardly any forest left—just vast fields of black land. The "black dirt," as it is commonly called, was ideally suited for the production of certain vegetable crops and provided the main source of income for most of the populace in the area. The muck averages 15 to 30 feet in depth, but in some sections it is 75 feet deep. These are not only the deepest mucklands in the State of New York but the deepest in northeastern United States and an extremely valuable agricultural resource to the present time. The soil has a high organic matter content and natural fertility which makes it very productive—one of the most productive soils in this country. The yield of onions per acre is approximately 350 hundred weight and sometimes considerably more. Reportedly at this time New York State produces one-third of all the nation's onions and one-half of those are produced in Orange County on its 8000 acres of black dirt.

Father had tried a number of jobs from dairy work and vegetable farming to bartending and one time held the job as foreman on the Town of Warwick Highway Department. He eventually got a job with the Lehigh and New England Railway Co. and was put in charge of loading onions onto cars at the Pine Island station for transportation to shipping houses. He really found his niche when through the influence of one John Cregan, a commission merchant, he became an onion buyer. From a period prior to World War I until about 1930 he was the largest produce broker in the area and was sometimes referred to as the "Onion King"—the first of a series of so-named. During those years he was in fact the only resident onion buyer of Pine Island and Little York. Onion growers in those days were almost totally dependent on the local buyer and there were only five or six major buyers in the entire county. The only other outlet was to ship by rail to the New York City commission merchants. This procedure was risky since the farmer never knew what he would get for his shipment and therefore was left "holding the bag." Perhaps this is where the phrase originated.

As a prominent onion buyer, Father was well known not only to the German community of Little York but also to the Polish immigrants of Pine Island and surrounding areas. At this time there existed a strong prejudice between the various nationalities, but "George Yungman, the onion buyer" communicated very well with all of them and developed many sincere friendships. During the late 1920s, as the large trucks appeared on the scene, more and more onion farmers delivered their produce directly to the city markets and virtually every farmer was in business, raising, buying, and selling. But George Yungman was especially affluent. He was in business and business was good. He also had a good wife and many healthy children who were also useful in helping to work the large acreage of his own onion farm. Father and Grandfather (George 4th & 3rd) formed a partnership and purchased more houses and property and also planted an apple and peach orchard (about 2000 trees) which is now the property of Walter S. Seely.

The Volga Germans were really beginning to prosper. They owned their own homes plus some acreage. They had friends around them and their church and their children had a parochial school. Life was good and they were happy. With affluence and automobiles the perspective of these "German immigrants" gradually changed. They became less clanish and more worldly. Also, after the parochial school was closed, and all children thereafter attended the public schools, the prejudice barrier was broken down and it was not quite such a disgrace if one of the young people married outside of the clan. The Volga German, like all other Americans, was forced into the American melting pot but the old habits and restraints were not quickly shed. It was not their nature to mix with people of diverse backgrounds or nationalities. Even in the 1930's, Pine Island (a Polish settlement which can be seen across the flats) was so far removed from Little York it was like going to another country to go to Pine Island—yet it was only a mile away.

The Polish immigrants started to settle in the Pine Island area about 1905 and had basically the same problems as the Volga-Germans. Gradually, more homes were being built and in 1912 they built a church (Catholic), and eventually a public school. They also existed on the "fruits" developed from the black soil. In spite of similar problems, the Poles and Germans had very little in common. But a new generation has made a difference, and since before World War II, Polish and German young people have intermarried with other nationalities and have even moved to other areas. During World War I very few of the boys of the Volga-Germans were drafted. However, during World War II many rallied to the call and served their country proudly. In our immediate family, five volunteered their services, two boys and three girls: Herman C., USAAF; Walter A., USAAF; Mary C., Waves; Susan M., Marines; and Rose, Nurse Cadet.

The early immigrants had a true appreciation for the blessings of liberty. The Volga-German Americans reportedly had more sons and daughters in the armed forces of the United States than any other nationality group in this country. Perhaps this was due to the fact that on the average their families were larger but it is more likely that they were ready and willing to defend a precious freedom. The "old timers" loved to reminisce and did not relinquish all their "Volga German" customs, but they felt no allegiance to either Russia or Germany—they were proud to be loyal Americans.

The Calgary Yagoders
by Sandra Stelter (1990)

"The boundary lines have fallen for me in pleasant places,
surely I have a delightful inheritance."—Psalm 16:6

I am a second-generation Canadian-born *Yagoder*. I have always been aware that my grandparents were Germans who immigrated from Russia to Canada in 1912. Both my mother's and father's parents left the same village along the Volga River, Yagodnaya Polyana, to come to the Western Canadian prairie city of Calgary, Alberta.

As I grew up in the 1940's and 50's, I learned that "a few hundred years ago a Russian ruler married a German princess who took other Germans with her to teach the Russians how to farm. These Germans were promised a certain number of years free from military service, but as the time ran out, many left Russia for North America." I always wondered if Catherine the Great was the German princess, but I could never find any reference to her bringing other Germans with her.

None of my history books said anything about Germans from Russia coming to Canada either. But that did not surprise me since Western society considered neither Russians nor Germans twentieth-century models. My family never denied they were German, but they did not flaunt it either. Experiences in both World Wars taught them to keep ethnic matters at home or at places like church where similar folk gathered. I knew that the largest ethnic group in the "other" segment of Canadian society was German, but it was understood that the two founding nationalities, English and French, were the ones with a place in history. It was enough to be living in a free and bountiful country.

Nevertheless, I knew my grandparents' culture was special and unique. There was the food—the *Mutta* or *Abun Klease* (cottage cheese or strawberry-filled dumplings), the *Kraut und Brei* (pork and sauerkraut served with very smoothly mashed potatoes), the *Rivel Kuchen* (sweet yeast dough with crumb topping). What a treat it was when my grandparents wrapped a *Gehenk Wurst* (ring of smoked sausage) in newspaper for us as we left for home. I was embarrassed when my classmates quizzed me about the *Krebble* in my school lunch (deep fried treats made from an egg-sour cream dough), but it never diminished my love for real homemade food made from simple basic ingredients.

Then there was the language—*Yagoda*, a German dialect with bits of Russian and a pronunciation other German-speaking people found difficult to understand. I longed to learn German, but my parents were not about to pass on something that had brought them embarrassment and pain. Learning English in school had been difficult for them and, furthermore, they knew their German was considered inferior by other German-speaking people.

I also knew that my church was not like others. We lived just south of the Blackfoot Indian Reserve near Gleichen, Alberta, halfway between Calgary and Medicine Hat, "the middle of nowhere" both then and now. It took us about two hours to drive thirty-five miles with our 1939 Ford pick-up to our "Country Church." Most of the congregation had Lutheran roots in the Old Country, but on the sparsely-settled prairies they found the Evangelical Church (American based with German-Methodist roots) accommodated things they had appreciated in the Volga Brotherhood. It was not just the German that made the services different. It was the whole form and style. The men sat on the right side of the church and the women on the left, children were scattered among the adults, mothers at the back nursed their babies. There were long hours of sitting through services I could not understand. I would often turn the hands on my mother's wrist watch ahead to try to make the 12 o'clock noon break arrive a bit faster. It helped if my grandma was visiting; she made knots in her white hanky to form interesting shapes like a baby in a cradle.

The afternoon *Versammlung,* which began after people had visited over their packed lunches, was more fascinating. There was hearty singing without accompaniment; men and women singing their parts on rousing songs like *Und wenn der Kampf Voruber Ist* (And When the Battle's Over). Unfamiliar songs were "lined out" by the leader. Three *Bruder* (Brethren) were called to the three chairs behind the pulpit; the one in the center chair spoke first. Meanwhile, one of the remaining two moved to the center chair preparing to be the next speaker. Throughout the service there were "seasons of prayer" when everyone knelt and all prayed at once, earnestly and very audibly. When the prayers subsided someone spontaneously began singing and soon all joined in. At the leader's word everyone rose from their knees and the service continued.

What was this culture I glimpsed through the taste of *Wurst,* the aroma of *Kuchen*, bits of dialect, and long afternoons of *Versammlung*? I always treasured seeing Grandma and Grandpa's picture of their church in Russia. I wondered about our relatives in Russia who had not been heard from since the 1930's. After high school I still checked history books, but was quite sure my people's past would remain fascinating but elusive. Grandpa said he had "left a bad country to come to a good one," so I knew we should concentrate on living with a due sense of responsibility here and now and not ask too many questions.

It was not until 1975 that the right series of circumstances triggered responses from my only set of living grandparents (on my father's side) on matters they had previously seemed reluctant to discuss. My own history came alive as they shared their past—recalling names and dates, producing documents and papers, telling stories of farming on the *Khutor*, on the ship crossing the Atlantic, and in their first homes in Canada. On my mother's side, the immigrant generation stories were never recorded; but their children (my mother, her sisters and brothers) have written down recollections of what it was like to grow up as first-generation Canadians. Their accounts, along with delightful conversations with other Calgary Germans from Russia, are the basis of the following glimpse of the *Yagoder* in Calgary. Whenever possible I have let them describe it in their own words.

Leaving the Old Country

When my paternal grandparents, John and Mary Schierman, were married in Yagodnaya Polyana (Yagoda, for short), in 1910, some from their *Dorf* (village) had been in America over thirty years. Their own personal decision to leave was the result of a strong desire for independence, a wish to have land of their own, apprehension as the time for Grandpa's compulsory service in the army approached, and general unrest in Russia. Grandpa turned twenty-one in November 1911 and was eligible for military service the following October. His application for a passport in January 1912 was refused. A second attempt through Yagoda men of position in Saratov gave him, Grandma, and their baby girl a six-month leave from the country after which he was to return for military service. Grandma's seventeen-year-old sister, Katya, planned to emigrate with them.

They packed a few clothes, a feather tick, and some pillows into gunny sacks. They prepared food, mostly bread and *Wurst*, to take with them in a small wooden trunk Grandpa had built. News of the sinking of the *Titanic* reached the colony and did not make the departure easier. Near the end of April 1912, with the traditional parting song, *Jesu Geh Voran* (Jesus, Lead Thou On), their family and friends sent them off by wagon to Atkarsk. There, along with others leaving for the new world, they boarded the train for the port of Libau, about 1100 miles northwest in the Baltic Province of Courland, today part of Latvia. At Libau, Grandma's sister Katya was prevented from continuing the journey; she was told she had an eye infection. She had to make the long trip back to Yagoda, hoping to come to Canada at a later date. Another concern was that baby Katya, usually a very cheerful little girl, began fussing. They felt she had probably caught a draft on the train ride to Libau when Grandma's sister was playing with her by an open window.

Immigrants continued from Libau by small boat to a British port. One family remembered that they had to take "a small dirty freighter to London. The freighter was loaded with animal hides, hanging from the beams. Not only was John's wife, Anna, seasick from the horrendous odor, but she was three months pregnant, and she was nursing Alex because no fare was charged for nursing children." The new language, customs, and surroundings were very different from anything they had ever known. My grandfather had his first ham sandwich in England. One family in London "saw the buses and said, 'Look, they go without horses!' When Alexander started to put jelly in his tea, the English waitress said, 'No, you put it on your bread!' " When the immigrant men and women were separated for inspection before boarding the "big boat" to cross the Atlantic, one German-Russian lady went hysterical because she thought there was a harmful plot against them (P. Coulter and B. Shierman, 1986).

Immigrants traveled third class (steerage) from various ports such as Liverpool, Glasgow, or Southampton. My grandparents' ship offered good service and accommodation. It was far above their expectations; some former immigrants had made the journey on cattle boats with terrible food and sleeping quarters. Grandpa and many others heartily ate the good food on board but suffered for it very soon with seasickness. Though Grandma noticed the good porridge, she had no appetite because by this time their baby was very ill. They were reluctant to seek help for Katya because some earlier immigrants had reported bad experiences with ship surgeons. When they finally did contact the doctors on board they were impressed with their helpfulness and kindness. But it was too late—the ship passenger list shows "Katharina Schiermann, 11 mo., died at Sea 20/5/12." It was her first birthday, May 7 by the Julian calendar still used in Russia at that time. (In the twentieth century, the Julian Calendar—used in Russia until January 1918—was thirteen days behind the Gregorian Calendar used in the West.)

The doctors, crew, and passengers were courteous and sympathetic. The baby was nicely dressed, the boat stopped for a short service, Katya was laid in a rubber pouch and lowered into the Atlantic. Although the *Yagoder's* view of death was that "her time had come," it was still very difficult. It bothered Grandma that the baby had not been buried on land, but someone directed her to the verse in the Bible (Revelation 20:13) that said the sea too would give up "the dead which were in it."

The trip continued; they passed towering icebergs in the North Atlantic. Ten days after leaving Glasgow they were among 637 passengers who landed at the Canadian port of Quebec City. Registers show that ships with Canadian-bound passengers held from 500 to over 1000 people and landed at such places as Halifax, Nova Scotia; Portland, Maine; or Boston, Massachusetts. The amount of cash each immigrant family brought with them is indicated. My father's parents landed with $40; my mother's grandparents had $50. Others bound for Calgary in 1912 had as little as $2. The most common route to Calgary followed the transcontinental Grand Trunk Railway system (GTR). My grandparents could not remember any places through which they passed; too much had happened since they had left Yagodnaya a month earlier. When they needed food along the way, they held money in the palm of their hand, trusting the merchants to take the correct amount. The whole journey from Yagodnaya to Calgary cost about 400 rubles for the two of them, approximately $200 at the time.

142

The New Country

One of the most striking features of the Calgary area is its the proximity to the Rocky Mountains. "On the second morning of the journey west from Winnipeg...as I stood near the window of the washroom of the sleeper, I got my first surprising glimpse of the Rockies, a sight which I will never forget. The sun shone brightly against the dazzlingly white snow-capped peaks of the majestic mountain range, the atmosphere being so pure and clear that, although still about 150 miles distant, they seemed just a short way off (C. Hoyler, 1951). In spite of the glory of the Rockies, the physical appearance of Calgary itself was less impressive. A 1911 visiting journalist reported: "Calgary has many things which appeal to the visitor, but he must be commercially inclined, as nature has not endowed it with any very wonderful natural charms or places of interest to boast of, and with the prevailing breezes, winds and chinooks, for which it is noted, and the extremely dusty roads in and out of the town during dry weather, much of the pleasure of sight-seeing is diminished, but what Chicago is to the Western States, Calgary is to Alberta" (F. Carrel, 1911).

As far as my grandmother was concerned, when they first saw the district that was to be their new home she only remembers, "Our hearts fell in our shoes." From the train station in downtown Calgary they crossed the Langevin Bridge to Riverside, the area where German-speaking residents had concentrated. Their first impression was so disappointing they wrote to their families in Russia discouraging them from following, inwardly resolving to go back themselves. Calgary had begun as a settlement at the confluence of the Bow and Elbow Rivers in 1875 when the whole area between Manitoba and British Columbia was still known as the Northwest Territories. (Alberta and Saskatchewan became provinces in 1905.) The short-grass southern prairies were considered too dry for grain farming, but the grasslands, particularly in the foothills of the Rockies, attracted ranching.

The major factor leading to Calgary's growth was the arrival of the Canadian Pacific Railway in August 1883. The new all-Canadian route connecting the prairies with eastern Canada meant people, supplies, and mail no longer had to use the Whoop-Up Trail bull trains that provided the only connection to the East through Fort Benton, Montana. Calgary soon developed into western Canada's railway distribution center. It was not uncommon at this time for developing communities to vigorously promote themselves. "It was an act of faith, an expression of confidence in the future." Advertising their city as "the gateway of the Last Great West...the most important city between Winnipeg and Vancouver" or "the Phenomenal," Calgarians demonstrated "boosterism" at its best. Immigrants in increasing numbers made their way to "one of the most discussed cities inside and outside Canada" (A. Artibise, 1985 and S. L. Bensusan, ed., n.d.).

People of German ethnic origin were among those who arrived, most of them coming from German-speaking settlements outside of Germany. They came from Galicia, from Volhynia, from Moldavia and other areas north of the Black Sea, and from the North Caucasus. And the *Yagoder* came—from The Volga, an area of German settlement on both sides of the Volga River near the city of Saratov. Their village, Yagodnaya Polyana, was the most northerly of the Volga colonies, about 60 verst (kilometers) northwest of Saratov on the *Bergseite* (the hilly side) of the river.

By 1891 an estimated 900 people of German origin lived in Alberta. The first *Yagoder* arrived in 1892, crossing the Rocky Mountains from Endicott, Washington, to the parkland between Calgary and Edmonton near today's town of Bashaw. Calgary's first *Yagoder* were four Poffenroth brothers, also from Endicott, who came in 1894 "looking for cheap land." By 1898, Calgary had fifteen German families (R. Scheuerman, 1977).

News of the city filtered back to Russia. "Three men came to Yagodnaya from Canada and asked if there were any people who wanted to go to Canada and advised that they would be their sponsors." As the American West filled and as new seed, techniques, and machinery made agriculture in the southern Canadian prairies more feasible, Calgary became the destination of more and more immigrants (P. Coulter and B. Shierman, 1986). Canada welcomed these German-speaking Russian immigrants. The ideal immigrant was one who could become an independent prairie farmer: "a stalwart peasant in a sheep-skin coat born on the soil, whose forefathers have been farmers for ten generations, with a stout wife and a half-dozen children" (C. Simpson quoted in D. J. Hall, 1977). *Use Leut* (our people) fit the description and came either directly from Russia or via the United States where some had accumulated machinery, money, and new-world farming experience.

The district in Calgary where the German-Russians settled was initially outside the city limits. North of the Bow River the bank abruptly rises to form the "North Hill"; but northeast of downtown, the escarpment swings north-ward in a crescent to enclose two lower levels of relatively flat land. The lowest land, near the river, was occupied first and became known as Riverside. By the turn of the century enough German-speaking immigrants had settled there for it to be dubbed "Germantown," complete with a Berlin Street (Second Avenue A North) and a Munich Street (7 Street NE). The new subdivision, Bridgeland, occupied the terrace north of Riverside—most of the area between Six and Eleventh Streets and Centre and Fifth Avenue NE. "A barbed-wire fence stretched from the hill down present day Six Street to Murdock Road or Centre Avenue and east to the Bridgeland district of today...the C.P.R. bought this section of land and divided it into lots. A corner lot sold for $75 and an ordinary lot for $50. However within three months lots jumped in price to $200 and $300 (Bridgeland Yeland Riverside Story, 1964). Bridgeland was annexed to the city in 1907, the older Riverside district in

1910. Over the years Riverside and Bridgeland fused into one community, the names sometimes used interchangeably. The area was also referred to as "Langevin."

By 1911 the Canadian Census showed that almost 4000 of Calgary's 43,704 inhabitants were of German origin. They formed the fourth largest ethnic group in the city—after the English, Scotch, and Irish. Most of Calgary's Germans before World War I had come from Russia and at least half of those were from Yagodnaya Polyana. *Yagoder* concentration was heaviest between Sixth and eighth Street and First and Fourth Avenues NE (H. Gutsche, 1993). Other Germans from Russia (e.g., from Norka or from Kraft) shared the district. "I was born in Calgary in 1906. My parents had come from Alexanderdorf. But I grew up speaking *Yagoda*. They were all around us!" (K. Fraser, n.d.).

By 1912 most of Calgary's essential services were in place. There was letter carrier service, an efficient street car service, an automated telephone exchange, electric lights, and a water supply. (The latter was a questionable service; two households in 1912 reported fish coming through the line!) The first of the world famous Calgary Stampedes was held in September 1912. New buildings such as the Hudson's Bay Company Store, the Palliser Hotel, the CPR Station, City Hall (complete with palm trees), and the Library (built with a Carnegie Foundation grant) were either under construction or newly completed that year. Building permit values hit a record high that was not again reached until Calgary became the center of Alberta's oil and gas industry in the 1950's. Between 1910 and 1912, Calgary showed more population and construction increases than any other city in Canada.

St. George's Island in the Bow River, just south of the area, had been set aside for a park. The city's main hospital, the General, was opened in Riverside in 1910. Many industries and the downtown area were within walking distance. The "flashy" new Langevin Bridge replaced the former wooden structure across the Bow River in 1910 and connected the area to the heart of the city. A street car track across the bridge followed Fourth Street North and First Avenue East to "the loop" at Twelfth Street NE.

Bridgeland, like the rest of Calgary, swelled with the arrival of immigrants. More homes were built in the district in 1912 than in any other year of its history. Most had cold running water and electric lights and used coal for heating and cooking. Riverside's commercial interests on Fourth Street north of the Langevin Bridge included the Riverside Hotel, a branch of the Dominion Bank of Canada, meat markets and grocers, dry goods and department stores, Chinese restaurants, a blacksmith, a Chinese laundry, a druggist, post office, tin shop, glass works, livery stable, and billiards. Bridgeland's area of commercial concentration began with meat and grocery stores and a cobbler on First Avenue near eighth and Ninth Street. Along with the other areas north of the Bow River, Bridgeland-Riverside was considered a second-class area in the city. But for the working man it was a very good place to live.

Settling In

My grandparents arrived on a Saturday, June 1, 1912. On Monday morning Peter Fox gave Grandpa a pair of overalls and took him along to work at the Cushing Brothers Door Factory. Grandpa put in a full day's work and was promptly hired. It was a typical labor job with a six-day week, ten-hour day, and 25 cents-an-hour pay. (If one was single the pay was about 20 cents an hour.)

In 1912 the CPR began building a railway car repair shop which was to be the major locomotive service center between Winnipeg and Vancouver. This massive complex, occupying over 200 acres 4.6 miles southeast of the center of Calgary, became Calgary's largest employer of immigrants. My grandfather was among the hundreds who in early 1913 took the street car to the new ships in Ogden (east Calgary industrial area) looking for work. But that day the whole group was turned back at the entrance by company security guards telling them no jobs were available at that time. Finding some way into the huge fenced yards, Grandpa persistently headed for the office. A supervisor who was coming from the mill shop to the car shop spotted him and asked, "What do you want?" "A job," Grandpa replied. "What can you do?" "Carpentry." And with that he had a job as a car repairer with pay of 25 1/2 cents an hour.

German women generally sought domestic work. Knowing no English, my greatgrandmother, Wilhelmina Rausch Schierman, went door to door in the well-to-do part of the city, pantomiming her services by falling to her knees on the porch to act out floor scrubbing. An employer often "became a close friend and helped much in the customs of this country" (W. R. Schierman, 1976). Considering the building boom, it is not surprising that most job opportunities in Calgary were related to construction, to the railway, or to various services. But not all *Yagoder* were laborers. "Scores of economic enterprises and businesses owned by German-Albertans are recorded: in Calgary, in 1904, both of the earliest settlers from the Volga region, Christian Paffenroth and Johannes Keiser, were very well to do: the former owned a large ranch, several other pieces of real estate and two hotels, the latter a large ranch. In 1908 there were already other owners: one owned a hotel, another a clothing store, some were partners in businesses, one in a real-estate firm, another in a meat sale company (A. Malychy, n.d.).

Life for my grandparents was definitely different in the bustling new city than it had been in Yagoda. One evening in the summer of 1912, a terrific boom shook the city. Some women were sure it was the end of the world! The newspaper substantiates that on July 17, 1912, there *was*, in fact, quite an event. "That night around nine o'clock, just after it got dark, there was at least ten thousand or twelve thousand people, I would estimate, gathered around the standpipe in East Calgary. Eugene Coste [who masterminded the plan] and his wife were there, and Whitey Foster was in charge of the valve control. At a signal from Mr. Coste, Whitey turned on the valve and he turned it on plenty, because coming out of this standpipe there was first a tremendous amount of dust, then stones and great big boulders, two or three pairs of overalls, pieces of skids—almost everything came out. There was a tremendous roar and the people started to back up. And there was almost a panic. Well finally Mrs. Coste was standing by with Roman candles and she was shooting these candles at the standpipe trying to light the gas. And away she finally went-with a terrible bang" (P. Mellon, quoted in T. Ward, 1975).

Bringing natural gas 170 miles by pipeline from Bow Island in southeast Alberta was but one example of the grand schemes of early Calgary entrepreneurs. They believed that bigger was better and, in terms of employment opportunities for the *Yagoder*, it definitely was. By 1912, Calgary had subdivisions as far as eight miles from city center in most directions—enough to house half a million people. There were 2000 real estate agents and 443 firms in the city. A famous British architect had been hired to produce an elaborate plan for a European-style city that would grow to a million. Calgary had set up a planning commission—a relatively new urban concept in Canada. But reality did not match optimism and Calgary's economic frenzy peaked. A recession in 1913, war in 1914, and the 1917 Bolshevik Revolution in Russia permanently shelved my grandparents' plans to return to Russia.

Church

The only church in Yagodnaya had been Lutheran, but in Calgary's early years a number of denominations established contact with German-speaking residents. A German pastor with the Dakota Conference of the Evangelical Church preached in Calgary as early as 1884. A German Baptist missionary from the U.S. performed the first German-Albertan marriage ceremony in Calgary in 1888. A Lutheran minister of the Canada Synod (later to become the Manitoba Synod) conducted the first Lutheran service in Calgary in 1891. A German Moravian missionary heading for rural areas east of Edmonton passed through Calgary in 1896. (T. Jesske, 1985 and A. Malycky, n.d.). An 1899 visit by a "traveling missionary" of the Missouri Synod of the Lutheran Church resulted in the formation of a German Lutheran congregation in Calgary in 1900. The parish included both Calgary and Pincher Creek and was under the care of the Lutheran minister at Missoula, Montana. Pincher Creek was almost 150 miles south of Calgary; Missoula another 300 miles south of Pincher Creek. The first minister was called in 1901 and early membership rolls indicate that approximately seventy percent of the Calgary members were *Yagoder*. By 1904 the church established a school and become a parish of its own, Immanuel Lutheran Church.

Immigrants brought with them religious preferences and practices not familiar on the North American Lutheran scene. One of the most cherished was *Versammlung*, gatherings of the Volga Brotherhood which since 1871

Yagodnaya Polyana Panorama

had drawn together like-minded lay people for teaching and encouragement. "The more spiritually minded assembled in private homes Sunday afternoons, evenings, and also on some week nights for additional devotional meetings" (W. Kroening, 1952). Some Lutheran ministers (in both the Old Country and Calgary) were interested in these meetings; others were not. Disagreements over *Versammlung* led some Calgary Germans to contact the Moravian denomination and in 1902 Calgary's first Sunday School for German children and a Moravian congregation organized. Most members "came...from Yagoda-Polyana, some from west of the Volga, others from east of the river" (C. Hoyler, 1951). They worshipped in a plain, modest structure built close to downtown Calgary. "The first pews were merely planks on supports with no back rests" and "must have been rather uncomfortable when the services lasted a long time" (F. Wiley, n.d.).

Some Moravian practices were unfamiliar to the Volga German Lutherans. But Calgary's first Moravian minister believed the Old Country Lutherans and the Moravians also had many similarities. "Their 'Volga Gesangbuch' of some thousand hymns contains many Moravian hymns as we sing them. It also contains the regular Moravian Litany. Many of the tunes are sung the Moravian way. It surprised a number of the Calgary people to hear the Moravian pastors when visiting them sing heartily their tunes. Not only that, but that they would humbly worship with them in their accustomed manner" (W. Kroening, 1952).

However, since the *Yagoder* had all been Lutherans in the Old Country, the attachment to that church remained very strong. The many different North American synods confused the people though, so some wrote to their pastor in Yagodnaya asking which one they should join. His first reply was that the Iowa Synod taught "the undefiled and pure doctrine of the Lutheran Church," and a second letter shortly after stated that the Ohio Synod could also be joined "without scruples." Subsequently, *Die Evangelishe Lutherische Sankt Johannes Gemeinde Zu Calgary* (St. John Lutheran Church, Iowa Synod) was established in 1909. About the same time an Ohio Synod congregation known as Zion was also organized.

Meanwhile, the Immanuel (Missouri) congregation continued but had difficulties. "It seemed to have revolved to a large extent around the use of the Missouri Synod hymnal vis-a-vis the Volga hymnal." The pastor "took a hard line for the Missouri Synod hymnal" (Rev John Herzer, 1913, quoted in C. Cheland, 1975), but the people clung to their dearly-loved *Wolga Gesangbuch.* In 1913 the congregation split with about half withdrawing to form St. Paul's Lutheran Church. This new group initiated an ambitious building project but soon had to abandon it when another split saw about half leaving to go to the Ohio church instead. Those remaining in the St. Paul congregation became the core of Jehovah Lutheran Church which formally organized as a second Missouri congregation in 1919.

At the peak of Calgary's boom in 1913, the Moravian congregation, "enthusiastic about the prospect of great expansion in that new suburban part of the city," erected a lovely brick building on the hill overlooking the Riverside flats, the Bow River and downtown Calgary. Bridgeland-Riverside also had other German congregations. There were the Methodists, the Seventh Day, the Baptists, and the "Ebenezer" congregation. Also, "during the year 1913, the Rev. C. S. Finkbeiner [of the Evangelical Church]...visited Calgary every month, and conducted services with a group of German people" (T. Jesske, 1985).

Pastors provided the immigrants with spiritual focus and encouragement and were the only link many had with the new country. My grandparents understood that immediately when they arrived in the city and their luggage did not. It was a minister who tracked it down for them. "The people in the beginning were very helpless where the English language was concerned. So they came to the minister with all their problems. If they were sick he had to fetch the doctor and interpret for them. When they had any kind of business transaction, they needed assistance to guard them against sharks in human clothing who often would take advantage of their ignorance. Sometimes property had to be purchased, or baggage went astray, or tickets had to be purchased. The minister sometimes had to write letters for them to the Old Country. Sometimes even love letters were sent" (F. Wiley, n.d.).

The church also kept the reading and writing skills in the old script alive among German young people. "We went to night school at Zion Lutheran every Tuesday and Friday. On Tuesday we got a lesson from the *Biblische Geschichten* and Friday we had to know it and write it out. Friday we got a new lesson for Tuesday. I've always been thankful for that" (K. Fraser, n.d.).

Schools

By 1904 a German parochial school with 60 to 70 children was operating in Riverside out of Immanuel Lutheran Church. By 1910, this school had 175 pupils and two teachers. However, minorities were judged by how readily they adapted to Canadian life and parochial schools were seen as a threat to assimilation. "If these children are to grow up as Canadian citizens they must be led to adopt our viewpoint and speak our speech....A common school and a common tongue are essential if we are to have a homogeneous citizenship" (D. Goggin quoted in N. McDonald, 1977).

Most German immigrants were aware they had come to a new country, and even before the German church school was shut down, many willingly sent their children to the English public schools. By 1909 public school classes in Riverside had grown to the point of necessitating a new Riverside Public School. By 1912 Bridgeland Cottage School had to be added to the district. In 1914 Riverside Bungalow No. 1 was built; in 1914 Bridgeland School (later known as Stanley Jones) was located up the hill north; in 1920 Riverside

Bungalow No. 2 was added; and in 1921 Bridgeland School was built in the northeast part of the district. "In the early days of Calgary, there were many old country people who came to Canada because of the wonderful opportunities here. The parents placed very high values on education, they encouraged their children to try to be better than they. The children, not wanting to hurt their parents tried a little harder for their education" (*Langevin School Community*, 1972).

"Grandfather was strict about sending his children to school. My mother (12 years old) was embarrassed going to school with six-year olds, so played hookey. When Grandfather found out, he gave in and told her to quit school, but she had to go to work. She got a job in a candy factory in Riverside. The boys did well and soon caught up to the children their age. When Uncle John came home from school he taught Grandfather what he had learned" (W. R. Schierman, 1976).

One early Riverside student observed, "With this double seating arrangement...we shared many things in common, some of which were not so welcome...the boys were happy when the weather was mild enough to permit them to have their hair cut as close to the scalp as possible. Also shed were the woolen or fleeced lined underwear that retained many things besides body heat, notwithstanding the claims that boiling the inner garments was the solution. Boiling was only a temporary solution for with the next new immigrants a more sturdy stock would appear. The boys had a picnic compared to the girls, for they really had long hair those days. They (the girls) also had pride and they would sooner endure rigid treatment and retain their hair even with the slight suggestion of a kerosene odor" (*Riverside-Langevin School*, 1964).

The Lord's Prayer was recited at the opening of the day. There were fire drills; all supplies were free. Recreational facilities including skating rinks were built. Medical services inspected pupils twice a year. Public school was grade 1-8 and the Alberta curriculum drawn up in 1907 included history, geography, reading and literature, spelling, composition, grammar, nature study, agriculture, arithmetic, and drawing. High school was mostly academic although 1916 revisions introduced compulsory manual training and household arts in grade 9 and 10 and a two-year commercial program to attract dropouts. Central Collegiate Institute (1908) was the city's first high school, but Crescent Heights (1909) would have been the one used by Bridgeland-Riverside students.

Teachers encouraged children to be proud of their new country. "My class occupied the south-east room, with windows looking out on the south hills of Calgary and the Rockies. I have never gotten over my first thrills at the sight of them and often in that room refreshed myself by a glance at them. Many times I called pupils' attention to their glories and to them as part of Our Canada (E. Patterson quoted in *Riverside-Langevin School*, 1964).

Farming

There was considerable movement in and out of Calgary during the early years. It was not unusual for *Yagoder* men to travel hundreds of miles, usually to places other Germans from Russia had settled, to get seasonal work. (In some ways this may have been similar to the travel they did in Russia to work on the *Khutor*.) In 1916 when news of a bumper crop in the Leader-Burstall area of southwest Saskatchewan reached Calgary, Grandpa and five other men saw the opportunity to earn extra money and each bought a wagon and two horses which they transformed by CPR to help farmers haul grain to the nearest rail line.

One of the main reasons the *Yagoder* had come to Canada was to search for reasonably priced land. "The yearn of farming never faded....Never lacking optimism, my father ventured to move back on a farm" (J. H. Schierman, n.d.). Some families moved to farms in the Carstairs-Acme area north of Calgary and commuted forty miles to continue work in Calgary. "Every day they took the train in to Calgary where street cars lined up at the CPR station to take people to their work destinations around the city" (W. R. Schierman, 1976). Not all who left Calgary went to farm. In 1919 when there was a CPR rail strike some left for places like Portland, Oregon, "looking for better employment opportunities" (P. Coulter, 1986).

The German Community

A strong sense of community existed among the Calgary *Yagoder*. While some immigrants arrived in Calgary destitute and in need through sickness or desertion of the head of the family, the *Yagoder* stuck together. "When I was five, an aunt died in childbirth. Uncle had six children and a new baby made seven now. So Mom and Dad took their three children to Uncle's place to help out a while" (W. R. Schierman, 1976). For those living in outlying areas, bonds of support continued with those in Calgary. "My uncles and aunts were very helpful during times of special need, especially harvest. In return they received potatoes and other garden vegetables, eggs and chickens, and pork and beef" (M. Rousch, n.d.).

In the Old Country it had been typical for families to share homes. My grandparents had lived with his parents, his unmarried sisters and brothers, his grandparents, his aunt and uncle and their family—all in two rooms under one roof. So when they came to Calgary it was common for families to live together. While having more than one family under one roof was "normal," it definitely did create problems. "I cried more water than I drank that year," my grandmother said referring to one of their many living arrangements in their first years in Canada. Women would disagree over kitchen use or over supplies. There were accusations, for example, that one woman had helped herself to another's barrel of sauerkraut in the cellar. Or there would be arguments over

152

child-rearing. Some of the children had vivid memories of the dominant or "bossy" man in the extended family. "Uncle always put the finger on me." Some *Yagoder* did not like this close-knit living. "Mother got lost on the boat and ended up in New York. Dad went to get her and they lived in the States for a while." Some of the family suggest the "getting lost" may have been intentional.

Acceptance by the Calgary Community

The river and the escarpment separated Bridgeland-Riverside geographically from the rest of the city, but the people's language and customs also separated them ethnically. "I think that all her life in Canada, mother-in-law only went to church and the grocery store. She read her Bible in German and cleaned house" (P. Schneidmiller, n.d.). At the same time though, the *Yagoder* did not resist or down play their new country or its dominant culture. A survey of German-Canadian creative literature in Alberta before World War I notes that it "is not preoccupied with the themes of loneliness or longing for the old homeland which characterize other non-English/French co-tempral and co-territorial literatures of Canada" (A. Malycky, 1978).

As for Calgary's response to the German-Russians, there was some resistance to any "hyphenated Canadians"; but generally there was acceptance. A 1902 promotional publication, *Gronlund's,* included references to Germantown "north of the city and just across the Langevin Bridge, where a large number of German-speaking Russians have settled and built homes for themselves. While in this country only a short time, they have gained for themselves a name for thrift, honesty and sobriety. The western Canadian immigration agent described Germans as an "excellent type of immigrant, sober, capable and industrious: quiet and law-abiding; possessed of a fair elementary education and only wanting the opportunity denied them heretofore to prove themselves creditable citizens" (H. Palmer, 1972).

Calgary remained, however, a predominantly Anglo-Saxon city in which unofficial Social Darwinism prevailed. Anglo-Saxons were firmly at the top and Natives, Orientals, and Blacks indisputably at the bottom. Northwestern Europeans fit somewhere in the middle and eastern Europeans a bit lower. The key to an immigrant's acceptance was his willingness to "assimilate," that is, willingness to accept Anglo-Saxon economic, political, legal, and educational institutions. This most *Yagoder* did—they knew Canada had many advantages and opportunities and taught their children to respect its institutions. As a result, Germans along with Scandinavians "were considered to be among Canada's best citizens since they were thought to be industrious and culturally and racially similar and thus readily assimilable." It was not until 1914 when Britain declared war on Germany (automatically putting Canada at war) that things began to get difficult for our people in Calgary. "German-Albertans plunged from the esteem of highly praised immigrants to the atmosphere of being suspected and in a sense made to pay for the behavior of Germany and the Danubian Empire" (H. Palmer).

Anti-German sentiment prevailed. No public German gatherings were allowed and German language church services were discontinued. There was friction within the German community too. "The Moravian Church had long been a pacifist church (although now the decision of whether or not to join in a conflict is left to the individual)....This caused hard feelings among some of the members" (T. Elliot, 1982).

A few days before my dad was born in February 1916, my grandmother remembers being ready to flee up the north hill to escape attacks of mobs gathering south across the river. "During the First Great War the feeling against Germans was intense. In Calgary large numbers of men were in training....A mob of more than 500, mostly soldiers, wrecked the White Lunch...the reason given for the riot was that the manager...had discharged a returned soldier and employed an Austrian in his place....The following evening, the mob was again on the warpath and within 20 minutes wrecked the Riverside Hotel which stood just across the Langevin bridge" (L. McNeill, 1975).

Calgary newspapers point out that the White Lunch restaurant owner had dismissed the soldier "because of his refusal to clean the floor of the place" and had hired the German because "it was impossible to get anyone else who would do this work and stick to the job." As for the attack on the Riverside Hotel, "from inquiries among the crowd, it seemed that the only reason for attacking the place was that it was 'owned by a German.' This applied apparently to the former ownership by Charles Poffenroth though the hotel is now owned by Alfred E. Ebbsworth of Blackie, an Englishman, and leased to John Rioux, a French-Canadian" (*Calgary Herald,* February 12, 1916).

Prior to the 1917 federal election, any German immigrants naturalized after 1902 were disenfranchised by the Wartime Election Act. Workers of "enemy-alien birth" were dismissed from work. Calgary citizens discussed whether or not there was a difference between Germans born in Germany and those born elsewhere. One *Calgary Herald* editorial came up with this guideline: "If you must expend your courage, do it on a real German instead of a German sausage."

My grandfather was one who got his job back by showing his Russian passport. But negative comments about "enemy aliens" or "Huns" continued in the press towards anyone with a "Teutonic" sounding name. The feelings of these years did not heal quickly: young people grew up learning not to outwardly identify themselves as German. "My how fast we learned not to even mention we spoke German. We were branded *Dutchmen.* Funny thing, many of these families were of German origin but would claim they were not. Since the 1914-1918 War, to be German was a barrier" (W. R. Schierman, 1976). In the 1921 Canadian census only 1.4% (876) of Calgary's 63,305 people identified themselves as of German ethnic origin.

That same year over half of the homeowners and landowners in Bridgeland were German: some blocks were entirely German occupied. Of Bridgeland homeowners, 35% were employed by the CPR, 18% were laborers, 16% were employed by city businesses (such as Burns Packing, Calgary Brewery, Cushing Brothers, Calgary Iron Works). Some 13% were tradesmen, 6% were drivers or teamsters, 8% were proprietors or clerks. By the 1920's Empire Meat, Lavine's Confectionery, Bridgeland Corner, Premier Grocery, Gerlitz Grocery, Bridgeland Drug, and The Modern Barbershop and Beauty Parlor were among area businesses.

Education and Religious Life

School brought the older generation into contact with the larger community in various ways. On the farm at Carstairs, the older German women were disgusted when Wilf Carther, a local cowboy singer, provided entertainment at one of the Christmas concerts. "Nuh," they shorted as he yodelled *O-de-ladie,* "He's making fun of the *Wibesleut*" (the old ladies).

Integration into the community also came through sports. Riverside was referred to as the "greatest sports centre in Calgary." Every spare minute we had away from school we played hockey or baseball...we won the City Junior Hockey championship in the 1943-44 season" (Reuben Rausch, n.d.). Some German-Russian youth went on to professional play—one of the most admired was Sweeney Schriner who had a long and outstanding National Hockey League career with the Toronto Maple Leafs. Donald Hartmann recalls that he coached the local youth teams on the ice rink below the General Hospital.

The *Yagoder* did not discourage the schools' promotion of Canadian and British tradition. "In 1936 the King and Queen came to visit Calgary. I can still see all the pupils of our school marching two by two up the North Hill and sitting on the grass waiting for the King and Queen (now the Queen Mother) to come. How thrilled I was when the motorcade came to where we were. What a beautiful Queen we had. After that I would cut out and save any pictures of the royal family I could lay my hands on. What a privilege to be born in this beautiful country of Canada" (H. R. Schierman, n.d.).

The declared objective of the educators had been "...to gather the children of different races, creeds, and customs into the common school, and 'Canadianize' them....Though they may enter as Galicians, Doukhobors, or Icelanders, they will come out as Canadians...." (D. Goggin, quoted in N. McDonald, 1977). This goal was realized in most Canadian-educated *Yagoder.* "I never considered myself anything but a Canadian" (S. Schriner, n.d.).

My grandmother, Wilhemina Rausch Schierman, summarized her religious upbringing these terms: "We grew up knowing what Good Friday, Easter, Pentecost, and Christmas meant. My father always explained these special days and satisfied our questions. I used to look forward to his story telling. He taught us how to pray. We prayed before and after each meal and at bed time. I found when I got older they were from a prayer hymn." After the War, most *Yagoder* belonged to St. John Lutheran (Ohio) and Jehovah Lutheran (Missouri). Some were part of Immanuel Lutheran (Missouri) or the smaller Moravian and Seventh Day Adventist congregations. "I also looked forward to attending the neighborhood prayer meetings held in *Die Halle*, the *Versammlung* Hall....At times my Dad would lead the Bible Study or play his horn in the wind instrument orchestra" (M. Rausch, n.d.). People from all various German churches participated in *Versammlung* (but not al the young *Yagoder* were in attendance—Galleli's Barn was just next door!).

When *Yagoder* moved to rural locations they tried to find a nearby German-speaking church. In the Leader area of Saskatchewan there was Peace Lutheran (*Friedens-Gemeinde*), St. John Lutheran, Zions Congregational, *Hoffnungstahl* "Valley of Hope" German Baptist, and Seventh Day Adventist Churches. About thirty miles southwest in the Burstall area there was Schmidt Lutheran, St. Paul's Lutheran, *Gnadenfeldt* Baptist, *Liebenthal* Baptist, and *Hoffnung* (Hope) Evangelical. Just across the provincial border in Hilda, Alberta, was Zion Lutheran, Evangelical Bethlehem Lutheran, Hilda Baptist, Salem Evangelical, Congregational, and Seventh Day Adventist Churches. In the Beiseker area and in the Cluny district there were Seventh Day Adventist Churches.

Children of farm families stayed with friends or relatives in Calgary when it was time to take Confirmation classes. One confirmand of 1932 remembers that his Dad gave the minister $15 to confirm him in English because he just could not seem to master the German. Confirmation was held on Palm Sunday every spring (P. Schneidmiller, n.d.).

"I loved going to church and Sunday School. We had to learn a new *Spruch* [Bible verse] each Sunday in Sunday School. When we learned a certain number of *Spruch,* we got a larger one with questions on the back. All these at first were in German" (H. R. Schierman, n.d.). Services were in German until the 1930's when some accommodation was made for the younger people. Not everyone agreed with the introduction of English; when Rev. Holfeld started English services at St. John Church, some said, "*Du bist fericht.*"

Employment

A 1936 study of German-speaking Albertans found that among Volga Germans in Alberta "the majority are still on the land, yet a fairly large number belong to Edmonton and Calgary's laboring classes" (E. Gerwin, 1988). Bridgelanders were laborers, tradesmen, teamsters, clerks, and proprietors around the city, but the CPR continued to be the biggest employer. "Special street cars took the men to Ogden early in the morning. In the evening when the men came home tired, dirty, and greasy, they could smell the different suppers cooking in each home as they walked down the street. It smelled so good" (M. R. Dippel, n.d.).

It was expected that children would contribute to the upkeep of the household as soon as possible. Although most children stayed in school until grade eighth, many had part-time jobs much earlier. "At the age of nine or ten, I used to deliver milk to customers at nine cents a quart. My mother had a cow that was milked twice a day. She used to go get the cow home early in the morning from the pasture which was south of the General Hospital, milk it, take it back to pasture, and do the same thing at night time. When I was thirteen, I also worked for Jenkins Grocery Store delivering groceries with a bike—at noon, 4 to 6 pm, and all day Saturday. I also sold papers six nights a week, 10:30 to 12 midnight, in front of the Paliser Hotel. At fourteen, I went to work at Bridgeland Corner Store delivering groceries and still selling *Albertans* at nighttime" (R. Rausch, n.d.). Some of the young people developed novel money-making schemes. "We caught pigeons down the manhole on Center Street Bridge and sold them to the Chinese for ten cents a bird. They loved to eat them" (J. Rausch, n.d.).

When there were difficult times such as a death in the family, the community was supportive. "When Dad died in the 1930's," remembered Grandmother Schierman, "we certainly had many wonderful friends who brought us food and helped in so many ways. Mom and we seven children lived rent and utility free with our grandparents. Mom had to go to work in homes of well-to-do people and I also worked for $10 a month for a lady in the neighborhood who was not well. Rev. Holfeld (the Lutheran minister) and the corner-store owner (a Jew) worked very hard to get financial help for Mom and after some months succeeded in getting widow's pension from the city. I think it was $42 a month. Also, that first Christmas the Red Cross helped us and the Salvation Army and the Fire Department brought to the house a food hamper and a toy for each child. I'll never forget that."

In the 1930's some young *Yagoder* men joined the many others who left town to look for work. "During the Depression, beginning around May, a cousin and I would ride the rails. A hundred or more boys would jump on by the Shamrock Hotel and head for Lethbridge and then on to BC. We would pick strawberries and work our way back to Fort Macleod. We would make about $200 a summer. They left you alone unless there was a forest fire. Then the Mounties said *Fight fires or go to jail*" (J. Rausch, n.d.).

Household Routines

Life in the 1920's and 30's was simple. "Seemed there was a system to the work. Monday—wash clothes, all on a washboard, all the whites boiled. This was an all day job. Tuesday—it seemed it took all day to iron with sad irons heated on the stove. Then the mending which was such a pile. This usually carried over to most of Wednesday and Thursday. Friday—sewing, churning butter, making cottage cheese, gardening. It seemed there was just so much to get done. Saturday was for cleaning the whole house, baking bread, pies. As usual there was company on Sunday afternoon. The noon meal after church was usually roast beef or chicken. Company was always a lot of fun" (W. R. Schierman, 1976).

Tidiness and cleanliness were important. "Dad had the barn so clean, we played house in it," recalls Marion Dippel. Outside around the doorway to the house, the ground was regularly swept. "Going to Grandma's house was always like going to a fairy land. It was so clean."

On the farm there was no running water. "We used catalogues for *nushnik papayah*," and "we would also save the paper wrapped around apples and oranges. We would carefully stroke them flat and quarter and stack them for the outhouse. "Young boys wore short pants in those days. Mom sewed for the three boys—shirts, pants, coats. Good parts from old adult coats were washed, pressed and used. I loved to sew and began sewing dresses for my three younger sisters at a very young age. Mom would buy enough of one piece of material to make all three. There were no patterns; you created your own. The boys wore black stockings and the girls wore fawn stockings. It seems the heels and toes always had holes. I also used to love to patch and darn sox. I was taught to make it as invisible as possible" (R. Rausch and W. R. Schierman, 1976).

"Shall I ever forget harvest time when the threshing gang came with the threshing machine, wagons, and the horses. Mom had been baking and cooking ahead of time. Little folks automatically stayed away from underfoot. The food at threshing time was tremendous and so good. Bowls and plates piled high with potatoes and meat, thick slices of homemade bread. For dessert—apple pie and cake. It would all disappear so quickly" (H. R. Schierman, n.d.).

Some social events in Bridgeland gave relief to the never-ending work. "Grandma was invited to many a bridal shower to provide entertainment while the ladies were getting lunch ready. She would dance on the table, arms folded at the chest, legs kicking out, while Mr. Gnam from down the street played the accordian" (W. R. Schierman, 1976). Others found enjoyment in homemade *Gavust* (home brew). "Things got pretty loud down there in the crawl space. One evening Mother locked Dad out. It was a rather chilly night!"

Medical Needs, Birth and Death

My grandparents' well-used copy of *Pfarrer Heumann's* German handbook (1922) included everything from suggestions of healthy living to advice on the care of sick children. It was filled with text and diagrams on parts and organs of the body and included, of course, advertisements for Rev. Heumann's tonics and remedies for everything—asthma, scabies, bed sores, worms, toothache, piles, nerves, corns, goitre, hernia, chilblain, insect bites, and burns (to name a few). Families were large. Advice for planning families was, "Nurse the baby as long as you can."

Medical services inspected school pupils. "It was found I was very underweight. The school had a program that any underweight children had to drink a half pint of milk a day. I was one of those 'privileged' kids who got milk to drink during the morning recess...[but] I hated milk! I would try to drink it, and just about choke. About the second or third day, Miss McKellar noticed the problem I was having. She saved the day by telling me to bring some ginger snaps and put some on my tongue and take a sip of milk and it would not be so bad. After school I rushed home and told Mom I needed some ginger snaps right now. She sent me to Jenkins to get some. You put a piece of cookie right on the center of your tongue and swished the milk through it. so my problem was solved. Did I gain weight? No way; I was underweight all through my school years" (H. R. Schierman, n.d.).

Doctors made house calls and hospitals were accessible, but the ill were cared for at home as long as possible. "I remember how sick Victor was and Mom used to make a daytime bed for him in the kitchen so she could watch him as she worked. I wax six and Victor was four. Mom and Dad knew it was Victor's end on earth, so told me to play with two-year old Martin in the front room and watch for Grandmother when she got off the street car. As I was looking out the window for the street car, I heard Victor say in a clear voice in German, 'Momma, Dadda, do you hear the angels? They are out the window and singing so nice.' So I too looked for the angels. Then Grandmother came and it became very confusing to me as now I was told Victor died and the angels took him to heaven. I still could not see the angels" (W. R. Schierman, 1976).

When there was a death, the body was put in the coldest room of the house. "I remember friends coming. The women helped make clothes for Victor and lined the little casket which the men built in the basement. The one bedroom was closed off and the body kept in there....While my dad was making the coffin, I went into the bedroom and tried to awaken him so that we could play together. He was two years older than I" (M. Rousch, n.d.). A bereaving household was identified by a dark bow hung by the funeral director on the front door. At first, all burials were in Union Cemetery; later Burnsland Cemetery was opened.

Childhood and Youth

To the children of the immigrants, Bridgeland was a closely-knit community. "My first recollections as a child were when I was about five. We always spoke German, so I knew no English. I remember calling cornflakes *fatza*. One morning I wanted *fatza* but there was none so Mom told me if I would go to the corner store and buy some I could have some. This was my first trip to the store alone. I was so happy to be so grown up. Mr. Gerlitz knew everyone in

After the Shower

Bridgeland and spoke the German language. But I could not say cornflakes and Mr. Gerlitz would not know what *fatza* was, so Mom drilled me on saying cornflakes. I said cornflakes that half block I had to go and when I got to the store and Mr. Gerlitz asked me what I wanted all I could say was *fatza*. Well the man could not figure out what I was saying so took me in his arms and went around the store and told me to point out what I wanted. I got the cornflakes and from then on remembered how to say it" (W. R. Schierman, 1976).

"When I was very small," recalls Helen Schierman, "Mom would sit me on her foot and lift me up and down saying, *Drus drus drillyah, dah bower hud a fillyah; dah fillyah spenged fac, the bower hud drac.*" (...the farmer had a colt; the colt ran away, the farmer had dirt.) Children were usually considered the woman's responsibility, but some men took a more active interest in their families than others. "I remember Dad holding me at church. The brethren said, 'Children are to be with the women.' Dad said, 'No, they are my children too,' and gave me a hug." "I do not ever remember hearing anyone say, 'What can we do?' " said Grandmother Schierman. "We created our toys out of leaking pots, pails, broken pieces of china." "I was happiest when around my big brother, following him all over, doing everything he did like rolling dirty tires, playing marbles, riding all kinds of horses, playing horseshoe, playing farms. We would make miniature farms, have sticks for fences and gates and make buildings....We loved playing church when the weather was not too pleasant. We had a two-story home and we spent a lot of time on those steps. We would imitate the services and prayer meeting. We tried to preach like the pastor and other men like Dad. And we would sing like the people; we would get soft, then loud, stomp our feet. We sure had fun" (E. Spady, n.d.).

"The neighborhood kids congregated together on the empty lot beside Jenkins Groceteria. Some of the games we played were *Runjy Brun; Giant Step; Green Light, Red Light; Anti-I-Over; Fox and Goose; Pump, Pump, Pull Away*, and many more. What fun we had. Then there were the times I enjoyed walking across Langevin Bridge to Grandfather's blacksmith shop where I would watch him shoe horses...Sometimes as I was leaving Grandfather would give me a nickel. Now I could buy an 'all day sucker.' I would practically run all the way home, but on the way, I would drop into Levine's Store and buy my sucker. They were large, and really did last all day. The inside was hard candy coated with chocolate. The exciting thing about these suckers was that with the store keeper watching, you took the silver wrapper off and if you had a slip of paper in yours you got another one free" (H. Schierman, n.d.). *Yagoder* were among those who worked to provide organized recreation in the community. These facilities included the YMCA which used the old #4 Fire Hall, the Ninth Street skating rink, and the BRAA (Bridgeland Riverside Athletic Association) skating rink.

July was Stampede parade time. "We would get up early and get a good spot to see the parade. My sister and I would go ahead and try to get a place on the steps of the police station. Mom and the younger boys would join us later. The Friday evening fireworks during Stampede week was a big thing to plan for. Marion and I would drag a pillow and quilt and sit with our backs leaning against the Church on the hill overlooking the river. More than likely, we'd even pack a lunch; I'd make myself liverwurst sandwiches. After all, we were a whole block from home and we just might get hungry" (H. Schierman, n.d.). When World War II broke out *Yagoder* men were among those who joined the services. Grandmother Schierman remembered the train loads of young men pulling out of the city, young men hanging out the windows singing *You Are My Sunshine*, mothers and sweethearts running after the train crying.

Bridgeland-Riverside and the Calgary *Yagoder* Today

Calgary today is an energetic city of 717,000 people. It is still famous for its booster spirit, as evidenced in the successful hosting of the 1988 Winter Olympics. Looking down from the North Hill today over the area to which my people came more than eighty years ago, I can still pick out the houses where my grandparents and great-grandparents lived. The straight compact rows of uniformly pitched roofs confirm that many of the homes built by the Germans from Russia before World War I will stand. Peaceful looking streets and avenues are shaded by lovely spreading trees which were only young saplings in the old pictures that record Bridgeland-Riverside's early days.

To the east, Tom Campbell's Hill is a protected natural area; motor bikes can no longer use it for test runs. To the west, St. Vladimir's Ukranian Orthodox Church and numerous apartments climb the hill; it would be harder to go sledding there now. To the north, the Ukrainian Catholic Church, the Russian Greek Orthodox Church of All Saints, and Stanley Jones School share the skyline of the escarpment where cattle once grazed. Our Lady of Perpetual Help Roman Catholic church hugs the northwest corner of the hill. To the south, Memorial Drive parallels the Bow River and passes over the site of the old Riverside Hotel. St. George's Island is home to the Calgary Zoo and Dinosaur Park. The 1910 General Hospital building, where I was born, has given way to newer additions and its parking lot has resulted in the demolition of homes and businesses (such as Bridgeland Corner) along the south side of First Avenue—now a busy street. The wooden utility poles lining it are no longer used as "home free" for children's games of *Hide and Seek*.

The Immanuel Lutheran building now a non-denominational church, is recognized by the city as a site of historical significance. The structure started by the break-away St. Paul Lutheran group is the foundation of St. Angela Catholic School. The beautiful brick Moravian building with its panoramic view of the city is now the home of the St. Matthew (formerly known as Jehovah) Lutheran congregation. The old Jehovah building became the Moravian church in 1945 and Bethel Korean Presbyterian Church in 1977 when the Moravians moved to another part of Calgary. Nearby St. John Lutheran Church occupies its original location with a new sanctuary. *Die Halle* is now living quarters. Galleli's barn is gone. Bridgeland Baptist Fellowship occupies the spot where the Zion Lutherans and, later, the Seventh Day Adventists met. Across the street, Salem Evangelical Church has expanded facilities. The Seventh Day congregation plans to build at the base of Tom Campbell's Hill.

The old "Sandstone Lady," Langevin School, burnt down in 1966. The new school built on the site is today a dynamic community school serving a large number of children from Calgary's Chinatown along with others from such diverse backgrounds as Spanish, Italian, Saudi Arabian, Ethiopian, and North American. Bridgeland's diverse and changing ethnic mix is illustrated by the history of buildings such as St. Stephen Ukrainian Catholic Church, which in turn has become a Polish Catholic Church, a Croatian Church, and now a Buddhist Temple. Some pre-World War I structures erected for combined commercial and residential needs still stand along Fourth Street and First Avenue—Reliance Block, Armor Block, DeWaal Building (formerly Poffenroth Block), Cannibale Block. Some were designated as Heritage Buildings, other fell victim to "newer is better," a modern misplaced version of the famous Calgary spirit.

Most Germans from Russia became naturalized Canadians by the 1920's and 30's. They sent their sons to war and became voting citizens. A few anglicized their names. The older people are still fondly referred to by their nicknames. In many cases, families were able to reestablish contact with relatives in Russia in the 1960's and 1970's, but now there are fewer in either Russia or Canada who can communicate in the common language that once spanned the miles—German. Most of the *Yagoder* who originally settled in the area are gone. The area is today inhabited more by Italians than by Germans; the Jenkins Store where my aunts used to play *Anti-I-Over* is now an Italian Center. *Yagoder* descendants have scattered to various parts of the city, to other communities, or to the farm. Those who stayed in Calgary rose above their label "squareheads from Bridgeland-Riverside" and earned themselves respected places in whatever their chosen trade, profession or business. One, Donald Hartman, served Calgary for twenty years as an alderman and for a short while as mayor. Over the years the *Yagoder* intermarried with other Germans from Russia and with other Canadians. With each generation the geographical scattering and socio-economic diversity continues. Today there are some second-generation 100% *Yagoder*, but it will be harder to find third-generation.

What do my own children have that is distinctly *Yagoder?* They rarely hear the *Yagoder* sounds, so much gentler than the heavily articulated "church" German. They do not live or worship in visibly different cultural styles as their ancestors did. Probably the only tangible link they have with their past is food. We still eat *Siesblina* instead of crepes and *Holupya* instead of cabbage rolls. We top Grandma's homemade noodles with *Schmeltzed Kraeva* (diced bacon bits and homemade croutons) and enjoy *Gamellah Tae* (camomile tea) with *Kraut Kuchen* (baked buns filled with steamed cabbage

163

spiced with lots of pepper). We stuff our Christmas turkey with *Finsel* (meat and potato dressing) and celebrate Good Friday with *Schnitzel Suppe* (fruit soup) and *Krebble*. Beyond that, the links with the past are only the stories, and pictures, and the memories of our peoples' simplicity and innovation that encourage us not only to stick to the basics but also to value creativity. By recording our people's experiences, lifestyle, and faith we preserve a tiny but fascinating porthole through which future generations will be able to view a world so far removed from their own. We leave a record of unique ways of teaching and passing on those truths that never change in spite of differences between generations. The advice of my great grandmother to a gossiping neighbor decades ago, for example, is still true: *Macheh mullah Boozehm auf—oo reech—dah kompt genuck schtungen aus!* (Smell your own bosom!)

So while our people's stories remind us to honor, respect, and be genuinely thankful for our heritage, they also urge us to seek that which transcends time, space, and culture. The challenge facing each generation is the same: **"Stand at the crossroad and look, ask for the ancient paths, ask where the good way is and walk in it."**—Jeremiah 6:16

Return to Berry Meadow
by Richard Scheuerman (1991)

Yagodnaya Polyana, "Yagada" for short, with the emphasis on the first syllable. Since the earliest days of my youth in the rolling Palouse Hills of eastern Washington State this Russian name has stirred wondrous fascination. The word was mentioned frequently in countless stories I heard from elders recalling life in an Old Country village near the lower Volga River. At some point I learned that Yagodnaya Polyana's namesake was a wild strawberry that grew profusely in meadows among the hillocks flanking the village. The entire region west of the Volga near Saratov, another exotic name flavoring Sunday dinner conversation at Grandpa Scheuerman's, was termed the *Bergseite* or "mountain side" by the German farmers who had tilled those gentle slopes since Catherine the Great had peopled that part of her domain with dependable colonists. Grandpa called her "the *Kaiserin*" and knew that she had been a German by birth before marrying into the Romanov dynasty. Her campaign to secure recently acquired domains for the sprawling empire prompted the proclamation of her historic Manifesto of 1763. This invitation enticed thousands of European peasants ravaged by the Seven Years' War and famine to settle on the Volga in exchange for free land, exemption from military service, religious liberty, and other benefits guaranteed "for eternal time."

Some 27,000 impoverished peasants, mostly Germans, accepted the liberal terms of Catherine's promise over the next four years of the campaign and endured the year-long trek to the Volga where they established about one hundred colonies. According to Grandpa, one family bore our surname, and they joined in a transport destined for the uninhabited steppe where they ultimately halted in an obscure meadow named for the white blossomed berry native to the area. According to the old timers of our town, the names of virtually all of our neighbors had been represented in that legendary journey two hundred years earlier. Another movement of *usu Leut* (our people) was undertaken a century later when one of Catherine's successors, Alexander II, decided to revoke the colonists' original terms of settlement in 1871 in a move reflecting a rising tide of Slavic nationalism. Thousands of these Volga Germans responded by emigrating to America, including the grandparents of most everyone with whom I had grown up. They settled half-way around the world in an area not coincidentally also known for its fertile rolling hills.

Our place was located between the tiny rural communities of Endicott and St. John in the heart of the steeply tumbled terrain for which the Palouse is famous. A small farm even by 1950s standards covering just a half-section, its virgin bunchgrass slopes had been turned and combed first by Great-grandfather Henry B. himself. My only direct knowledge of the man was through family stories and the image on a cardboard backed photograph from Russia showing a heavily bearded fellow with benevolent eyes sitting next to his comely wife, Marikia, whose slight smile speaks of forbearing mien. His son Karl, my grandfather, regularly visited the farm long after his retirement but he especially enjoyed being there during August's sweltering hot "thrashing weather." We would sit in a grain truck perched for view as Dad harvested some of the finest crops around with a growling mechanical dinosaur of speckled red skin that slowly ate its way through rolling seas of wheat. The high yields produced year after year reflected an agrarian sense in both men that had been passed down over centuries from the viridian fields of Hesse and Volga steppelands to the Palouse Country.

Grandpa was a citadel of understanding. Fully aware of the struggles his family had endured in Russia and frontier Kansas, he did not allow the siren sounds of memory to romanticize our people's history. He encouraged me to ask questions, to listen and read for answers. While Psalms and Proverbs were his favorite readings, a few years of schooling here had introduced him to selections of Tennyson and Wordsworth which always remained with him. About that time a social studies teacher at school and local historian Anna Weitz introduced me to several books indicating that Grandpa's fanciful stories about queens and empires were rooted in important historical events. I learned that during Catherine the Great's reign control over the lower Volga shifted recurrently among Russia, Turkey, and various local tribes of Mongol origin. With Genghis Khan now entering the picture, more exotic images of past family adventures filled my young brain. That our ancestors had been part of imperial Russia's empire building plan to secure this vital region cast their role with new significance. As I matured the interest nurtured by childhood curiosity and encouraged by family and teachers turned more critical in an attempt to distinguish fact from fantasy.

I set about to visit every person in our neighboring towns of Endicott, St. John, and Colfax that I knew had been born in Russia. Often assisting in this peculiar pursuit were my parents, Don and Mary Scheuerman, and aunt and uncle, Evelyn and Ray Reich. Aunt Evelyn was an indefatigable family genealogist while her husband was known throughout the area as a great storyteller. As is often the case in rural America, among one's most special friends at any age are senior citizens who welcome opportunities to reminisce. The moment we would breathe the name "Yagada" a gleam would flash in most hosts' eyes and a smile would transform their smoothly weathered faces. Work at school or on the farm usually filled my weekdays but many Saturdays and most Sundays were spent in town to afford a great field for filling my curiosity and imagination. For years Saturday mornings usually began with mowing Grandpa Reich's lawn. He was not really our grandfather but bore the name out of both the respect his kindness engendered and the fact that he was a grandfather to several cousins about my age who lived just far enough away to avoid mowing duty. Reflecting pride in place and possessions, every edge of his lawn had to be neatly trimmed and all caked grass thoroughly removed from beneath the mower with a paint scraper after each cutting. Sometimes his neighbors and lifelong friends August Markel and Conrad Schmick would join us when the work was nearly ended. A glass of hand pressed lemonade usually awaited us inside Grandpa Reich's small kitchen where the interrogation would begin. I never could tell whether the other two were more interested in refreshment than my questions but it was clear that they enjoyed both. I knew by observation in his home that Conrad's preferred drink was a cruel concoction of fortified port and Jack Daniels, the very smell of which often sent guests into another room. Having come to America as young adults between 1902 and 1907, all three men could tell me about life in the days when work was measured in literal terms of horsepower and freedom by distance from the tsar.

Before lunch, time usually remained to visit others in the neighborhood for the same work and rewards. My cousin Clifford and I worked up enough gumption one day to visit the oldest man in town, Phillip Ochs. Though also a Russian German and thought to be a relative through some vague connection, so many unusual stories had surrounded his life from tales of Indian fighting to horse thieving that we had some cause to fear his presence. Overcome by boyish curiosity, we made our way to his backyard where he regularly sunned in the afternoons. Half expecting a concealed six-gun to shoo youthful meddlers away, we instead were disarmed quickly by his cordial welcome. He spoke beneath an enormous gray felt hat that seemed a permanent fixture regardless of the weather and he also evidenced scarcely the hint of an accent detectable in most others we knew of his generation. Through Phillip we entered the world of a Wild West experience little known to even most of his contemporaries. The Volga German immigrant farmers that began arriving in large numbers in America around the turn of the century tended to be a reserved lot. Phillip, however, had joined the original vanguard that brought our people by wagon to Washington Territory in 1882 before the later influx. We found that Indian fights and rustling genuinely had been part of his pioneering experience. But with forthrightness he also confessed to us his own responsibility for being caught up in some of the regrettable episodes. Far better that we boys stick to mowing lawns and minding our parents. Somehow his saddled yarns did little to support that advice in our minds. But those special moments that summer day grew in meaning to me as Phillip passed away soon afterward. The abruptly closed entry to his fellowship and reminiscences caused me to deeply grieve the passing of our brief friend.

Death is no stranger in any rural immigrant community where elderly residents value self-reliance. Many steadfastly withstand the best and well intended efforts of their adult offspring, often living elsewhere, to relocate or enter retirement homes. For this reason, the *Whitman County Gazette* still regularly prints reminders on Thursdays through its obituary column that another "native of Yagada, Russia passed away at the home" somewhere in the vicinity. But even the circumstances of their passing often contributed to a fuller appreciation of their lives. Family and friends from distant places assembled in great numbers for their funeral services in local Lutheran, Congregational, and Adventist churches. I missed considerable schooltime in my youth because I sang at these funerals. In the few years there that witnessed my transition from boyish soprano to settled baritone, these occasions, deemed a morbid duty by my friends, afforded me an opportunity to meet an ever widening circle of first-generation Yagaders. After the eulogy and music we would silently adjourn to Mountain View Cemetery for a brief service where the deceased's body was committed to the secure company of others facing eastward in the direction of their native land and of their Lord's promised coming. The living would then gather at the church parish house where stories of the Old Country and a potluck feast were traded for science class and school hot lunch. For at least another hour I would listen to spirited arguments on disputed family relationships, hilarious anecdotes on nickname origins, and recounted sagas of trans-Atlantic crossings. All the while everyone enjoyed the finest ham casseroles with breaded egg noodles, potato sausages, and dulcified fruit kuchens.

Sunday mornings usually offered renewed opportunities to learn about our people's heritage but from the women's perspective. When I was growing up our church conducted separate services in German and English. The former were held for the benefit of the many immigrants living in our area who retained German as their language of worship. On occasion another cousin, Ann Schierman, and I would sing a familiar German hymn like *"Gott is die Liebe"* or *"So Nimm Denn Meine Haende"* which always engendered appreciation from the parishioners despite our understanding of German that was based entirely on phonetics and an occasional use of the word *nichts*. A decade before, these sturdy souls had worked side by side with their grown children to lay the foundation and raise the immense arches that with prayer and sacrifice supported a church of Old World design renowned for its beauty throughout the synod. The peculiar color scheme of turquoise, lavender, and Prussian blue embellished with lustrous gold enfolded pews and furnishings of lacquered birch and alder. As was the custom in Russia, the men and women sat on opposite sides. Having already attended German Church on such days I would also take advantage of these times to garner my parents' permission to skip the main service and visit my great aunts who lived together in a large white clapboard house adjacent to the church. My delight was upon entering their kitchen through the back porch since Aunt Lizzie Repp invariably was making doughnuts every time I arrived. The room would be heavy with the smell of sweet dough and I loved listening to the exploding crackles each time she dropped the soft forms into the hot golden pool. I never really knew if her baking of these treats was merely a weekly event on Sundays at 11:00 a.m. or a special treat for an appreciative nephew.

Aunt Lizzie's countenance was kindness and this spirit characterized her every graceful move, gentle voice, and easy smile. Equally loving but imbued with a healthy dose of wit and earthy wisdom was Aunt Mae Geier. Both sisters had been born in Yagada and had emigrated with my great-grandparents to America in 1888. Lizzie was among the eldest of the children and both could recount endless details of pioneer life. Their first years in this country were spent in Rush County, Kansas, where many of our people settled in the Great Bend, Otis, and Bison areas. Aunt Lizzie had a fondness for remembering the beauty of her native land and told of family outings to the wooded glens around their village in search of wild strawberries and succulent mushrooms. Aunt Mae was a living family index preserving dates and names of special significance in her lifetime. Whether I asked when they landed in New York (April 27, 1888), at the Endicott railroad siding (March 7, 1891), or at points between, she could instantly respond with the month and day and subsequent research confirmed her accounts. Less amenable to substantiation were her insights, often rendered in hushed tones, regarding village hexers who had not left their powers in the Old Country. It was an evil business still practiced in these parts and she knew all the details including the sinister consequences. At those moments Aunt Lizzie might politely shrug and change the subject or ask me to bring some more doughnuts from the kitchen.

Aunt Lizzie was the only one among the surviving children of my great-grandparents who could definitively respond to questions about our ancestral lineage. One morning our visit touched on this subject as she had been carefully recreating the village of her youth in my mind. She had lived in a single-storied frame structure just north of the imposing white Lutheran *Kirche*. I wanted to know the full name of her Grandfather Scheuerman. As was the custom in my own time, her family usually had joined her grandparents for Sunday dinner. Sitting in her faded maroon overstuffed chair she reached back to savor a distilled reminiscence of those moments at the length of nearly a century. "His name was Pete," Aunt Lizzie said after a long pause and while the sunshine danced through her open laced curtains she hummed for me one of the children's songs he had taught her from the tempo of his knee. Every effort to stretch memories back further proved futile though she and Aunt Mae were well versed in the legends of our people's original trek to the Volga in 1766. "The Queen Catherine herself came down to visit our folks when they landed in Russia; she was a German by birth and wanted to hear her native tongue," Aunt Mae volunteered. I have not found any official references to the incident but it is a story I later heard recounted in other oral histories and is entirely plausible.

Most Sunday afternoons found our family gathering at the home of Grandpa Scheuerman who was the patriarch of a vast clan connected by his six children and his five sisters, most of whom also had large families. Only his elder brother, Yost, did not have children of his own but he often joined the weekly gatherings. Dinner conversation over the inevitable meal of roast beef with boiled potatoes, carrots, and parsnips usually was devoted to the newest infant grandchild (there always seemed to be one), prospects for the wheat crop, or government interference in farming. When the women cleared the table and the men adjourned to the living room for televised sports or a few hands of the favored local card game, pitch, Uncle Yost and the others of his generation were fair game for adolescent inquiry. In later years when he and others like him from the community relocated to rest homes in the neighboring towns of Colfax and Ritzville, I would go periodically after Sunday dinner with Grandpa to visit these special ones. Again we would share in song and fellowship but never left without a few questions about the life in Yagada. Uncle Yost died before I began my historical research in earnest but his name in itself offered a valuable clue in the quest to trace our ancestry across two transcontinental migrations while confronting the twin challenges of obscure origins in Germany and inaccessible records in Russia.

Uncle Yost's name was unique in our community. As was the custom in virtually all Volga German families, individuals were often known by names other than those given to them at birth. Families with eight or more children were not uncommon in Russia and since relatively few new people came to the villages, commonly used first names became widespread. Yagada likely had dozens of Mary Repps, Adam Morasches, and other people sharing the same name. To solve this confusing problem, the Germans resorted to an elaborate system of nicknames that assisted them in distinguishing one another in conversation. Certain names might be given to persons of peculiar frame— *Knooga* (Boney), *de dick* (the Fat) or *Kuoybah* (Cow Leg). Others were classed by distinctive characteristics, many not adulatory, such as *Rahmbadya* (Cream Chin) and *Knebelya* (Little Club); some by colors, *da bleu* Wilhelm (The Blue), *Schwartza Pete* (Dark Pete), *Rud Phillip* (Red Phillip); and still other agnomens like *Haarnase* (Hairy Nose), though quite descriptive, must have proved somewhat embarrassing. Some individuals were known by some commodity they could raise, or could not raise, as was the case with *Huhnkil Hannas* Gerlitz (Chicken John), *Arbuza* Schmick (Watermelon), and *Moslanga* Reich (Sunflower). Still others were associated with animals: *Krommageeglel* Kromm (Crooked Rooster), *Haas* Lautenschlager (Rabbit); or clothing: *Galotja* Pfaffenroth (Small Coat) and *Rudarmel* (Red Sleeve). Occupations were often indicative of one's nickname as *Badelya* Scheuerman (Small Bottle) ran a liquor store and *Kringelsbacker* Pfaffenroth was a village baker.

This system of nicknames also involved distinctive designations for certain extended families when the surname was shared by all. Accordingly, a person with the last name Schmick might belong to the *Linkeya* (Left) clan of Schmicks or to the *Lutwisch* (Ludwig) Schmicks in addition to having his or her personal nickname. Many other family clans were identified in a similar manner: the *Homba* Morasches, *Shuska* Bafuses, and *Kutcher* Klewenoes. We belonged to the *Yusta* Scheuermans but others in the community belonged to the *Watchka* and *Kosack* branches. We were not supposed to get along well with the *Watchkas* though no one seemed to remember why in my time. The peculiar name of our clan intrigued me. *"Yusta"* was too close to "Yost" in my mind to be mere coincidence but whether the word was rooted in a nickname, given name, or some forgotten place seemed beyond knowing. We again faced the dead end of memories limitations and unavailable documentation preventing the identification of any ancestor by whose name our family was still known.

A not uncommon experience when conducting oral histories among Yagaders was vigorous disagreement among participants regarding the true name of an acquaintance all had known well in Russia. Frequently nobody outside the immediate family really knew for sure. Chuckles invariably erupted when discussing another aspect of clannishness reflective of the village's isolation. Cutting entirely across blood relationship was identity based on the two halves of the village. Those living south of the church were called the *Kalmooka* while all to the north were *Totten*, names apparently given originally for pejorative purposes stemming from the marauding Kalmyk and Tatar tribes that once inhabited the area. A late evening foray into the other's sector was often sufficient cause for attack by youthful ruffians that sometimes turned bloody. The situation could prove particularly troublesome for young men during courtship when venturing across town meant running the gauntlet in a test of devotion.

A critical piece of family genealogy eventually came from an unexpected source. In the early 1970s a handful of individuals with an interest in preserving our ethnic heritage had met in Greeley, Colorado to form the American Historical Society of Germans from Russia. One of the prime movers in this historic effort was remarkable Emma S. Haynes who was known internationally for her research on the *Russlanddeutschen.* Her father had pastored a church in Odessa, Washington when she was a young girl so we both shared a Northwest connection and soon became acquainted through AHSGR's first president, David Miller. I learned that she had worked with Volga Relief Society in the 1920s which grew from an organization in the Pacific Northwest to a national movement among Russian Germans to provide food and clothing to the famine ravaged population on the Volga. Emma Haynes was the last person from North America known to have visited the Volga German villages before the region was closed to Westerners in 1928. But she had not visited Yagodnaya Polyana. Emma was fluent in German and had served as one of Hermann Goering's translators at the Nuremburg War Crimes trials. She remained in Germany after the war and lived with her husband in Oberusel near Frankfurt a.M. where she continued her indefatigable research in Russian

Maria Scheuerman and Her Table

German history. Several years after we first became acquainted through the mail she wrote to inform me of an unusual discovery. While poring through aged documents in the Buedingen Castle library she chanced upon a thick yellowed register titled *Einwanderliste von Yagodnaya Polyana aus Hessen*. Penned in the flowing hand of Yagada schoolmaster Georg Kromm, the document represented the first complete listing known to exist of every individual who had participated in the historic 1766-1767 trek from Buedingen to Yagodnaya Polyana.

My first reaction upon inspection of a copy was that the names on it resembled my hometown's telephone directory. From Appel to Weitz the names of these eighty families were well known to everyone in western Whitman County. Clearly, they did not just come together a century earlier through random resettlement on the Volga steppe. They had come as a group over two centuries earlier and, since the dutiful Kromm was careful to note German villages of origin and vital statistics, we realized that many of our families had lived next to each other in tiny Hessian *dorfs* since time immemorial. I quickly paged through the alphabetical entries, compiled by Kromm in 1912, to see if any Scheuermans were included. My eyes fell upon Hartmann and Elisabeth Scheuermann who were natives of Ober Lais in the Vogelsberg district near Buedingen. They were both in their forties and brought seven children on the epic journey eastward at the same time our nation was undergoing the birthpangs of independence. Four of the children bore the given name "Johann" but the second eldest's middle name was Jost. Quickly calculating that he must have been born about 1749, I realized that while this information was invaluable to the reconstruction of our family lineage, a remaining "missing link" in our Yusta clan still eluded us since Johann Jost's son would have been too old even in the early years of the nineteenth century to be Aunt Lizzie's Grandfather Peter. A phantom ancestor was yet to be found in order to bridge the gap but the prospects for such a discovery grew dimmer with each passing year and no more break-throughs.

Continued weekend visits with other community elders provided insights into other aspects of daily life in Yagada. Mrs. C. P. Morasch explained to me the process of making cloth from the fibrous stalks of flax and hemp and Martin Lust would sing the Bible verses he was taught in school as a child. Elizabeth Fox, known throughout the community for her hilarity, recalled the weekly gossip sessions at the great spring that rushed from the hillside behind the church to feed the brook bordering the east side of the village. Women gathered there daily to wash clothes and draw fresh water. Adam Lust and Adam Kromm shared details about the church holiday traditions. The rigors of life from a student's perspective in Schulmeister Kromm's classes at the German school were well known to John Holstein as well as the saga of his family's peregrinations across Europe and South America before they came to the States in 1911.

These stories and countless other accounts of life in a Volga colony during the previous century painted a vivid picture of a seemingly idyllic existence. Yet the fact remained that these souls and thousands like them had chosen to leave. Over time I sought to explore the complexities of life in both worlds and the exigencies that led many to abandon what was memorialized as precious, stable, and beautiful. Patterns of conflict became evident as inquiry turned to factors initiating a decision to immigrate. The reasons provided did not support a simple explanation. Some of the first to leave Yagada shared distinctive religious convictions associated with others who were among the first to begin emigrating from the Volga colonies in the 1870s. These had participated in the Brotherhood movement which was a phenomenon among the laity to renew spirituality and piety within the established Lutheran Church. Not coincidentally, the first Yagaders to Endicott were members of the Brotherhood and formed the Congregational Church though a Lutheran parish was established soon afterward. As a high schooler, I joined a circle of like-minded friends my age for a weekly interdenominational Bible study in the spacious home of Conrad and Christina Moore whose grandson, Jim, was one of my classmates and the leader of our fellowship. Heirs to the Russian Brotherhood tradition and old enough to be our grandparents, Mr. and Mrs. Moore not only tolerated our teenage antics and never ending choruses of "Kumbaya," but effused a youthful enthusiasm themselves that combined with a spiritual vibrancy to give visible expression of their faith. Elders like the Moores taught by the example of their life that pietism does not necessarily seek withdrawal from the world, but can affirm faith through a life of service in joy to others.

For other immigrants the primary motivation to leave was economic. As with other Volga colonies, the population of Yagodnaya Polyana had mush-roomed during the middle decades of the nineteenth century. The village that had known only 2,922 inhabitants in 1834 swelled to 9,061 in 1912. (Descendants of the original colonists had also established the daughter colonies of Schoental and New Yagodnaya in the 1850s on the Jeruslan River east of the Volga.) Since distribution of land among the males was based on periodic census revisions, the increasing population forced a concomitant decline in allotted acreage from over twenty at the beginning of the century to less than four in the Yagada area by 1900. Recurrent crop failures in 1884, 1889, 1892, and 1897 provided the impetus for many to leave during these years.

Adam P. Morasch recalled a particularly wet fall in 1908 when as a young man he was growing increasingly pessimistic over prospects for a stable future. Political tensions were in the air after the 1905 Revolution and leftist sentiment was openly expressed on the streets of the regional capital, Saratov. When the futility of one more menacing storm front heavy with rain threatened the family's unharvested rye, Adam cast aside his scythe and decided to join his friends in America, where he arrived with two quarters in his pocket. Years of hard labor in the new land coupled with fiscal conservation enabled him to

174

acquire over 1200 acres of prime farmland in the Palouse by middle age. He married Katherine Schmick, an acquaintance from his childhood in Russia, and the two reared a large family. One of their grandchildren, Lois Jean, became my wife and I shall never forget my first trip into her grandparent's basement following Adam P.'s passing. Reflecting an Old World frugality born of necessity, the fruit room downstairs was well stocked with canned peaches and Blue Lake beans, brown paper sacks that had held decades of groceries lay neatly arranged under a long table, countless yards of used white string hung suspended from nails, every tool had its place, and rows of old German books brought from Russia lined a corner bookshelf. Most were hymnals and religious works covered in cracked leather bindings, but several copies in a buff-colored binding looked new. I pulled out one of the clothbound books to find an illustrated guide to the alphabet in archaic German script. Grandma Morasch informed us that he had purchased a copy for each of his six children with instructions for them to learn the basics of *usu Leut's* mother tongue.

The relationship of Lois's grandparents to each other taught us much about marital values affirmed by the Yagaders. Grandpa Scheuerman's wife had died when I was only ten and I had not known them well as a couple. But I came to know Adam and Katherine Morasch as a couple in a most enduring sense. The only time I remember not seeing them together was in German church when the adults kept to their Russian custom of all men sitting on the right side with the women on the left. Otherwise, they seemed inseparable. From family outings to the Snake River to hoeing cabbage rows in the garden, they lived as one and in earlier years Katherine had even spent time in the fields alongside her husband. To be sure, a traditional division of labor existed for the major tasks of the Volga German's year in Russia or America. But whether butchering hogs or planting potatoes, completion of the task would not have been possible in the prescribed manner without the husband and wife full partners in the activity. An abiding affection and transcendent mutual respect also pervaded their relationship. Brashly reminded in jest by her husband of some humorous incident they had both experienced half a world away in Russia, Katherine would smile coyly and nod quietly until offering an alternate interpretation of disputed events. One sensed in their presence that while she would never question his authority, family decisions were in large part based on her counsel. And at this date when Grandma Morasch approaches her 102nd birthday, Grandpa ever remains "Mr. Morasch" to those outside the family. Reference to one's spouse by first name among members of their generation was generally confined to the privacy of the home where manner of both conduct and conversation promoted intimacy. For Mr. and Mrs. Morasch this relationship endured for over sixty-five years.

As others in the community learned of my interest in our people's heritage they periodically called with information of discoveries they thought might be helpful in my research. In this way Ramon Huntley shared copies of century old letters from Russia that his family had safeguarded for generations and

Clara Litzenberger opened the contents of an old steamer trunk containing treasured memorabilia from a mutual relative, Adam Schmick. Among the most unique items was a scarlet Russian peasant shirt embroidered in yellow and festooned with white porcelain buttons. Clara and I spent countless hours around her kitchen table speculating on the fate of those who remained in Yagodnaya after the First World War and the Russian Revolution. Although she was fifty years my senior, Clara never lost a youthful curiosity and rejoiced every time we uncovered some new fragment of our people's story. An avid reader, she taught me to realize the relationships between our history and great world events as diverse as Catherine's ascension to the throne in 1762 and Lincoln's Homestead Act of 1862.

Mollie Bafus phoned one day to report that she had found a photograph of Yagodnaya Polyana while going through some of her late husband John's things. The glossy print measured eight by ten and was dated 1914. A sweeping panorama of the village clearly showed the church and belfry, German and Russian schools, the market center, nearby spring, and other prominent landmarks. Family residences were clustered in blocks with decoratively carved beams framing massive wooden gates opening to the farmyards adjacent to the houses. To enter these gates into the world of the Volga German *Hof* was to experience the rustic sights, pungent barnyard smells, and children's chatter known daily to village residents. I sought to know this Old World universe of corporeal solidity where most Volga Germans spent the majority of their lives. Such knowledge, however, would only be held by someone who had been old enough to fully participate in the work year before leaving. Since the borders were closed following the outbreak of World War I in 1914, I inquired after German services one Sunday who had been both a farmer and among the last to leave Yagada. Someone suggested I direct my questions to venerable Conrad Blumenschein who drove every week the sixteen miles between his home in St. John to Endicott to attend services.

I had long admired Mr. Blumenschein because his presence exuded a distinctive spirit of inner resilience. He was a handsome man, stout, and the kind of person whose visage you sensed would never change regardless of personal circumstances. His powerful handshake was commentary to his life but like so many other elders he also knew that manly strength was ultimately based on faith in God. I made some comment after that church service about the unusually dry weather we had been experiencing recently. Yes, he recalled, they had known such times on the Volga when the dreaded *Hoehenrauch* wind from the south threatened to parch the crops. He had seen a Russian peasant prostrate himself in a withering field shouting pleas for the Lord's help. "I am not sure it brought our deliverance," he observed, "but such prayers are always heard." Mr. Blumenschein was a profoundly courteous man whose manner of speech reminded me more of a statesman than a Palouse farmer and the afternoons I spent with him around his kitchen table remain among my most pleasant memories. On several occasions that summer I was given the special opportunity to question him and a man of equal stature, his lifelong friend Conrad "C. G." Schmick, about the customary farmstead layout in Yagada and the annual cycle of field operations. They plotted designs in great detail with remarkable similarity. Each family's *Hof* resembled a deep rectangle measuring roughly 120 by 200 feet and divided nearly equally into a streetside *Fehderhof* (outer yard) and *Hinnerhof* (inner or back yard). The *Fehderhof* contained the family home, typically a three-room structure with a thatched or tin roof, and an open area dividing it from the wagon shed, horse and cattle barn, sheepfold, hogsty and chickencoop. A small fruit orchard, the ever present berry bushes, granary, and large vegetable garden comprised the *Hinnerhof* which was fenced to protect it from any wandering livestock.

Through oral histories about village life and agriculture in the Old Country with Yagaders like Conrad Blumenschein and C. G. Schmick, immigration and settlement patterns also emerged from their recurrent references to places like Longmont, Colorado; St. Maries, Idaho; and Calgary, Alberta. The demographic data that George Kromm had appended to his emigrant register of 1766-1767 indicated that 1,620 souls had left Yagodnaya Polyana by 1912 for North America. Allowing generous latitude for the few families that were diverted to Argentina due to entry restrictions, that the enclaves of Yagader settlement in the greater Northwest could account for that large number seemed unlikely. Visits to these other areas in the 1970s confirmed that Kromm's estimate was either too liberal or that significant numbers of our people resided elsewhere in North America. AHSGR began to hold annual conventions in the early 1970s and these gatherings soon grew into veritable national Russian German reunions featuring guest speakers from around the world and presentations on our people's folklore and history in an atmosphere of spirited *Gemuetlichkeit*. At the first such meeting I attended in Boulder, Colorado in 1972 I finally met Emma Haynes, David Miller, and others instrumental in the organization's founding including famed H. J. Amen who was nearing his hundredth birthday. Mr. Amen was one of the principal figures studied by author James Michener for his composite sketch of the hardworking Volga German immigrant Hans "Potato" Brumbaugh in his sweeping historical novel *Centennial*. I also came to learn of the excellent research conducted by Barry Lust, Don Vogt, Colleen Rose, Robert Lust, Harland Eastwood, and others who had contributed significantly to our understanding of Volga German settlement in the Pacific Northwest.

The conventions provided a forum to share perspectives and information as well as become acquainted with others in the United States and Canada who claimed Yagodnaya Polyana as their ancestral village. In this way we came to identify large enclaves of *usu Leut* in Alberta, the Midwest, and the East. We became fast friends with sisters Susan and Ann Yungman of the Little York-Pine Island Yagada community of southeastern New York State. We speculated from family legend that Great Grandmother Litzenberger, a victim of the difficult trans-Atlantic crossing, lay buried in an unmarked grave in the Pine

Island area. We had not been aware that a group of our people had established themselves in vegetable farming in that scenic part of the Empire State. Similarly, we came to appreciate the most generous hospitality of the Rudy Schmicks, Theodore Schmicks, and other residents of Preston, Maryland where many of our people built prosperous farms on the red earth of the Chesapeake Peninsula. Other Yagaders like my Great Grandfather Henry B. Scheuerman made it as far as eastern Kansas after their initial arrival where they started businesses or began farming. Unlike Henry B., most prospered there and many like his brother Peter remained to form Yagader communities on the prairies. My cousin Bill Scheirman is Peter's grandson and for at least fifteen years I have received from "W.L.S." not less than one mailing, usually heavy enough to require more than a single stamp, every six weeks apprising me of family news as he has tirelessly ferreted out relatives on four continents. He has selflessly shared his discoveries with all who are interested in this special heritage as has our cousin-colleague Mrs. Leon Scheuerman of Deerfield, Kansas who first established the connection between our family in Russia and the ancestral lineage in Germany. In Canada the Alfred Poffenroths, Elsie Untershulz, and Roy Kaiser of Calgary; the John Scheiermans, Sandra Stelter and the Albert Stugarts have added immeasurably to our knowledge of the Volga German experience in Alberta and British Columbia.

Few events at the many outstanding AHSGR conventions have been more memorable than my introduction to Catherine "Kedda" Luft in a San Francisco hotel lobby in 1977. With flaxen white hair and slight stature, she could have passed for Aunt Lizzie's twin sister except that she possessed Aunt Mae's sense of humor and a memory for detail I have never known in another human being. Devoted to faith and family, this gentle spirit had traveled from her home in Sheboygan, Wisconsin in the company of her equally remarkable daughters Esther and Miriam who visibly tired in their attempts to keep up with the schedule of diminutive "Kedda." We spent hours going over plats of city blocks in Yagodnaya with Kedda identifying the locations of dozens of families as she squinted to point out their locations on a copy of Mollie's treasured photograph. She knew tales of wolf attacks, folksongs which she sang beautifully, folk medicine cures, and clarified many enigmatic nickname origins. (Her own was traced to the sound of her first name when stuttered by a nervous young suitor at their front gate in Yagada.) She could quote the most appropriate Scripture verse to illustrate a pithy point but not until later did I learn that she had committed to memory every Psalm and most of the Gospels. Kedda was delighted to know that I had married Katherine Morasch's granddaughter as she and Grandma Morasch had been girlhood friends in Yagada.

Captivating interviews with special people like Catherine Luft, Conrad Blumenschein, Elizabeth Repp, C. G. Schmick, and Alec Reich seemed to pose as many new questions about our people's plight as were answered. Almost all the first generation Yagaders had left parents, brothers, or sisters behind in Russia. As Kromm's statistics for 1912 indicated, less than one in five residents of the village had elected to emigrate. Most lost the opportunity to leave with the outbreak of the First World War in 1914 and the subsequent border closures. Russia's failure in the war with Germany invited widespread hostility directed against the German farmers on the Volga who never attained majority status in comparison to the number of Slavic peoples living in neighboring villages throughout the region. The Bolshevik Revolution of 1917 was not generally supported by the enterprising Volga Germans but a division in public sentiment was evident even in villages like Yagodnaya Polyana. That communism ultimately prevailed among the Volga Germans was not an indication of broad popular support but of militant support channeled by Bolshevik revolutionaries to rural malcontents in exchange for pledges of future position. These circumstances led to the brutal Russian Civil War in 1918-1921, the disastrous and contrived famines of 1921-23, the ruthless collectivization of agriculture and Stalin's war on religion in the 1930s, the Second World War, and exile to Siberia in 1941.

The shock of any one of these tragedies that brought recurrent pillaging and murder would render incalculable personal loss and social dislocation in a village so encysted in Old World stability as Yagodnaya Polyana. That these scourges were visited with such rapidity and savagery led to quixotic expressions when I asked the frequent question to community elders, "What ever became of our families that remained in Russia?" The initial response was often silence and raised eyebrows followed by a shaking of the head. Only fleeting references in the few letters that made it out of the village during the inter-war period gave any hint of what actually happened. Extracts included such lines as "Please take pity on us dear Uncles and send us food or we shall not be long on this earth" (1928), "We are now writing to you from Siberia" (1929), "Sometimes the rains flow down our streets, other times the streams run red" (1930), "Where our parents are now is known only to God" (1933), and "Do not ask anymore about Heinrich's whereabouts, he is to remain in the house without windows [prison?]" (1935). One could only speculate about the horrors associated with each obscure reference to changes in the circumstances of these oppressed people. Most elders remembered that when these letters arrived, often months after being postmarked, families would gather together on Sunday afternoons to share the news and cry that so little assistance which they offered was getting through. They also recalled that what little correspondence was exchanged ceased entirely in 1939 when war broke out again in Europe. The long foreboding silence would last nearly three decades. An overwhelming sense of helplessness cast a pallor on their spirits that fostered an intense antipathy towards any kind of authoritarian rule.

In 1968 a strange letter arrived at the Endicott post office. Postmaster Taft Hergert, whose parents were Yagada born, studied the peculiar square envelope bearing blue Russian stamps and addressed crudely to a "John Jungmann, Whidman County, Washington, America." Judging from the various cancellations on the envelope it had made an extended journey in vain to the nation's capitol and other points searching for the correct Washington and Mr. Jungmann. Taft directed the letter to Endicott's John Youngman, an immigrant of 1913, quick-witted and salty in temperament, who did his best to make sense out of the letter's contents. An Ernst Jungmann living in the village of Peschanoye near Pavlodar in the Soviet republic of Kazakhstan was venturing to find his relatives in America. Since the author recognized there would be many John Jungmanns among Yagaders, he astutely identified the individual by a nickname that could be borne only by a single person with that surname: "Harness John." Our Mr. Youngman had known a distant kinsman by that name who had lived briefly in Endicott before the war but he relocated subsequently, perhaps to Spokane. John's daughter, Paula Morasch, shared this information with me in the hope I might have encountered such a family in my research. Though I had not, a quick search through the Spokane telephone directory revealed several Jungman family listings and on the second or third try an Emily Jungman responded to our story with intense interest. Not only had Harness John been a member of her family, but her namesake was a lost aunt who had been exiled east of the Urals with the entire German population from Yagada in 1941. Through later correspondence she learned that this aunt was still living near Pavlodar and was overjoyed at the thought that the family was now permitted to establish contact.

Return to the Volga for the Siberian German exiles, however, was out of the question. Legislation annulling their official designation by Stalin as "spies and diversionists" was enacted by the Supreme Soviet in 1955. However, we learned later that this statute was never publicly announced and it specifically denied Soviet Germans the right to resettle in the former Volga villages. I also wrote to Ernst Jungmann several times in order to ascertain what had become of our other Yagada families. Had they randomly been spread across the endless reaches of the Siberian taiga or were they still clustered together there in Kazakhstan which conjured up images of desert sands and Mongol tribes? Not unsurprisingly in that period which was witnessing Breshnev's consolidation of power, the political climate had returned to conservatism and suspicion after the brief hiatus under Krushchev. Ernst's answers were vague and he seemed unwilling to respond directly to my queries regarding the fate of specific families about whom we had long wondered. After several pleasant exchanges I concluded that communication in writing would never reveal the answers to these questions. Apparently only a personal meeting could end the years of futile speculation. Unfortunately, both Pavlodar and Saratov were closed cities to Westerners.

An opportunity for Lois and me to travel throughout Europe and the USSR came in the summer of 1976 when graduate studies at Pacific Lutheran University enabled me to conduct research on Volga German religious history at Keston College's Institute for the Study of Religion and Communism near London. This work was supported by the Lutheran World Federation whose president, Dr. Carl Mau, was then initiating an historic effort to reestablish ties with the remnant Lutheran Church in Russia. Headquartered in Geneva, Switzerland, LWF was involved in delicate negotiations with the German and Soviet governments on this sensitive matter. The eventual restoration of the Church to legal status in the USSR was due in large part to the skillful diplomacy and spiritual vision of Dr. Mau. Coincidentally, he had also spent his youth in tiny Endicott, Washington where his father had pastored the local Trinity Lutheran parish in the 1930s.

That summer of 1976 Lois and I ventured across the English Channel on a brief excursion to Germany in search of the legendary Vogelsberg district in Hesse. Our forebearers had lived in the placid villages of that hilly region for countless centuries before descending on the *Sammelplatz* of Buedingen to begin their migration to Russia in the summer of 1766. I especially wanted to find Ober Lais, the tiny hamlet that Kromm's register had indicated was our family's ancestral village. An exhaustive search through the maps of the Keston's library produced a contemporary rendering in detail of Hesse which had confirmed the town's existence. Days later Lois and I were driving past historic Buedingen Castle and through neighboring Schotten where Henny Hysky, curator of the Vogelsberger Heimat Museum, kindly assisted us in finding more information about Yagodnaya Polyana that Georg Kromm had the foresight to send to the local press in the early 1900s. She also directed us to Ober Lais which we found to be a sleepy village of not more than a few hundred inhabitants. I strolled into the only store in sight and asked in halting German where the nearest Scheuerman lived. The proprietor dispatched a lad of about ten to lead us down a cobblestone street one block to the residence of an elderly gentleman whose bushy eyebrows and squinting smile reminded me of my grandfather. He introduced himself as Johann Scheuermann and welcomed us inside a spotless home connected in "L" fashion to the livestock barn in typical Old World fashion.

Surely we were related in some way and the indeterminable distance mattered little to our gracious host who related family lore that stretched back to Vogelsberger obscurity as dim as his unlit kitchen. Our name, for example, had nothing to do with the conventional thinking that the German word *Scheuer* had something to do with a stream or brook. We were originally "Schauermann" which denoted in the distinctive local dialect a shearer, likely of sheep that were herded in these parts ages ago. So my father had been right after all when he repeatedly reminded me as a boy those cold winter mornings to tend the lambs because sheep raising was "in our blood." We were also shown the old cemetery in adjacent Unter Lais where generations of family members have been buried and also saw the sagging remnant of the village's original eighteenth century Evangelical Lutheran Church. Likely Hartmann and Elizabeth had taken their last communion before departing for Russia at this very place. Although the story of the famed trek eastward was known to area residents, nobody we met there knew anything about their fate. We shared what we knew at that time and received precious gifts from our new friends. Among our most prized were a confirmation certificate depicting the old church and a commemorative booklet on regional history that would provide fascinating insights into our people's German origins.

One month later we joined a tour group organized by Peter and Anita Deyneka that was traveling to Soviet Central Asia that August and with Novosibirsk on our schedule we made arrangements to meet Ernst Jungmann at that city's airport. To our bitter disappointment, however, soon after arriving in Moscow we were informed that "special circumstances" required a change in our itinerary and that Bukhara, an ancient city in the desolate Kuzyl Kum desert, would be substituted for Novosibirsk. When pressed for a fuller explanation, our Intourist guide answered that a Soviet trade exhibition was being held in the city that month and all hotel space for foreigners was simply unavailable. A week later when viewing from an aerial tram the beautiful city of Alma Ata against the backdrop of the imposing Tien Shan mountains of China, I found myself in the company of a Soviet tourist from Novosibirsk. I inquired about the trade show but he reacted in surprise. He was a city official and had just been there but no such event was underway in Novosibirsk. I have always felt that in some measure my correspondence with our Pavlodar kinsmen was responsible for this frustrating change in plans.

What could have happened that caused a government to go to such lengths to conceal events that had transpired over a generation earlier? Moreover, the deportations had involved the German residents of all villages in the former Volga German Republic. This meant that the voices of ten of thousands of displaced souls effectively had been silenced for decades through a conspiracy of terror in the East and ignorance in the West. My anger over this failure to finally connect with our long lost kinsmen only fueled my desire to fill what Sovietologist Robert Conquest had termed the "memory hole" that had long characterized our people's exile into oblivion. Not until five years later did we discover that Ernst and his family had traveled all the way from Pavlodar to Novosibirsk to patiently await our arrival in vain all day at the airport. Details of that sad event and our first glimpse into the dramatic story of *usu Leut's* Siberian fate were not of my doing. They came in the harvest season of 1981 when an indomitable foreigner visited tiny Endicott in fulfillment of a lifelong vow.

My most indelible memory of Friedrich Lust is of him standing in a sea of winter wheat on the Don Lust ranch west of Endicott where we were harvesting at the time. A prophet borne westward, he seemed out of place there in his bluish green suit surveying the vast golden expanse that moved in the wind before him. With a white handkerchief headband protecting him from the hot July sun, Friedrich plucked a brittle spear and crushed it between his palms in a gesture that spoke familiarity with the land. As the breeze carried off the bearded chaff to reveal the plump kernels, he remarked that the whitened sheen visible in the distance reminded him of a harvest scene on the Volga. I looked at him with a combination of respect and compassion—feelings that grew in intensity as I came to more fully understand both his story and that he planted other seeds as well. We had learned only days earlier the jubilant news that a visitor was coming to Endicott from Germany after having just arrived in that country from Siberia. An aunt whom he had never seen, Katrillsie Morasch, was nearing her ninetieth year but doing well living by herself in Endicott. Friedrich Lust was the son of her sister and his mother had made him promise years earlier to personally seek out her family in America with the message that her abiding love for them had never faltered despite the many decades of imposed silence. Friedrich's mother had long since died but there could been no better emissary of faith and love than him. Through Mrs. Morasch's hospitality and the generosity of his newly found cousins Bud Smick and Robert Smick, Friedrich discovered a little bit of the Old Country he had known in his youth.

He experienced all he could in the few days he remained there by talking with community elders and reestablishing broken family relationships, attending and speaking at church services, and dining with long lost relatives who included my wife's family. He visited aged Yagaders in area rest homes who laughed at his stories and rejoiced that such a *junge Mann* (Friedrich was in his fifties at the time) could speak flawlessly in the distinctive Hessian dialect that even they had tainted with Americanisms. I was particularly impressed by his most casual manner in every new setting of asking at some point, "And how is it with you and the eternal?" I noticed that to the elders this was a natural question that generally elicited a confirming response regarding matters of ultimate destiny. To those of younger generations this query often evoked perplexity. But Friedrich was a sower of the Word, whose only Bible for years had been written entirely by hand. He would use any occasion to verbally affirm that the fundamental values of our people were spiritual and that life in a Western materialistic society was no less a threat to those principles than the militant atheism of communism. He contended that without a resolute and evidential faith resident in an individual's life, personal and family welfare would ever be at risk. Friedrich's life was a testimony to this profoundly simple and sacrificial creed.

During those summer days we shared in the harvest field I finally was able to glimpse the fate of our people who remained in Russia after 1917. Although my German was no better than his English, we found in Russian a second tongue that seemed adequate, and perhaps appropriate, means of communication. Mine was a limited remnant from a stint in the Air Force heavily seasoned with useless military vocabulary. My comprehension was sufficient, however, to visualize through Friedrich's poignant descriptions the horrors of family separations when as a child his family was forcibly relocated to a collective farm miles from Yagodnaya Polyana. He also described the brutality of heavy labor in the fields for days on end often devoted to tillage

183

Garden Scarecrow

operations deemed improper by his father and others for both care of the fertile but fragile land and for producing optimum yields. Friedrich also knew firsthand the tragic days of September, 1941 when the Volga villages were systematically surrounded by Red Army units and the civilian "enemies" herded into trucks and wagons for transport to the rail center across the Volga in Engels. They were told that the relocation was a temporary measure, lasting perhaps only a few weeks, undertaken in their best interest to safeguard the rural populace from the advancing Wehrmacht. This deception, however, worked the double curse of preventing their provisioning with either winter food supplies and clothing. As armed young *Komsomoltsy* and their officers yelped orders to bewildered families, the adults worked day and night to close their homes and prepare for the journey eastward. Tears were shed by young and old alike for favorite family pets forbidden to accompany the families, as well as for the faithful workhorse teams that still formed the backbone of most field work. Friedrich remembered the painful parting with a favorite mare he nuzzled for the last time before being turned loose to fend for herself. The fate of every living thing seemed jeopardized in the cataclysmic wake of approaching armies and banishing of entire village populations. Stalin later pridefully characterized this grandiose operation as "a great social experiment." For Friedrich and other Volga Germans the event began a maelstrom from which they would not emerge for many years.

Despite Friedrich's best efforts to describe the terror of such events that had been burned in the mind of a twelve year old boy, the full impact of some incidents defied my imagination and perhaps could have been known only to one who had experienced that black period of our people's past. The trains that steamed slowly eastward from the Germans' beloved Volga lumbered for days along branch lines south of the Urals since the main trans-Siberian route was used primarily to transport soldiers and war materials. Delays were frequent and the exiles' bewilderment grew as the way headed deeper across mysterious deserts of flame-colored doom. For Friedrich's family, not unlike the experience of other Yagaders, the long anticipated end of the wearisome railroad journey in Kazakhstan did not mark their ultimate destination. It did bring more trauma for the Lust family, however, as Friedrich's father, Phillip, uncles, and older brothers were marched off for wartime service in the *Trudarmia* or Labor Army. Treated little better than slaves, several did not survive the brutal conditions of their service. A few weeks later Phillip was crushed to death in an accident when moving between cars in a railyard. His bleeding body was unceremoniously carried off and buried in an unmarked grave.

Young Friedrich continued northward for countless miles with his mother and sisters in a truck caravan until they entered the legendary Siberian taiga belt. After enduring several more days the road deteriorated to mere ruts and amidst cries of children in the chill fall air the remnant was then assigned to horse-drawn wagons that followed rugged trails deeper into the forests until finally halting on the edge of the obscure and impassable Tara River. Here the pitiful band was ordered to assemble on the frozen ground and either build makeshift huts or occupy any of several crude dwellings that were clustered in the vicinity forming the village of Urgol. The place was a tiny settlement of former kulaks, prosperous farmers who had resisted collectivization a decade earlier. Because they had endured similar exile at that time, some of the inhabitants offered shelter to the newcomers after overcoming their initial paranoia of invading Germans. With food in short supply for everyone, however, the spectre of famine appeared within weeks. In desperation, they turned to eating yellowed grass pulled from under the frozen crust, boiled tree bark, and even shoe leather. Many could not endure the deprivation and Friedrich lost one of his sisters. Circumstances there in subsequent years during the war were little improved since the land was unsuited to agriculture. In time Friedrich and others managed to join other Yagaders who had found less severe conditions on collectives in the Kachirskii district north of Pavlodar.

Friedrich vividly recalled the countless nights before the fire in their tiny home where his mother would find strength in the retelling of stories gleaned from old letters about life in America. Some members of their family had prospered in that distant place which sounded like another planet to a boy whose brief life had known so much pain. His mother remembered the name of the town in which one sister, Katrillsie, was thought to live—Endicott, State of Washington. When foreign correspondence privileges were again permitted, Friedrich's family was able to reestablish contact with her in the 1970s but he was in no position at that time to even apply for an exit visa. In the absence of an ordained clergy, many of the faithful like Friedrich had become lay pastors who refused to comply with laws prohibiting Christian teaching to youth. For his persistent and successful efforts in this offense, Friedrich was sentenced to five years in a strict regime prison. Given the choice not long after his release of a renewed sentence for his effective witness or emigration to the West, Friedrich elected to safeguard his family's future by moving to Germany. Presently residing among other recently resettled Volga Germans, he remains active in the struggle to institute full religious freedom in the land of this century's most martyred church—the Soviet Union.

Friedrich's dramatic story provided the impetus needed to launch a publication entirely devoted to the history of our ancestral village. The idea had long been considered, borrowed from other village researchers like our friends Elaine Davison (for Kautz) and Jean Roth (Walter) who formed a cultural network of detectives within the AHSGR organization. I was sure that others across the country who shared an interest in Yagada would be fascinated by Friedrich's story. For years I had stuffed the top drawer of a file cabinet with the order forms from every person who had ever purchased my first effort at penning our history, *Pilgrims on the Earth: A German-Russian Chronicle.* Paging through the contents today I find little reason to be proud

186

of the stiff prose of a nineteen year old but the title ever remains an appropriate epithet, taken from Hebrews 11:13, for a people whose identity is so closely linked to migrations. For thousands of others today like Friedrich Lust, the movement continues. Public response to the newsletter venture far exceeded expectations thanks to special guidance in the project by Manny Poffenroth of Spokane, Oshkosh's Amelia Noebel, Gloria Root of Colorado Springs, and other local correspondents who resided in areas of our people's choosing across the United States and Canada. Lois constituted the typing staff, my parents the mailing department, and the kitchen table our production line. Subscriptions numbered in the hundreds within weeks and grew as interest burgeoned contemporaneous with the national "Roots" phenomenon. Continued strong support for the project is gratifying now that it enters its twelfth year and continues in wide circulation under the able editorship of Bill Scheirman in Kansas.

Issues regularly carry special features of general interest, the most recent being a fascinating account by Roberto Kornshuh Bierig on the South German drummer dove that Yagaders brought to Argentina and still raise there. Also featured are copies of letters from Russia and other primary sources in translation and a "Family Finder" for genealogists and those seeking lost relatives. We settled on the somewhat difficult title *Usu Leut vo Jagada* (Our People from Yagada) after learning of similar AHSGR affiliated newsletters. Several incorporated in their names their distinctive colloquial expression for "Our People" (*Unser Lait*, etc.). Such spellings like that of the Yagaders' *usu Leut* make some of our high German purist friends cringe from the assault on their language's proper *unsere Leute*. As a recent article in the newsletter pointed out, however, these Volga German dialects which are still spoken in some parts of North America and Russia are considered the only living vestiges of a bygone era. They have been extensively studied by historical linguists who find them the least acculturated remnants of conversational German from eighteenth century Hesse. Lois's grandmother and Friedrich Lust could read a Vogelsberger's letter from that distant time with greater ease than a resident of Schotten itself today.

Three years after Friedrich Lust's first visit to Endicott, I found myself sitting in Mollie Bafus's living room listening to an equally stunning story about the Volga after 1917. Again a life quest to find family had brought this meeting to pass as Paulina (Bafus) Schmidt was also making a pilgrimage halfway around the world to find her late husband's brother—Mollie's husband John—who had also passed away a few years earlier. Another recent Soviet emigre, this stalwart woman of proud posture betrayed no hint of the tragedies that had marked her life. She had the same smooth waxen complexion that readily identified her as one of us but beneath her auvelian features lay a lifetime acquainted with incredible sadness. I had asked our former neighbor on the family farm, Renata Lautenschlager, to serve as a translator for my visit with Paulina. Renata had participated herself in a dramatic escape from East

Germany as a child shortly after Soviet occupation turned into totalitarian domination. Her unusual sensitivity to Paulina's plight helped open the path to the shrouded memories of an earlier life that could not be discussed casually. We moved from news of family members here and in Kazakhstan to her recollections of a childhood in Yagodnaya facilitated when Mollie produced the special photograph of the village. We learned, however, that Paulina's memories of the place were fragmentary. When she was a young girl her father had been imprisoned for being a kulak in Stalin's campaign to liquidate that class because he possessed too much livestock—a horse and two cows. In desperation her mother had to relocate the family to a neighboring village where they lived with relatives.

Her father did not share in the fate of thousands of others similarly charged whose fate was never learned. He appeared one day many years later at their doorstep following his release. A mere skeleton in rags, not even his wife recognized him. By that time Paulina was married with two children of her own but due to the arrest of her husband on other fabricated charges at the height of Stalin's purges in the 1930s, he was taken away never to be seen again. Paulina and the children were banished with others to an Arctic labor camp near Archangel. Frozen forever in her mind was the first disheartening view of their new home: snowy rows of hoveled residences behind a foreboding rime-encrusted gate. Here they faced confinement behind barbed wire fences except when laboring under armed guard in brigades to cut timber deep in the evergreen forests. Realizing that life under such brutal conditions would inevitably bring death to her young daughters, Paulina risked her own life one night by dashing with them from the woods to the nearby city port. Within minutes the guards released vicious German shepherds which tracked them down and effectively prevented their escape. To this day, she whispered with the glint of tears in her eyes, that breed's bark strikes terror in her heart. With a mother's sacrificial love knowing only deliverance or death in attempting it under such circumstances, Paulina resolved again to escape this Titan's labyrinth of winding trails with murderous men and savage canines. Given better timing after weeks of planning, they huddled in heartpounding anticipation for the right moment to break successfully for freedom. After anonymously boarding a passenger vessel in the port several miles away, a sympathetic ship's officer overlooked her lack of proper identification papers and allowed them steerage to Leningrad.

The beautifully silhouetted skyline of pre-war Leningrad's domed cathedrals and magnificent buildings befitting the former imperial Russian capital belied the famine that again stalked the nation. Huddled for months in a tiny chill apartment on the outskirts of the city, Paulina lost one of her beloved daughters to starvation while the other was rescued from the pestilence only because of the timely arrival of a food parcel from her relatives in America. She resolved to one day visit that distant land and the people by whose goodness they had been delivered. Her visit to Endicott in 1983 was in fulfillment of that pledge. The tragedy that befell most Volga Germans remaining in Russia, however, delayed the trip for over forty years as Paulina soon found that fleeing the country was even more of a challenge than escaping the grips of an icy Arctic prison. Her hegira back to the Volga was undertaken just before Hitler's panzers raced into the Russian heartland and she then was assigned to one of the many transports hauling its human cargo eastward to a nebulous destiny. Old enough for impressment into service with the Labor Army upon arrival in Central Asia, Paulina was forced to entrust care of her only remaining child to a group of older women continuing northward. Ironically, her brigade was soon directed back to the Volga region for bridge building near the front which cost the lives of many fellow workers. Not until the war ended was she able to be reunited with her daughter and for the first time in their troubled lives establish some semblance of stability living near other resettled Yagaders in Kazakhstan.

I sat transfixed by Paulina's gripping narrative related in measured tones but with great difficulty at certain painful moments. The challenges I had known in youth underwent a redefinition. In the security provided by two loving parents in a familiar and hospitable place, I had never really encountered any manner of personal problem in an elemental sense and had understood hate only in abstract terms. This godly woman's daily acquaintance with such hardships imposed only because of her family's nationality steeled her spirit in ways I could never fully appreciate but which were evident in Paulina's Christian witness. As we parted company on Mollie's doorstep a verse from Peter's first epistle came to mind: "That the trial of your faith, being much more precious than of gold that perisheth, though it might be tried with fire, might be found unto praise and honor and glory...." Every time I have encountered that verse since then my thoughts return to that gentle woman of inner strength I met that day. She represents but one of thousands whose lives throughout the apocalyptic events experienced this century in communist Russia give living and victorious expression to the meaning of the word "overcome."

Emigres like Friedrich Lust and Paulina Schmidt began arriving in West Germany in the late 1970s because of relaxation of the Kremlin's rigid emigration policy. The guiding force in America behind the increasing world pressure for this change was the distinguished senator from Washington State, Henry M. Jackson. Although of "west side" Norwegian extraction, Senator Jackson knew well the Volga German constituency of the eastern Washington farm belt and was fully informed on the details of their history. His grasp of our heritage was eloquently expressed to Lois and me during our biennial visits to the capital accompanying Corps of Discovery student delegations on field trips to the East Coast. Though best known as an international champion of human rights and Soviet Jewish emigration, Senator Jackson worked steadfastly to secure these same privileges for Germans living in the USSR as he came to better understand their plight. The landmark 1974 Jackson-Vanik

Amendment linking Soviet-American trade to emigration was specifically written for these purposes notwithstanding the senator's awareness that his own state as one of the nation's leading grain exporters stood to lose more than most others if the Soviets chose non-compliance. The thousands who subsequently found freedom in Germany and Israel are living testimony to the rare courage and historical insight displayed by a statesman who chose principle over profit and to whom Volga Germans worldwide owe so much.

In the spring of 1987 our parents were stunned with the announcement that we were moving back to Endicott. Nestled in the eastern foothills of Washington's Cascade Range, the Wenatchee Valley is among the most scenic parts of the Pacific Northwest. A dozen years there in the public schools and a rewarding career teaching history at the community college had introduced us to a wide circle of good friends. Continued work on the story of *usu Leut,* however, had been done at arm's length for years as we made periodic holiday trips to Endicott and never missed the harvest season. With a sense that something remained there to be done, I accepted an administrative and teaching position in the newly formed Endicott-St. John School Cooperative which was a creative educational alternative to the school consolidations that were causing many rural communities elsewhere to lose their identities. Under this new approach, schools would be maintained in both communities under a single administration. Endicott's superintendent, Dr. Bill Schmick, had himself just recently returned to his hometown after distinguished careers in the foreign service and California public education. His diplomatic background had prepared him well to undertake such change in small towns jittery over their future. With mixed feelings and tears shed over a recently completed dream home, we struck out eastward on the journey to our own native village exchanging shopping malls and college lectures for Sunday potlucks and hall duty. Yet satisfaction came in working daily with the children of friends we had known for life in a community where continuity was a hallmark. In church, for example, Pastor Schnaible had baptized, confirmed, and married Lois and me while Dr. Hardy had delivered us as well as our first-born daughter, Mary Katherine.

While the challenges confronting rural America were evident in the closed businesses and recently vacated houses around town, we were also impressed by the determination of our old friends to confront this debilitating trend. A successful campaign spearheaded by Mayor Tom Byers returned a doctor, after Dr. Hardy's passing, and had reopened a grocery store, while our energetic new Lutheran pastor, Reverend Stan Jacobson, led a cooperative effort of local churches to sponsor several Russian emigre families. Their resettlement in Endicott and adjustment to smalltown America required his mobilizing a small army of volunteers to repair long abandoned houses, organize food drives, and make sense out of Green Cards and government medical coupons. But we also noticed another force quietly at work in the life of the town. While nearing the twenty-first century, I was surprised to find so

190

many Russian-born souls from the previous one still contributing meaningfully to community life. Mollie Bafus made her annual visits to middle school social studies classes clad in the embroidered black headscarf and brown woolen shawl she brought from Russia, and Jake Schmick at ninety-seven still greeted everyone on his daily outings to the post office. Yagada-born Lizzie Scheuerman, who arrived in 1910 speaking the Spanish she picked up in the village's Argentine daughter colony, still made sure that anybody even remotely related had one of her priceless afghans to fend off a winter shiver, while Carl Litzenberger regularly stopped to sample the freshly applewood smoked German sausage in the local market to ensure a "good dew." Many of their generation seemed ageless as I recalled being a guest in their homes as a boy posing questions about the Old Country.

For all the hours spent interviewing, reading, translating, and letter writing, answers to two of the most perplexing questions challenging our research still remained elusive. The identity of our ancestor who linked family progenitor Hartmann Scheuerman to Aunt Lizzie's "Grandpa Pete" was still a mystery. The matter of what dramatic events transpired in Yagodnaya Polyana during the Thirties and in those fateful days of September, 1941 was shrouded in speculation as well. Some sinister force seemingly had snuffed out the very existence of that once vibrant place and cast its inhabitants beyond some "great gulf fixed" into an unreachable Hades. Friedrich Lust's testimony was from the perspective of one living on a distant collective farm when those events had transpired while Paulina Schmidt spent time in an Arctic prison and elsewhere on the Volga. Paulina had mentioned, however, that a rumor circulated among Yagaders in the Pavlodar region that a native of the village had managed to return to Yagodnaya Polyana as a veterinarian. She was believed to be living there now but correspondence was discouraged because it might draw unnecessary attention to the tenuous presence of a Volga German among people intent upon blotting out their memory. Clearly, the only way to ascertain the true facts was to somehow personally visit the place. The prospects, however, remained unlikely since no Westerner had been allowed there since the delivery of Volga famine relief under President Hoover in the 1920s. Unlike some of the other original Volga colonies apparently obliterated or abandoned after the German villagers' exile, Yagodnaya Polyana did at least remain on current maps of the region under its original name. What exactly was there and what secrets its residents held remained securely locked, however, behind an insurmountable wall of restrictions on travel in the Soviet Union that regulated even the presence of its own citizens in the area.

Opportunities to breach the barrier of silence seemed no closer in the summer of 1990 when we took a temporary leave of absence from the school district for me to serve as associate director of the Institute of Soviet and East European Studies in Wheaton, Illinois. Institute director Anita Deyneka was a longtime family friend coincidentally from Washington's Wenatchee Valley whom Lois and I first had met on the ill-fated expedition to the Soviet Union in 1976. We remained in close communication over the years as we knew the work the Deynekas conducted to be of vital importance to all peoples of the Soviet Union. Rev. Peter Deyneka, Jr. was president of the Slavic Gospel Association which had ministered through an international radio and literature delivery network to the spiritual needs of the persecuted church in the USSR since 1934. I came to Wheaton to direct a Soviet educational project cooperatively undertaken between the institute and the Russian Ministry of Education. Remarkable changes were in the wind under glasnost which had inaugurated such new endeavors. This one was especially noteworthy since ministry officials earnestly sought to understand American approaches to curriculum development and instructional improvement and study Christian perspectives in moral education.

In July, 1990 AHSGR held its annual convention in Sacramento, California and while preparing to address a ballroom crowd on the origins of Volga German settlement in the American West, my good friend Allyn Brosz of Washington, D.C. who served as the session's moderator handed me a startling letter from Dr. James Long of Colorado State University. He had established contact with a professor in Saratov, Russia, Dr. Igor Plehve, whose field of specialization was Russian German history. Saratov had remained the political and economic hub of a region that in 1921 had been designated by Lenin the Autonomous Volga German Socialist Republic—the first such entity of its kind in the new nation. Furthermore, the letter indicated that the professor offered definitive confirmation that the long sought nineteenth century census revisions did in fact exist. This intelligence alone had eluded the best efforts of special task forces of international archivists and genealogists commissioned to determine the disposition of such documents in the Soviet Union. On my return home I immediately fired off a letter to the professor with copies of material I had written on the Volga Germans and word that I might have occasion to visit the USSR that fall on institute business.

The following September I traveled to Washington, D.C. to help host a delegation of Soviet educational officials we had arranged to bring to the United States. One particularly intrepid and winsome fellow named Oleg insisted on experiencing more of America than capital area tours. While I had expected the general requests for shopping excursions and theatre tickets, his were quite specific and a bit more challenging to meet. He needed a rubberized neck brace, incandescent insect electrifier, and a trip to see New York City's Greenwich Village immediately. I replied that the first two could probably be handled, but a trip to New York City during their brief stay would require myriad arrangements for travel and lodging at a time when our agenda was heavy with official business. Before entirely dismissing the possibility, however, I risked asking for a special personal incentive. Somehow I would get him to New York if on our reciprocal visit to Moscow in October he would arrange my travel to Saratov. I would take my chances on Yagodnaya Polyana once getting that far. His hearty laugh and sly smile told me he could pull the right strings and a handshake sealed the bargain. I returned to Illinois to find a telegram on my desk with a concise message from the Soviet professor: "Will be glad to meet with you in Saratov during your trip."

One month later I found myself trailing my Russian comrade as he hurriedly fought our way through the cacophonous caverns inside Pavelyetsky Railway Station near the heart of Moscow. I kept expecting something to go haywire at any moment but thanks to Oleg my visa had "Saratov" prominently typed on the destination line and I soon recognized the same name in Cyrillic suspended from the high iron arm of a signpost in front of a waiting train. With not more than ten minutes to spare we were off by night, one of the limitations imposed on my travel, and settled into a good night's rest lulled to sleep in our comfortable cabin by flashbacks of stories heard in my youth and the muffled clatter on this road back in time. I knew this place to which we were headed as well as any Yagader. Saratov had been often described to me by our Russian-born informants. About forty miles southeast of Yagodnaya Polyana, this great Volga city was visited at least once or twice a year by most families who made the trip for special purchases and to transact banking or other official business. But I knew the streets and sights of Yagodnaya even better through the composite memories of so many old friends who had taken the time to patiently recall with obvious pleasure countless details of village life. For their sake I hoped also to travel those last forty miles from Saratov.

The gently rolling panorama of spacious awe that greeted us the following gray morning reminded me of the many photographs I had seen of endless Russian steppelands in *National Geographic*. Recently harvested grainfields were separated by thickly branched arbors from chestnut fallow lands stretching to the horizon. Now leafless in full fall, many groves along the railroad revealed within their frosted lace a habitat of innumerable hanging baskets built by birds I assumed were related to orioles. The mood of haunting beauty was enhanced by a pallor of solitude across the landscape. Even by late morning we rarely spied a soul on the muddy roads along the route. Fenced country cemeteries densely packed with distinctive Orthodox crosses often suddenly appeared against the somber October sky and little activity was seen in the neighboring villages through which we regularly passed without stopping.

The first indication that we were finally entering the land of *usu Leut* came when the steel wheels carrying our car announced a forthcoming stop in low shuddering tones. Slowly the train rumbled to a rest next to a railway station directly opposite our window. Perched above the broad double-doored entrance was a weathered wooden sign bearing the word "ATKAPCK" which I recognized as Atkarsk, the place where scores of our people had boarded trains for the first leg of their journey to America. Yagodnaya Polyana could not be more than twenty miles to the east but I had to settle for a look out the opposite side of the train across the sepia expanse and the hope I could somehow venture there over the weekend.

An hour later we began entering the littered outskirts of Saratov, a city of some 900,000 bordered by the massive Volga on the east and a sea of smoking hovels in the morning air from all other directions. Soon we entered the city proper and rolled to a stop along an elevated concrete ramp at the train station. We were warmly greeted upon alighting from our coach by Dr. Plehve, a man in his late thirties and obviously delighted we could meet, as well as a journalist firing questions about local nationality problems and policies I had hoped would be avoided in public. Our host tried to deflect the inquiries and succeeded in postponing the session until he could acquaint me with the local political situation. He also told me he had visited Yagodnaya Polyana once several years earlier and that he might be able to arrange a visit there on the morning of my scheduled departure in two days. I readily assented. We then set out in a yellow Lada with one of his associates to tour what was once the Volga German capital.

I soon learned that the residents of the city, who are overwhelmingly Russian and Ukrainian, fear that their region is still under consideration for a restored Volga German Republic. Alternative locations in Kazakhstan, Kirghizia, and Kaliningrad have not been accepted by an all-union commission charged with resolving the matter and most Soviet Germans, one of the country's largest ethnic groups, favor restoration of republic status for political and cultural reasons. Although most now reside in Soviet Central Asia and Siberia, many are known to prefer returning to their old homeland on the Volga. Consequently, some citizens of the Saratov area fear the possible expropriation of their homes, enterprises, and other property.

The heart of old Saratov remains the former German Street district. Since German associations with area place names have remained a sensitive subject since the war, the street is now called Nevskii Prospekt. Strolling down the broad thoroughfare was like walking into a bygone world. Its length is entirely closed to traffic and has the appearance of a great European mall with the only modern feature being electric street lights crowned with clusters of clear glass globes. Two rows extending for a half-dozen blocks illuminate the entire area at night in a soft yellow. As the city escaped the ravages of the Second World War, imposing four-story structures from the previous century rise up on both sides of the boulevard in a variety of continental styles reminiscent of some scene from Budapest, Vienna, or other great European city. Among the most prominent buildings is the enormous corner steepled conservatory, its spires soaring over one hundred feet, that would seem more at home overlooking the Rhine than the Volga. Noticeably absent, however, was the hubbub of activity one would expect in the heart of such a metropolitan area. Strangely, the crowds quietly passed by with people poking in and out of store fronts to gaze or stand in lines while waiting to procure life's necessities. Where commercial banks and exclusive merchandisers once were located were found meat shops and costume jewelry stores; former luxury hotels contained dimly-lit apartments and cluttered bookstores. Not one that I visited had a single book on the region's German heritage although there was a rare availability of books on city and area history due to the celebration of the anniversary of Saratov's founding as a frontier military garrison in 1590.

Saratov has been home to many figures of national and international significance during the subsequent four centuries. Among other notables who have lived or studied here are the literary figures Radishchev and Chernyshevsky, government officials like Stolypin and Kalinin, and the first man in space, Yuri Gagarin. The city maintains several museums to commemorate the achievements of these individuals as well as a general city museum that does have a small exhibit on the German colonies. This building is located several blocks north of the Slaviskii Hotel where I stayed. A very good facility by Soviet standards within steps of the Volga shoreline, it features a large restaurant and receiving center for Volga cruise ships that ply these waters all summer between Volgograd and Nizhni Novgorod (formerly Gorky). A large bridge connecting Saratov and Engels could be seen a short distance upstream and seemed to stretch for miles to the opposite shore. Sunset Sunday evening painted an unforgettable panorama of dappled rose across the blue-grey water beneath my window.

As our excursion continued the next morning, my hosts explained that a great debate continues about the origin of the city's name though a consensus of scholarly opinion credits its etymology to two Tatar words: "sari" (yellow) and "tai" (hill). The name possibly referred to the hill Sokolova that looms above the city. The Tatars were one of several Mongol tribes that remained in the region following the invasion of Asiatics under the khans in the thirteenth century. Centrally located on the great Mother River of Russia, Saratov soon came to serve as the political and economic center of the region. Its original Russian military fortification knew recurrent challenges at the hands of local tribes. The famed Cossack raider Stenka Razin attacked the fort in 1617 as did Emelian Pugachev in 1774 during his ill-fated attempt to claim Catherine's throne. Saratov survived each crisis, however, and steadily expanded along the west bank of the Volga. In 1780 it was designated the regional center for civil government which brought a new wave of residents who were reinforced after the formation of the Saratov Gubernia as an administrative district in 1797. The phenomenal success of the German colonists agricultural enterprises after an initial period of difficult adjustment also boosted the economic development of the region and great wooden granaries soon appeared along the waterfront as Saratov became the major grain exporting center on the lower Volga.

Stretching nearly sixty feet in the center of the Nevskii Prospekt mall today stands a massive panorama in oils depicting historic scenes in chronological order from the sixteenth century to the present. I looked to find the arrival of the first German immigrants pictured between the defeat of the Turks and Pugachev's Rebellion but this historic moment escaped the artist's brush. Another impressive anniversary display a few blocks away was an enormous three dimensional diorama of the Saratov waterfront with an adjacent matching scene showing the present arrangement. Noticeably absent in the contemporary view were the great Catholic and Orthodox cathedrals and the beautiful Lutheran Church—all victims of Stalin's campaign again religion in the 1930s. In their places were the cold gray cubic structures that stood as monuments to the brutality of previous regimes which stifled religious expression and creativity. My friend took me down a back alley to see what remained of the Catholic Cathedral which in the rear still revealed its original grand lines and pillars. The front had been entirely torn off and replaced with a dead square entry. My guide shrugged his shoulders and decried the effort as "vandalism." The Lutheran Church was completely destroyed as were several of the city's most historic Orthodox Cathedrals. The most prominent one that remains, however, the Starii Zobor, is a testament to the genius of architects who combined both Eastern and Western Christian motifs in a design unlike anything I had ever seen. The entryway resembled a broad walled conservatory of jeweled glass on top framed by flowing letters in Old Church Slavonic painted white. For the first time in nearly half a century, its symphony of bells began to be heard again recently as every hour is announced in melodic tones and a special chorus of harmonies is rung from the belfry each Sunday.

A remarkable collection of European art that is largely unknown abroad was seen in Saratov's Radishchev Art Museum. This striking building of red brick with an entry framed by sandstone columns was designed by famed architect Ivan Strom and opened in 1885 and was the first public art museum in Russia. It was established by Alexi Bogoliubov who had given his personal art collection to the city eight years earlier in order to promote wider appreciation for fine arts and to immortalize the memory of his grandfather, Alexander Radishchev, whose family was of the nobility and owned a large estate in the Saratov district. Radishchev spent several summers of his youth near the city before leaving his mark on Russian reformist thinking by writing a scathing indictment of Tsarist oppression in his 1790 classic, *A Journey From St. Petersburg to Moscow*. Its publication resulted in his exile to Siberia but inaugurated a new era of revolutionary writing and action. His grandson, Bogoliubov, was an artist who shared many of these ideas and also acquired a substantial collection of Russian and Western European paintings, antique furniture, malachite urns, and Delft porcelain which today fill several spacious galleries in the museum. Rare sixteenth century German painted glass is displayed in a room with Peter the Great's statue and an enormous canvas of Catherine the Great appears upstairs above the main entrance. A smaller one nearby is a less flattering portrait of the empress in later life. A regal mass of gray hair flows around her slightly tilted face showing a sunken mouth but eyes still brightly exuding a royal confidence.

During our stroll through the museum I learned that Dr. Plehve shared my passion for learning the full story about all that had happened to our people after the Russian Revolution and was equally committed to providing help for family history researchers. I inquired about the holdings of local archives and was impressed with both the depth of his knowledge and the extent of the collections. In addition to his teaching responsibilities at the university, he had labored for months to compile an exhaustive list of all original Volga German colonists from extant eighteenth century records housed in both the Saratov and Engels archives. He had also assembled copies of the colonies' 1834 census revisions including the one for Yagodnaya Polyana. Access to the original documents was severely restricted but possible given enough time and the approval of the archive director. Unfortunately, neither could be arranged on the weekend of my visit. Dr. Plehve offered, however, to bring his copies of records in handwritten Russian to my hotel room the next evening if that would be of any help. The question seemed rhetorical as no one in the West had even known for sure that such records survived the ravages of revolution and war.

He appeared at the appointed time bearing a heavy black leather satchel which carried hundreds of pages of census lists arranged in file folders by village. I desperately wanted to retrieve them all for the sake of the thousands worldwide who yearned to understand more fully a heritage so long denied them. But lacking a photographic memory and copy machine I was compelled to confine my investigation to the families from Yagodnaya Polyana. Further complicating my efforts was the difficulty in readily comprehending German names handwritten in Russia. As he had other business that evening, I thanked Igor heartily for entrusting the documents to me and promised to return them to him in the morning since our trip to the village was still planned. I rolled up my sleeves before the small birch desk and opened the file to see the names Bafus, Blumenschein, Fox, and Lust all on the first page. A quick glance through the stack provided other names I had known from youth and confirmed in my mind the records were genuine. I pulled the last page to read that in 1834 a total of 2,922 residents inhabited Yagodnaya Polyana in 286 families. Returning to the beginning I then began copying down by hand as many names and vital statistics as possible before my mind would demand rest from the weekend's hectic schedule. In the course of putting down hundreds of names I realized that I could complete only a partial listing at best in the allotted time but determined to be accurate with what entries I could record. The periodic designation *novorozhd* next to certain children baffled me until I deduced by their ages that these persons were among those for whom this census was intended. These were the "newborn" whose names would not have appeared on the previous enumeration of 1816 and therefore need to be added for tax purposes and land redistribution. Similarly, individuals who had died during the interim were also indicated.

There were frequent entries with my own surname as was the case with all others in the village of prolific and isolated Germans that had grown dramatically since the trek of the first families sixty-eight years earlier. When I encountered family entry number eighty-eight, however, my heart stopped.

197

The Berries of Berry Meadow

The father's name was Yost Scheuermann and he had been among those who had died since the last census at age sixty-five in 1820. Doubtless this was Johann Jost, the son of Hartmann and Elizabeth who had joined his parents as a boy on the historic trek to the Volga and whose name was included in Kromm's emigrant register of 1767. Even more startling was the name and age of a grandson. Fifteen year old Peter was certainly the man who in later life taught Aunt Lizzie those children's songs from his knee. The dates all coincided with what fragments of information we had scraped together from oral histories. Peter's father, we learned for the first time, was named Heinrich which only seemed appropriate. It was the same name given to my great-grandfather, the man who ultimately brought our family to America. Our "missing link" had finally been found. I worked throughout the night with renewed vigor from this discovery trying to make sense of crude transliterations from German that must have knotted the brows of any Russian census-taker. "Gomshtene" was really Holstein, "Ryech" was our Reich, and the name of our Kleweno cousins was spelled "Klyevyeiau."

Another document revealed that Johann Jost arrived in Russia with his family on September 13, 1766 aboard a ship named the *De Pyerle* under the command of a Captain Thompson. It was one of three ships that brought the colonists who would establish the village of Yagodnaya Polyana. The following September Johann Jost was listed as being eighteen years old in 1766, son of Johann Hartmann and Elizabeth Scheuermann, with six other children: Konrad (21), Johann Heinrich (14), Hans Heinrich (12), Johann Heinrich (8), Balthazar (2 1/2), and a daughter, Elizabeth. Clearly visible on the right hand margin of the manifest was their village of origin in Germany—Nidda. But tragedy apparently struck the family while enroute to the Volga, however, as the name of little Balthazar did not appear on the roster of original Yagodnaya inhabitants. At some unknown place along the windswept thousand mile trek deep into Russia a small group of foreigners paused to lay a family's youngest child to rest in the new homeland. Having pored over the documents for many hours by this time, I also paused for a brief rest as the first glint of sunlight peered over the horizon but I quickly fell into dreamtime about the memories I had stirred.

A knock at the door that seemed just moments later signalled the beginning of my final day in Saratov. After a breakfast of oatmeal and cabbage, a combination I had only known Lois's grandfather to enjoy, I met my university hosts for the hour's drive to Yagodnaya Polyana and the fulfillment of a lifetime dream. We tore through the city at the same breakneck speed I had come to expect in Soviet cities and prayed that an accident I also anticipated someday would not occur today. We soon moved onto a highway at a more leisurely pace encountering several small communities and undulating landscapes similar to the terrain we had passed by train two days earlier. Our discussion turned to the problems of Soviet agriculture though the best commentary enroute was the rusted hulks of feed mills and grain elevators that resembled castles of cracked concrete surrounded by sprouted moats of careless spillage.

We passed stubble fields and an immense congregation of ochre sunflowers bowed with heavy heads that would provide no harvest offering this late in the year. The murky gray skies we had known for several days, however, soon dissipated into a ceiling of lucent turquoise. Climbing the kind of gentle rise for which the colonists named this side of the Volga the *Bergseite,* we spotted a sign in large white letters against a Prussian blue background for Yagodnaya Polyana that directed us eastward off the main highway onto a severely cratered road. This route deteriorated into a deeply rutted lane in three miles as we began descending steeply through an autumn gilded cowl of quaking birches protecting this tranquil valley. Visible among the peeling white *beryozky* was an endless aisled carpet of humble moss and frosted woodland flora where Aunt Lizzie and her friends once collected wild mushrooms and strawberries. In the distance appeared the outskirts of my trip's ultimate destination, Yagodnaya Polyana, an obscure Russian village yet sacred to the memory of thousands.

Half-way down the slope leading into a substantial community we slid to a stop on ground greasy with morning sunmelt. I wanted to compare the scene to a copy of Mollie's picture that I had brought for this very purpose. Straining to find a familiar physical landmark, I thought we either had the wrong village or that the negative had been reversed when the print was made years ago. I proceeded along for some time in geographic vertigo until realizing that the print was fine but what I always had understood to be east in the picture was actually the opposite direction. Suddenly everything fit into place as we parked the car near what appeared to be the village's major crossroads. The dry goods store that we just passed now revealed itself to be the old Russian school where C. G. Schmick, Conrad Blumenschein, and so many others had grudgingly studied as boys. A block south of where I stood was a two-story building of fading aqua bearing the unmistakable lines of the German school where after enduring a single day of Schoolmaster Kromm's discipline, Martin Lust never returned. The structure now apparently served civil functions. Several youngsters chased a flock of gabbling geese in its adjacent lot and their school nearby appeared to be one of the newer and largest buildings in the community. It was surrounded by a wire fence anchored by blue posts and positioned where the Henry Appel home had once stood.

This orientation meant that the cream colored brick structure crowned with a red star rested where the splendid Lutheran Church had been located. Our Grandma Scheuerman had been baptized here and hundreds of our people took their last communion within its walls before tearing themselves away for the journey to America. Many held the parochial certificates just signed by Pastor Schilling that today were keepsakes for families back home. So much for the Pollyannaish hopes that parish records miraculously survived in some attic sanctuary of the original building. The place before us did not appear more than twenty years old but did remarkably approximate the architecture of its predecessor minus the four-tiered entry tower once crowned with cross-laden cupola. The number of side windows and tin-roofed gable design appeared identical to the former church. Two passing women braving the mired streets confirmed its recent age and informed us that it presently served as a community recreation and meeting hall. They viewed us with some suspicion but spoke freely when we explained the nature of our mission. They reported that a few Germans had even moved back in recent years without volunteering any specifics.

Knowing that my great-grandfather's home was directly across the street from where the church had stood, I approached the house that was occupying that place to see a red-scarfed bundle of black ambling among some chickens behind a crude fence of upright poles. Responding to the Russian of one of my companions, an elderly Ukrainian woman turned to peer at our strange faces before breaking into a helpful smile. The conversation shifted into Ukrainian when both realized they were natives of the Novodruzovskaya region. She was among the first people to reinhabit Yagodnaya Polyana after the German farmers had been deported. She came as a refugee from the Ukraine where their entire kolkhoz had fled en mass in the wake of the Nazi onslaught into that region. Upon arriving in Yagodnaya Polyana only weeks after its virtual abandonment they found only a few families in which German women married to Russian husbands had been permitted to remain. The deserted households were already showing signs of disrepair and pilfering but as in other Volga German villages they were readily occupied by peasants streaming to the area. She herself was soon redirected to work on a cattle farm twenty kilometers away but returned to the village when she retired not long ago. When asked how many Volga German families had managed to return to Yagodnaya Polyana she estimated about a dozen with several residents in the immediate vicinity. One elderly couple in fact had just arrived and were living with their daughter's family behind the community building. We posed together for a picture and offered our thanks before heading toward the house. With afternoon commitments back in Saratov and an early evening departure time, I knew this next visit would likely be my final opportunity to ascertain the story of Yagada's interwar fate.

We clumsily stepped single file in each other's footprints to cross the quagmired road separating us from an elevated sidepath while two red-sweatered boys dawdled in the mud. The only visible means of transportation under such conditions was an occasional wagon drawn by ponies bearing the traditional *duka* arch yoke reminiscent of a scene from Dostoyevsky's *Poor Folk*. Several men glared at our curious dress and my camera, making each muddied step a bit more uneasy. Within moments I heard rushing water and after crossing a rapidly flowing brook the muffled roar of Yagada's fabled spring emerged from a steep sidehill enmeshed in brambled bowers of overgrown bushes and vines. Surely this was where Grandma Morasch and

Kedda Luft exchanged family news and future dreams as hundreds of women gathered daily for fresh water and clothes washing. They ultimately settled in Endicott and Sheboygan, respectively, and saw each other but once in their adopted country though they never forgot an enduring friendship that grew from this special place.

A few moments later we traipsed up an earthen driveway to the back of an attractive home of plastered white exterior with blue framed windows. Standing next to a woodpile near the entryway was an attractive middle-aged woman with whom my hosts briefly spoke. I thought I caught a familiar name as she led us inside somewhat indifferently after we left our shoes of muck in the entry. I again heard the name inside the kitchen as she introduced us to her parents: Georg and Maria *Scheuermann*. They caught my expression and when I told them my name we were all dumbfounded for a moment. The elderly couple took us into a small living room divided from the kitchen by a flowered curtain where Maria reclined on a couch specially prepared for her use with a stack of pillows and warm quilts. She said her maiden name was Schneidmiller and seemed pleased when I replied that Yagada families by that name were well known to me in Washington and Idaho. Georg reported that he was of the *Kosack* clan of Scheuermans but that we were surely distant cousins through our common German emigrant ancestor. A member of our *Yusta* branch was living just down the street. He and Maria were still getting reacquainted here since arriving from Peschanoye in Kazakhstan just three weeks earlier. That fact led me to ask if they had ever known my wife's cousin, Friedrich Lust. Know him?! He was a favored nephew whose lay ministry among our people in Central Asia had been well known to many Volga Germans.

Their retelling of the tragic events in Yagodnaya Polyana through the fall of 1941 meant dredging up painful memories made little easier by the emotional impact of my sudden appearance minutes earlier. I chose to temper my questions accordingly but readily learned that I was in the presence of two people who had fully experienced the travesty of the innocent village's rapine. They had witnessed the expropriation of everyone's property and the slaughter of those who resisted; they had both known starvation during the famine Stalin had imposed upon their people, his brutal suppression of their Christian faith, and heard the announcement in the village that fateful fall morning beginning the deportation. Only a handful that survived all these plagues had managed to return where they all had taken place. Their descriptions of these events especially affected one of my Russian companions who listened incredulously to events of national significance entirely new to his educated ears.

The disruption of life across the country following the 1917 Russian Revolution and Civil War coupled with poor harvests in the early 1920s brought famine to the Volga and Yagodnaya Polyana. Grain reserves were shared widely but were soon depleted. Hundreds perished in the area before relief from America arrived. The most pitiful casualties, Georg recalled, were children who shriveled into living skeletons with bloated bellies. Like Paulina Schmidt, circumstances during the next decade were little improved for Maria who experienced exile and family loss before the mass exile. When she was a young girl in 1931, her immediate family had been banished beyond the Urals in the midst of Stalin's collectivization which began in Yagodnaya about 1930 and consolidated all land holdings in the area into two huge collective farms. Both Maria's parents soon died in the East and relatives back home arranged for her and a brother to return. As brutal as these conditions were, other farmers who resisted expropriation of their property were often shot outright and buried in mass graves in the cemetery overlooking the village. The fact that some of the perpetrators were Germans themselves remained a source of community shame. Soon after the Russian Civil War concluded in 1921 the region was occupied by the Red Army which established a local soviet or workers' council in every village with sweeping legal authority. Placed by the army as chairmen and representatives within the soviets were handpicked local Bolshevik Party sympathizers who tended to constitute the shiftless element that clings to any community and stands to gain the most at the expense of somebody else. These feckless firebrands who had increasingly become the bane of the Volga villagers during the Civil War soon bullied their way into positions of local authority.

These same malcontents facilitated the war against religion in the village when ordered to do so by party officials in 1928. The local Lutheran pastor, Reverend Arthur Pfeiffer, continued to serve his local parish despite repeated threats on his life and family's welfare until the church was closed with his arrest about 1934. No one dared appear at his trial for fear of further reprisals against him or themselves and the courageous man who had served Yagodnaya for many years was sentenced to ten years in prison. After his release he continued to minister unofficially since the Lutheran Church in Russia was formally dissolved in 1938. Pastor Pfeiffer sought out his former parishioners and relocated to the Pavlodar area where his unofficial ministry flourished before retiring to Moscow where he died in the early 1970s. His wife, Zhiganova, still lives in Moscow.

I groped to understand in gallant naivete how local resistance had not somehow prevailed when their beloved church was threatened or why an invisible underground had not sheltered innocents facing arrests and exile. Georg explained the horrific circumstances in one word: terror. These lamentable events had not occurred haphazardly but seemed part of a complex diabolical plan to systematically reduce the local populace into compliant subjects forced to bury their own convictions. Acquainted for generations with the intricacies of agriculture rather than tactics of terror, the German farmers were like sheep among wolves that tore assiduously and ruthlessly at the cultural vitals of religious conviction, private farms, and inseparable family. Beleaguered by starvation, shock, and loss of blood, they faltered and

203

ultimately collapsed into a withdrawn silence. But the periodic stirrings that kicked against the beasts of oppression only to renew bloodshed were not death throes. While the heart of the body numbly succumbed in compliance, it ever breathed the memories of another life that knew faith, pride, and love which survived even in the face of exile to the desolate wastelands of the East.

Many of the troops assigned to the relocation in September, 1941 were scarcely out of their teens as the government seemed to be using younger recruits for such service while older men were sent to the front. NKVD agents had gone door to door just days earlier ostensibly to compile a roster of all residents fluent in German who could serve as translators if such work became necessary during the war. In retrospect Georg realized they were deceptively at work drafting the village's deportation list from which there would be no escape unless a German woman had taken a Russian spouse. With a population of about two thousand, Yagodnaya had only a handful of families that fit this category. Officials had returned to the village later in the week with the announcement that since the German army's advance was threatening the region, transport vehicles would arrive in three days to facilitate their "evacuation" and that armed guards were posted all around the village to prevent any unauthorized exit. The Russians feared that given the choice, many Volga Germans would remain to face the conditions of life under Nazi occupation rather than entrust themselves to further treatment at the hands of proven enemies. A widespread rumor held that the Germans were racing to the Volga to liberate lands already peopled by their *Aussiedler* countrymen.

Again powerless to mount an alternative response, the villagers' panic settled into chaotic preparation for the move. The weather was turning colder and required careful selection and packing of necessities since the orders allowed only baggage that could be readily carried by the family. Brass samovars and white linen skirts were cast aside in favor of wooden soup spoons, black crusted loaves of rye bread, and pleated woolen coats. Tattered German Bibles, often hidden in secret places, appeared on the select pile while precious feather bedding locked in wooden chests, deftly used spinning wheels, and even heirlooms from the legendary eighteenth century trek would remain in Yagodnaya Polyana to face an equally uncertain fate. This new journey eastward knew none of the sanguine anticipation of that earlier time. Though some of the smaller children looked upon the tumult of those three black days with wide-eyed interest, their elders knew this event was not of their choosing and some guessed that they would never return.

At the appointed time a battalion of trucks rolled down the western approach to the village and began loading operations that took hours to complete. Men and women alike wept at the prospect of leaving a beloved home giving little mind to the proddings barked by the drivers and men assigned to this bitter task. Despite the agonies of recent years extraordinary force was sometimes needed to tear heart from hearth. Some soldiers looked upon the scene with sympathy as old women were pulled away from their doorsteps to the cold confines of a truckbed. Other troops evidenced no little animosity against the villagers whom they had been propagandized into believing were fifth columnists poised to rise up in support of the German invaders. By late afternoon a caravan extended for miles along the road leading across the westward hills sheltering their once secure domain and holding the bones of departed loved ones in the plaintive cemetery near the top of the rise. In another hour they reached Saratov where they waited endlessly in a holding compound before being ferried across the Volga to the railhead in Engels. From that point they began an exhaustive ten day journey to Kazakhstan with occasional stops for replenishing supplies of bread, potatoes, and water. Traveling with other Yagader families the bulk of the contingent was assigned to a collective farm in the Kachirskii region north of Pavlodar. They gathered to form a new community at Peschanoye while a group of rural Ukrainians equally dispossessed by war's approach began occupying their old homes back on the Volga.

Among the many topics covered that day none was more meaningful than the reason this family and others like them had returned. After an earlier lifetime of travail they had established an ordered existence in Kazahkstan but in old age Georg and Maria apparently were risking it all again by moving back to Yagada. The renewed presence of Volga Germans in the old colonies threatened to fuel fires of local prejudice that recurrently had been directed against them . Maria's response to my question was laconic. This was home. Yet increasingly clear through our morning's conversation was that "home" connoted more than mere place. She spoke eloquently about the faith spawned here and memories from which her people had drawn strength during "the dark times." And despite the limitations, life today in the village even amid a sea of strangers had certain advantages to an indefinite residence in Central Asia. For one thing, she explained emphatically, the sky was again blue here and rolling earth black—the way God has fashioned His creation. Even decades of communism could not blot out these happy features which stood in marked contrast to the monotonous brown smears of the horizon, adobed homes, and what few hills did exist where they had lived before.

They were glad to be here at almost any cost as when adopted children sometimes overcome seemingly insurmountable obstacles to be reunited with a natural parent. For me the all too brief introduction to the mother colony would have to suffice while they were committed to residence with a maternal memory. Our momentary diversion from their incredible chronicle to more interpretive matters brought to mind an observation by Henry Wallace that seemed to embody this ethic: "Many of the most lively, intimate expressions of spirit spring from the joyous, continuous contact of human beings with a particular locality....If life can be made secure in each community there will flower not only those who attain joy in daily, productive work well done, but also those who paint and sing and tell stories with the flavor peculiar to their own valley, well-loved hill, or broad prairie."

As we sat in Georg and Maria Scheuermann's tiny living room listening to the saga of their lives and this remote part of such a vast country, I was annoyingly returned to present reality by our driver's recurrent motions to his watch. My Russian friends courteously left the room to allow us a few private moments before parting. The stories related by these two tempered souls had given me far more than I could ever offer them. They had finally shed light on the lives of all *usu Leut* whose fate in this troubled country had long eluded our knowledge. I could do little more than impart manifold assurance from so many others across the ocean that they had not been forgotten during all those years of sufferings and in these uncertain days still remained in our prayers. A kind of catharsis permeated our fellowship as two worlds briefly met in the place both had begun. On the road back out of town I looked in vain for the clumps of wild strawberries that had given Yagodnaya Polyana its name and realized that the question of their presence I wanted to ask was one of many I had missed. If they were anything like the domestic species in our garden back home they were connected by long living runners firmly tied to a parent plant deeply rooted in prairie soil. Whether their absence was due to overgrazing, errant spraying, or simply preference for sunny exposure, I could not tell but preferred to accept the latter explanation.

My knowing the fate of that isolated village which soon disappeared behind us had grown in importance in recent years as when a son or daughter seeks the assurance of a parent's welfare in later life. I reflected on the affirmation of cultural values among members of my own generation back home that had been born of experience in this place. Perhaps my outlet for these expressions was a quest of historical research while for others cultural identity was evident in more subtle but equally meaningful ways. Many have found renewed fulfillment in an active church life rooted in our people's evangelical heritage. Some of my contemporaries also now assume responsibility for the annual wurst-making bees and vie for the most consistency with Old Country culinary standards. For others whose circumstances have led to life in the city, applications of hard work, honesty, and fiscal conservatism learned from their elders have fostered prosperous businesses nationwide. For many who remain in the rural Endicotts, Bisons, and Prestons, identity is implicit in a farm life that weaves pastoral tapestries of living hues on well-tended fields. While methods of planting, cultivating, and harvesting have changed over the years, each has required an intimate agrarian savvy carefully nurtured through generations of life with the land.

A guest in our home might find my wife's preoccupation with a bright strawberry motif in the kitchen to be either quaint or overdone. I have always known, however, that it has more to do with a special place of timeless cultural rendezvous than with Lois's fondness for red. Now into a second century in this life, her Grandma Morasch still asks for news about that distant village of her childhood as if little has changed there. To many it remains an ethereal Brigadoon where family and friends still gather wild berries that cover the gentle slopes surrounding a German village on the Volga named Yagodnaya Polyana.

SELECTED BIBLIOGRAPHY
Books and Pamphlets

Bauer, Gottlieb. *Geschichte der Deutschen in den Wolgakolonien.* Saratov, 1907.

Beratz, Gottlieb. *Die deutschen Kolonien an der Unteren Wolga.* Saratov: H. Schellhorn u. Co., 1915; sd ed., Berlin: Verband der wolgadeutschen Bauern, G.m.b.H. 1923.

Bonwetsch, Gerhard. *Geschichte der deutschen Kolonien an der Wolga.* Stuttgart: Verlag von J. Englehorns Nachf. 1919.

Bryan, Enoch A. *Orient Meets Occident: The Advent of the Railways to the Pacific Northwest.* Pullman, Washington: The Students Book Corporation, 1936.

Burgdorff, H. George. *Erlebnisse als Missionar oder Reiseprediger in Russland.* Hillsboro, Kansas: M. B. Publishing House. 1924.

Collard, Rev. Ernest and others. *Peace Lutheran Church Fiftieth Anniversary, 1909-1959.* Tacoma, Washington. 1959.

Duin, Edgar C. *Lutheranism under the Tsars and Soviets.* 2 vols. Ann Arbor, Michigan: University Microfilms. 1975.

Durant, Will. *The Reformation: A History of European Civilization from Wyclif to Calvin, 1300-1564.* New York: Simon and Schuster. 1957.

Eckhoff, Rev. R. H. and others. *Seventy-five Blessed Years, 1890-1965.* Zion Lutheran Church Anniversary Booklet. Tacoma, Washington. 1965.

Eisenach, George J. *A History of the German Congregational Churches in the United States.* Yankton, South Dakota: The Pioneer Press. 1938,

Eisenach, George J. *Pietism and the Russian Germans*. Berne, Indiana: The Berne Publishers. 1949.

Eisenach, George J. *Das religiöse Leben unter den Russlanddeutschen in Russland und Amerika*. Marburg an der Lahn, W. Ger.: Buchdruckerei Hermann Rathmann. 1950.

E(rbes), J. and P. S(inner). *Volkslieder und Kinderreime aus den Wolgakolonien*. Saratov: Buchdruckerei Energie. 1914.

Fairchild, Henry Pratt. *Immigration*. New York: John Wiley and Sons, Inc. 1925.

Foege, Rev. W. and others. *Emmanuel Lutheran Church 75th Anniversary*. Walla Walla. 1963.

Forty-fifth Annual Reunion of the Association of the Graduates of the United States Military Academy. Saginaw, Michigan: Seemans and Peters, Inc. 1914.

Gieseke, Rev. H. J. and others. *A Brief History of Zion Lutheran Church (Missouri Synod) at Endicott, Washington*. 1941.

Giesinger, Adam. *From Catherine to Krushchev*. Battleford, Saskatchewan: Marian Press. 1974.

Groschupf, Rev. John and others. *The Story of Fifty Years: A Brief History of the Emmanuel Lutheran Church, 1889-1939*. Spokane, Washington. 1939.

Hansen, Marcus Lee. *The Immigrant in American History*. Cambridge: Harvard University Press. 1940.

Haxthausen, August von. *Studien über die inneren Zustaende des Volkslebens und insebsondere der laendlichen Einrichtungen Russlands*. Hanover, 1847-1852. (Translated by Eleanore L. M. Schmidt: *Studies on the Interior of Russia*. Chicago: University of Chicago Press. 1972.)

Hedges, James Blain. *Henry Villard and the Railways of the Northwest*. New Haven: Yale University Press. 1930.

Height, Joseph S. *Paradise on the Steppe*. Bismark, N. D.: North Dakota Historical Society of Germans from Russia. 1972.

210

Hellman, Walter H., Ed. *Fifty Golden Years: The Story of the Northwest District of the American Lutheran Church, 1891-1941.* Dubuque, Iowa: Wartburg Press. 1941.

Klaus, Aleksandr Avgustovich. *Nashii kolonii: Opyty materialy po istorii i statistike inostrannoi kolonizatsii v rossi.* St. Petersburg: Tipografiia V. V. Nusval't. 1869.

Koch, Fred C. *The Volga Germans: In Russia and the Americas, From 1763 to the Present.* University Park: Pennsylvania State University Press. 1977.

Krause, Revs. A., H. Rieke, G. F. Pauschert and P. Groschupf. *Denkschrift zum Silber-Jubiläum des Washington Distrikts der Ev. Luth. Ohio Synode, 1891-1916.* Columbus, Ohio: Lutheran Book Concern. 1916.

Lavender, David. Land of Giants: *The Drive to the Pacific Northwest, 1750-1950.* Garden City, New York: Doubleday and Company. 1958.

Luebke, Frederick C. *Immigrants and Politics: The Germans of Nebraska, 1880-1900.* Lincoln: University of Nebraska Press. 1969.

Mecca Glen Memories. Ponoka, Alberta: Mecca Glen Centennial Committee. 1968.

Meinig, Donald W. *The Great Columbia Plain: A Historical Geography, 1805-1910.* Seattle: University of Washington Press. 1968.

Malcky, Alexander. German-Albertans: *A Historical Survey.* Calgary, Alberta. n.d.

Nelson, E. Clifford. *Lutheranism in North America, 1914-1970.* Minneapolis: Augsburg Publishing House. 1972.

Ochs, Grace Lillian. *Up From the Volga: The Story of the Ochs Family.* Nashville: Southern Publishing Association. 1969.

Pallas, Peter Simon. *Reisen durch verschiedene Provinzen des russischen Reiches in den Jahren 1768-1774.* St. Petersburg, 1771-1776.

Pissarevskii, Grigorii G. *Iz istorii inostrannoi kolonizatsii v rossii v XVIII v. (Po neizdannym arkhivnym dokumentam.)* Moskva: A. I. Snegirevyi. 1909.

Pissarevskii, Grigorii G. *Vnutrennii rasporiadok v koloniiakh povolzh'ia pri Ekaterine II.* Varshava: Tipografiliia varshavskago uchebnago okruga. 1914.

Protokoll der im Jahr 1889 zu Saratov abgehaltenen 16-ten combinirten Synode der bei den Wolga-Präposituren. Saratov: Prapositur der Wolga. 1889.

Raugust, W. C., R. Hoefel, Rev. A. Rehn and Rev. A. Hausauer. *History of the Pacific Conference of Congregational Churches of Washington, Oregon and Idaho, 1897-1964.* 1964.

Riasanovsky, Nicholas V. *A History of Russia (Second Edition).* New York: Oxford University Press. 1969.

Sallet, Richard. *Russian-German Settlements in the United States.* Fargo: North Dakota Institute for Regional Studies. 1974. Translated by LaVern J. Rippley and Armand Bauer.

Schleuning, Johannes. *Die deutschen Kolonien im Wolgagebiet.* Berlin, 1919. Reprint. Portland, Ore.: A. E. Kern & Company. 1922.

Schmidt, David. *Studien uber die Geschichte der Wolgadeutschen.* Pokrowsk, A.S.S.R. der Wolgadeutschen: Zentral-Vöker-Verlag. 1930.

Schnaible, Rev. Fred and others. *A History of Trinity Lutheran Church, 1887-1975.* Dedication Anniversary Booklet. Endicott, Washington. 1975.

Schul — und Küster-Schülmeister Instruction in den evangelischen Kolonien des Saratovschen und Samaraschen Gouvernments. Moscow: Evangelisch-Lutherischen Consistorio. Undated.

Schwabenland, Emma D. *A History of the Volga Relief Society.* Portland: A. B. Kern & Company. 1941.

Sheatsley, C. V. *History of the Evangelical Lutheran Joint Synod of Ohio and Other States.* Columbus, Ohio: Lutheran Book Concern. 1919.

Snowden, Clinton. *A History of Washington: The Rise and Progress of an American State.* 6 Vols. New York: The Century History Company. 1909

Stelter, Sandra. John and Mary Schierman: *A Family History,* Russia 1890-Canada 1977. Vernon, British Columbia, 1977.

Stumpp, Karl. *The Emigration from Germany to Russia in the Years 1763 to 1862.* Tübingen, Germany: by the author. 1973.

Stumpp, Karl. *The German-Russians: Two Centuries of Pioneering.* Trostberg, Germany: A. Erdl. 1967. (Translated by Dr. Joseph Height).

Thomson, Gladys Scott. *Catherine the Great and the Expansion of Russia.* New York: Collier Books. 1965.

Villard, Henry. *The Early History of Transportation in Oregon.* Eugene: University of Oregon Press. 1944.

Volz, Jacob. *Historical Review of the Balzerer.* York, Nebraska. 1938.

Wagner, Rev. Albert F. and others. *Emmanuel Lutheran Church Diamond Anniversary.* Ritzville, Washington. 1965.

Weitz, Anna. *History of the Evangelical Congregational Church, 1883-1963.* Endicott, Washington. 1963.

Williams, Hattie Plum. *The Czars Germans: With Particular Reference to the Volga Germans.* Lincoln, Nebraska: The American Historical Society of Germans from Russia. 1975.

Winsor, Henry J. *The Great Northwest: A Guidebook and Itinerary for the use of Tourists and Travellers Over the lines of the Northern Pacific Railroad.* New York: G. P. Putnam's Sons. 1883.

Wirsing, Dale R. *Builders, Brewers and Burghers: Germans of Washington State.* The Washington State American Revolution Bicentennial Commission. 1977.

Yungman, Susan M. *Faith of our Fathers.* By the author. 1972.

Zorrow, William F. *Kansas: A History of the Jayhawk State.* Norman: University of Oklahoma Press. 1957.

Züge, Christian Gottlob. *Der russiche Kolonist.* I. Zeitz und Naumberg: Wilhelm Webel. 1802.

PERIODICALS

Davidson, Elaine. Ed. "Autobiography of Wilhelm (William) Frank," *Unsere Leute Von Kautz,* I (May, 1979), 17-21.

Dudek, Pauline B. "Further Notes on the Wagon Train from Nebraska to Washington," *AHSGR Journal,* II, No. 3 (Winter, 1979), 44-46.

Esselborn, Karl. "Die Auswanderung von Hessen nach Russland," *Heimat im Bild,* 1926, 83-104.

Flegel, Art and Cleora. "Research in Hesse," *AHSGR Work Paper* No. 13 (December, 1973), 21-27.

Haynes, Emma S. "Germans from Russia in American History and Literature," *AHSGR Work Paper* No. 15 (September, 1974), 4-20.

Haynes, Emma S. "Researching in the National Archives," *AHSGR Journal,* II, No. 1 (Spring, 1979), 4-7.

Hoezler, Johann. "The Earliest Volga Germans in Sutton, Nebraska and a Portion of their History," *AHSGR Work Paper* No. 16 (December, 1974), 16-18. (Translated by Art Flegel).

Kromm, Georg. "Die deutschen Ansiedler an der Wolga," *Schottener Kreisblait,* Redaktion, Druck und Verlag von Wilhelm Engel, Schotten. Germany, Nos. 15-17, 21 (February, March, 1910).

Moeller, Theodore C., Jr. "The Development of Lutheranism in the Pacific Northwest with Specific Reference to the Northwest District, the Lutheran Church-Missouri Synod, Part I," *Concordia Historical Institute Quarterly,* XXVIII (Summer, 1955), 49-86.

Oregon-Washington Distrikt, Synode-Bericht, 1901 (Missouri Synod). Translated by K. Lorenz, 1901. At the District Archives, Portland, Oregon.

Rempel, David G. "The Mennonite Commonwealth in Russia: A Sketch of Its Founding and Endurance, 1789-1919," *Mennonite Quarterly Review,* XLVII (October, 1973) and XLVIII (January, 1974)

Roth, Jean, "Walla Walla, Washington," *Unsere Leute Von Walter,* I (June, 1978), 15.

Saul, Norman E. "The Arrival of the Germans from Russia: A Centennial Perspective," *AHSGR Work Paper* No. 21 (Fall, 1976), 4-11.

Saul, Norman E. "The Migration of Russian-Germans to Kansas," *Kansas Historical Quarterly,* XL, No. 1 (Spring, 1974), 38-62.

Schlommer, Harm. "Inland Empire Russia Germans," *The Pacific Northwesterner,* VIII (Fall, 1964), 57-64.

Stärkel, Johannes. "Johann Wilhelm Stärkel aus Norka unter der Fahne Pugachews," *Friedensbote* (November, 1901), 685-688.

Stumpp, Karl. "Verzeichnis der ev. Pastoren in den deutschen und gemischtenvor allem in Städten-Kirchenspielen in Russland bzw. der Sowjetunion, ohne Baltikum und Polen," *Heimatbuch der Deutschen aus Russland,* 1972, 276-389.

Verhandlungen des Washington Distrikts (Ohio Synod), 1891-24, Columbus, Ohio. At the Archives of the American Lutheran Church, Dubuque, Iowa.

Wagner, Ernst. "Auswanderung aus Hessen," *Auslanddeutschtum und evangelischen Kirche Jahrbuch,* 1938, 24-33.

Würz, Wilhelm "Wie Yagodnaya Polyana gegrundet wurde," *Heimatbuch der Deutschen aus Russland,* 1962, 65-66.

NEWSPAPERS

Calgary Herald. Calgary, Alberta.

Endicott Index. Endicott, Washington.

Hays City Sentinel. Hays City, Kansas.

London Times. London, England. February 1, 1876.

Lutheran Standard. Columbus, Ohio. 1887-95.

Palouse Gazette. Colfax, Washington.

Ritzville Journal-Times. "Adams County Pioneer Edition," September 15, 1949. 1950.

Russell Record. Russell, Kansas.

Topeka Daily Blade. Topeka, Kansas. December 13, 1875.

Walla Walla Weekly Statesman. Walla Walla, Washington.

PUBLIC DOCUMENTS AND PAPERS

Church Anniversary Bulletins of the American Lutheran Church. At the North Pacific District Archives, Seattle, Washington.

Hesse, Acten des Geheimen Staats-Archives, XI, Abhteilung, Convolut I. At the Hessen State Archives, Darmstadt, West Germany.

Kromm, Georg, Ed. *Einwanderliste von Yagodnaya Polyana (aus Hessen).* At the Vogelsberg Museum in Schotten, West Germany.

Russia, *Polnoe Sobranie Zakonov Rossiiskoi Imperii. Sankt Peterburg, 1649-1916.* At the Hoover Library and Institute, Stanford University, Stanford, California.

Oliphant, J. Orin. Unpublished papers. At the Holland Library Archives, Washington State University, Pullman, Washington.

Oregon Improvement Company. *Annual Business Reports. 1881-1890.* At the Suzallo Library, Special Collections, University of Washington, Seattle, Washington.

U. S. Bureau of the Census. *Thirteenth Census of the United States: 1910. Abstract,* 1912.

U. S. Bureau of the Census. *Religious Bodies: 1916,* Part I. *Abstract,* 1919.

U. S. National Archives. *Manifests of Vessels arriving at New York, 1820-1897. S. S. Ohio* (to Baltimore) (November 23, 1875), *S. S. City of Chester* (July 10, 1876), *S. S. Donau* (August 5, 1876), *S. S. Mosel* (October 24, 1876), *S. S. Frisia* (December 8, 1876), *S. S. Hungaria* (May 15, 1888), *S. S. Wieland* (June 5, 1878), *S. S. City of Montreal* (January 6, 1876).

Weitz, Anna B. Unpublished papers. At the Holland Library Archives, Washington State University, Pullman, Washington.

ORAL HISTORIES

Adler, Jacob. Tekoa, Washington, January 2, 1973.

Bafus, Mrs. John. Endicott, Washington, April 29, 1980.

Blumenschein, Mr. Conrad. St. John, Washington, May 6 and 13, 1980.

Engelland, Hazel (Tannatt). Lacey, Washington, April 20, 1978.

Eichler, Art. Yakima, Washington, June 31, 1979.

Gradwohl, Mr. & Mrs. George, Jr. Walla Walla, Washington, March 18, 1978.

Greenwalt, Mr. & Mrs. John. Quincy, Washington, April 2, 1976.

Koch, Peter. Portland, Oregon, June 15, 1977.

Kromm, Elizabeth. Lacrosse, Washington, June 10, 1979.

Lautenschlager, Mr. & Mrs. Leo. Brewster, Washington, April 17, 1980.

Litzenberger, Henry. Deer Park, Washington, May 4, 1980.

Luft, Catherine. Sheboygan, Wisconsin, June 15-19, 1977.

Lust, Martin. Colfax, Washington, April 7, 1975.

Markel, August. Endicott, Washington, June 19, 1970.

Meininger, Jacob. Tacoma, Washington, April 4, 1978.

Miller, Jacob. Tacoma, Washington, April 4, 1978.

Morasch, Mrs. A. P. Endicott, Washington, March 4, 1980.

Morasch, Mrs. C. P. Endicott, Washington, April 23, 1971.

Ochs, Ed. Cashmere, Washington, March 17, 1977.

Ochs, Mr. & Mrs. Dan. St. Helena, California, February 16, 1974.

Ochs, Leta. Endicott, Washington, April 23, 1971.

Oestreich, Mr. & Mrs. Roy. Ritzville, Washington, April 1, 1978.

Poffenroth, Mr. & Mrs. Alfred. Calgary, Alberta, July 5, 1977.

Rehn, Jacob. Tacoma, Washington, April 4, 1978.

Reich, Alec. Endicott, Washington, April 2, 1969.

Repp, Elizabeth. Endicott, Washington, April 1, 1971.

Rieke, Mr. & Mrs. H. H. Cashmere, Washington, October 10, 1975.

Scheuerman, Karl. Endicott, Washington, December 10, 1969.

Scheuerman, Una Mae. Endicott, Washington, June 8, 1975.

Scheuerman, Mr. & Mrs. Walter. Bashaw, Alberta, July 1, 1977.

Schierman, Dave. Walla Walla, Washington, July 9, 1972.

Schierman, Mr. & Mrs. John. Vulcan, Alberta, July 2, 1977.

Schmick, Conrad G. Colfax, Washington, April 14, 1969.

Schneidmiller, Mr. & Mrs. William. Walla Walla, Washington, April 13, 1980.

Weber, Jacob. Quincy, Washington, April 17, 1980.